DANTE METAMORPHOSES

PUBLICATIONS OF THE UCD FOUNDATION FOR ITALIAN STUDIES

General Editor: John C. Barnes

Dante and the Middle Ages: Literary and Historical Essays, ed. J. C. Barnes and C. Ó Cuilleanáin

Dante Comparisons: Comparative Studies of Dante and: Montale, Foscolo, Tasso, Chaucer, Petrarch, Propertius and Catullus, ed. E. Haywood and B. Jones

Dante Metamorphoses: Episodes in a Literary Afterlife, ed. E. Haywood

Dante Readings, ed. E. Haywood

Dante Soundings: Eight Literary and Historical Essays, ed. D. Nolan

Word and Drama in Dante: Essays on the "Divina Commedia", ed. J. C. Barnes and J. Petrie

J. Petrie, *Petrarch: The Augustan Poets, the Italian Tradition and the "Canzoniere"*

M. Davie, *Half-serious Rhymes: The Narrative Poetry of Luigi Pulci*

T. O'Neill, *Of Virgin Muses and of Love: A Study of Foscolo's "Dei Sepolcri"*

G. Leopardi, *Canti*, with an introduction by F. Fortini and translations by P. Lawton

U. Fanning, *Gender Meets Genre: Woman as Subject in the Fictional Universe of Matilde Serao*

G. Talbot, *Montale's "Mestiere Vile": The Elective Translations from English of the 1930s and 1940s*

Pasolini Old and New: Surveys and Studies, ed. Z. G. Barański

Italian Storytellers: Essays on Italian Narrative Literature, ed. E. Haywood and C. Ó Cuilleanáin

B. Reynolds, *Casalattico and the Italian Community in Ireland*

BELFIELD ITALIAN LIBRARY

Dante Alighieri, *Vita nuova*, ed. J. Petrie and J. Salmons

Lorenzo de' Medici, *Selected Writings*, ed. C. Salvadori

Niccolò Machiavelli, *Mandragola*, ed. E. Haywood

Carlo Goldoni, *La locandiera*, ed. D. O'Grady

Luigi Pirandello, *Il berretto a sonagli*, ed. J. C. Barnes

Eugenio Montale, *Selected Poems*, ed. G. Talbot

DANTE METAMORPHOSES

Episodes in a Literary Afterlife

edited by
ERIC G. HAYWOOD

Published for
The Foundation for Italian Studies
UCD, National University of Ireland, Dublin

FOUR COURTS PRESS

Published by
FOUR COURTS PRESS LTD
7 Malpas Street, Dublin 8, Ireland
Email: info@four-courts-press.ie
and in the United States for
FOUR COURTS PRESS
c/o ISBS, 920 N.E. 58th Avenue, Suite 300, Portland, OR 97213.

© Foundation for Italian Studies, UCD,
National University of Ireland, Dublin, 2003

A catalogue record for this title is available from the British Library.

ISBN 1-85182-662-9

Publication of this book was assisted by financial help from:

The UCD Academic Publications Committee
The National University of Ireland

Printed in Great Britain by
Antony Rowe Ltd, Chippenham, Wilts.

PREFACE

Another title for this book could well have been "Dante: Five Centuries of Abuse". It tells the story of how the *Commedia* (together, occasionally, with some of Dante's minor works) was appropriated throughout the ages and across Europe by a variety of authors for a variety of reasons and to various effects. In so doing it demonstrates (not for the first time) how "globalization", at least in the cultural sphere, is an older phenomenon than we perhaps realize. Almost from the very moment it was written, the *Commedia* was fashioned into the universal language of (Western) culture— though paradoxically it was by being provincialized that it became universalized, as authors of differing nationalities cut it down to size to adapt it to the changing demands of time and place. In fifteenth-century Spain it served, through the episode of Francesca and its Castilian imitation by Íñigo López de Mendoza, to fathom the depths of courtly love. In fifteenth-century Florence it and its author were tied to the fortunes of successive regimes and made to mirror the needs of competing "state" ideologies, from the civic *engagement* promoted by the early Humanists to the political quietism and cultural imperialism sponsored by Lorenzo de' Medici. In sixteenth-century Ferrara, on the other hand, Dante and his work were conscripted by Ariosto to make light of the Florentine aspirations to cultural and political hegemony and further those of Ferrara and the Este instead. Later, with Campanella, the *Commedia* came into its own again, so to speak, as a paragon of Christian and Catholic poetry and poetics, though at about the same time, in Reformation England, Dante was lined up with those who wished to defy the authority of the Pope in Rome (and occasionally with those who sought to uphold it). Some two and a half centuries later he was once again made to perform the same task, as the *Commedia* was Englished with Anglican zeal by Henry Francis Cary, just as in Milan it was "Lombardized", with even greater liberty, by Carlo

Porta, in an effort to "bring it down" to the level of the people while "elevating" dialect to the level of literature. George Eliot, for her part, wove sentiments and images of it into her novels, as she sought to illustrate, through Virgil-like figures, how morality may be sanctioned in a godless society. Finally, the Romantics, and after them d'Annunzio, taking a fresh look at Francesca, made her the embodiment of tastes and passions in many ways quite foreign to Dante. Opening with Francesca in Castilian garb, the book thus comes full circle, closing with her in Decadent transfiguration.

The essays have been set, as far as possible, in chronological order and they merit being read in sequence, as each one expands upon those that come before, though of course each also stands on its own. They are the outcome of public lectures given, as part of the annual Dante Series, at UCD in 1993, 1994 and 2001, by scholars who, although not all strictly speaking professional Dantists, have all found, in the course of their research into other writers and periods, that Dante's universal presence cannot be ignored and must be accounted for. Professor Nicholas Round is in the Spanish Department in the University of Sheffield, Professor Corinna Salvadori the Italian Department in Trinity College, Dublin, and Dr Eric Haywood the Italian Department in UCD, while Professor Enzo Noé Girardi was formerly in the Facoltà di Magistero, Università Cattolica di Milano; Mr Nicholas Havely is in the English Department in the University of York; Dr Edoardo Crisafulli, formerly on the staff of the UCD Italian Department, is now a cultural promotion officer in the Ministry of Foreign Affairs, Rome; Dr Verina Jones recently retired from the Italian Department in the University of Reading; Dr Andrew Thompson lectures in English in the Department of Humanities and Science, University of Wales College, Newport, and Dr Deirdre O'Grady is in the UCD Italian Department. The UCD Foundation for Italian Studies apologizes to them for the long delay in the publication of this book. It is gratified to note that none of them perished while waiting to be published. The book's editor is grateful to his colleagues Deirdre O'Grady and John Barnes for their invaluable assistance at various stages of the editorial process.

All Biblical references in English are to the Douay Bible, and all references to the works of Dante are based on the following editions, which in the notes are indicated by the abbreviations shown here:

Vn	*Vita nuova,* edited by D. De Robertis (Milan–Naples, Ricciardi, 1980); also in D. Alighieri, *Opere minori,* 2 vols in 3 (Milan–Naples, Ricciardi, 1979–88), I, i, 27–247
Conv.	*Convivio,* edited by F. Brambilla Ageno, 2 vols in 3 (Florence, Le Lettere, 1995) *La "Commedia" secondo l'antica vulgata,* edited by G. Petrocchi, revised edition, 4 vols (Florence, Le Lettere, 1994)
Epist.	*Epistole,* edited by A. Frugoni and G. Brugnoli, in D. Alighieri, *Opere minori,* II, 505–643

The following abbreviations are also used:

Inf.	*Inferno*
Purg.	*Purgatorio*
Par.	*Paradiso*
Enc. dant.	*Enciclopedia dantesca,* 6 vols (Rome, Istituto dell'Enciclopedia Italiana, 1970–78)
RVF	*Rerum Vulgarium Fragmenta* (Petrarch's *Canzoniere*)
Of	*Orlando furioso*
DNB	*Dictionary of National Biography,* edited by L. Stephen and S. Lee, 22 vols (London, Smith and Elder, 1908–09)
STC	*A Short-title Catalogue of Books Printed in England, Scotland, and Ireland, and of English Books Printed Abroad, 1475–1640,* compiled by A. W. Pollard, G. R. Redgrave and others (London, Bibliographical Society–Oxford University Press, 1926)

CONTENTS

LOVERS IN HELL:
INFERNO V AND ÍÑIGO LÓPEZ DE MENDOZA

Nicholas Round

In the loosely generalizing mode associated with literary "back-ground" we commonly refer to Dante's "universal" quality. By that, presumably, we mean two things: first that his poetry, especially the *Commedia*, gathers within itself a great summation of medieval knowledge and belief; secondly that it has registered with generations of readers as both impressive in itself and relevant to their own concerns. But to read Dante, or even a tiny portion of Dante, closely is to think of poetic language as language at a growing-point. Language grows, we may say, when some bit of knowledge, of cognitive substance, becomes focused through some piece of linguistic substance, creating a new resource of meaningful speech. In Dante that happens all the time: the focusing of many knowledges, their pressure to become effective as new meaning, the achievement of that outcome in a language whose power to mean more seems inexhaustible. The effect is exhilarating, and one is grateful for that. It is also awesome in its blend of intensity and scale. It is not merely the length of the *Commedia* that has led to its being appreciated, typically, on the strength of particular excerpts and episodes. It is the sheer, daunting responsibility of engaging with it at length.

My own engagement here with *Inferno* v—perhaps the most routinely gone-over of all such episodes—may seem part of the problem, not the solution. There is perhaps some better hope of a gain in understanding from my other concern, with one of the earliest Spanish poets to make their own discovery of Dante's output and of its potential meaning for themselves. The two elements of that discovery, of course, are hardly to be separated. Thinking about any discovery is made easier if we can represent the thing discovered in terms that are already in some part familiar.

As to the uses to which it is then put, these tend to answer the perceived needs of discoverers, rather than any view of what the object of discovery might itself demand. In these respects intercultural discovery functions along much the same lines as target-oriented translation. Yet among translations there is also a source-oriented mode: it arises when the textual authority of the source clearly overrules the demands contingently placed upon it by the target culture. A similar authority can make itself felt too in other kinds of cross-cultural influence. Dante in the later Middle Ages was influential precisely as a latter-day *auctoritas*. The outcomes which stem from such cases of major literary influence are thus characteristically diverse and intermediate, ranging between exploitation of the source for purposes of one's own and deference to those purposes which first informed it.

That, in very general terms, was what happened in the early fifteenth century, when Spanish—or more specifically for present purposes Castilian—poets discovered Dante. There is good ground for thinking that the discovery mattered to them. By the mid-century there were Catalan and Castilian translations of the *Commedia*, as well as versions of such commentators as Pietro Alighieri and Benvenuto da Imola.[1] In Francisco Imperial's early-fifteenth-century *Dezir de las siete virtudes*, and again some fifty years later in Diego de Burgos's *Triumfo del Marqués de Santillana*, Dante appears as the poet's supernatural guide to a complex allegorical vision. These appearances in the role which he had once assigned to Virgil reflect the immense prestige enjoyed by "el seráfico Dante" (as Juan de Mena called him in the 1430s).[2] They

1   Translations: Dant Alighieri, *Divina Comèdia: versió catalana d'Andreu Febrer*, edited by A. Gallina, 6 vols (Barcelona, Barcino, 1974–88); J. A. Pascual, *La traducción de la "Divina Commedia" atribuída a D. Enrique de Aragón: estudio y edición del "Inferno"* (Salamanca, Universidad, 1974). For versions of commentators see M. Á. Pérez Priego, "De Dante a Juan de Mena: sobre el género literario de 'comedia'", *1616: Anuario de la Sociedad Española de Literatura General y Comparada*, 1 (1978), 151–58 (p. 156).

2   On Imperial see D. W. Foster, "The Misunderstanding of Dante in Fifteenth-century Spanish Poetry", *Comparative Literature*, 16 (1964), 338–46 (pp. 340–41). The text of Diego de Burgos's *Triunfo del Marquémay* may be read in *Cancionero castellano del siglo XV*, edited by R. Foulché-Delbosc, 2 vols (Madrid, Bailly-Baillière, 1912–13), II, 535–59. On Mena (commentary on Stanza 37 of the *Coronación*) see F. Street, "The Allegory of Fortune and the Imitation of Dante in the *Laberinto* and *Coronación* of Juan de Mena", *Hispanic Review*, 23 (1955), 1–11 (p. 6).

also exemplify one of several ways in which Castilian poets were beginning to imitate his work. Yet most modern critics would reject the view that the literary response to Dante in fifteenth-century Castile was in any sense epoch-making. Many would go further, arguing that in practice the Castilians got their responses to him wrong.

There would indeed be problems about regarding Dantean influences in this period as decisive. The voices arguing such a case tend to be those of early-twentieth-century Italian critics like Sanvisenti and Farinelli, with whom we should perhaps discount a certain measure of cultural nationalism. Arguably we might wish to do the same with Pierre Le Gentil's attempt, half a century later, to trace some supposedly Dantean elements to French allegorical models. Yet the French influences are certainly there. So too are the classical precedents which Florence Street and María Rosa Lida saw as authoritative in Juan de Mena's work. Dante as a poetic model has his place in a complex and sometimes contradictory pattern. Peter Russell's assessment would appear to have the balance right: Dante, while powerfully attractive to many Spanish writers of the time, influenced them less profoundly than has sometimes been thought.[1]

But here the second strand of received opinion cited above merges with the first. The real question, as David Foster wrote in 1964, "is not whether Dante was read and interpreted but how". To which a chorus of voices—some more bluntly than Foster's, but his among them—has replied that it was not done very well. More than a century ago the Comte de Puymaigre dismissed the alleg-orical design of Mena's *Laberinto de Fortuna* as "chaotic and meaning-less" by comparison with Dante. In Post's *Medieval Spanish Allegory* (1913) Santillana is described as "utterly unable to attain the delicacy that surrounds the conceptions of the *dolce stil nuovo*", while of Mena it is said that "the Italian's essential nature must

---

1   On the views of B. Sanvisenti (1902) and A. Farinelli (1920) see F. Street, "The Allegory of Fortune", p. 6; also R. Lapesa, *La obra literaria del Marqués de Santillana* (Madrid, Ínsula, 1957), p. 128. On P. Le Gentil (1949) see R. Lapesa, *La obra literaria del Marqués de Santillana*, p. 129 and N. Salvador Miguel, *La poesía cancioneril: el "Cancionero de Estúñiga"* (Madrid, Alhambra, 1977), p. 137. On the classical background see F. Street, "The Allegory of Fortune", pp. 10–11 and M. R. Lida de Malkiel, *Juan de Mena, poeta del prerrenacimiento español* (Mexico, Colegio de México, 1950). On Dante as *auctoritas* see P. E. Russell *Temas de "La Celestina"* (Barcelona, Ariel, 1978), p. 230.

always have remained an impenetrable enigma to the Spaniard."
Even for Rafael Lapesa the outcome of the "inevitable" comparison
with Dante is to crush (*aplastar*) Santillana's *Infierno de los enamorados*.[1] The latter part of this essay will provide an opportunity to
review that judgement. Meanwhile, we should at least note the
contrast of such views with Santillana's reputation in his own day
as Dante's closest reader and chief promoter among Castilians.
"Que si tengo fama y soy conoscido," Diego de Burgos makes
Dante say, "es porque él quiso mis obras mirar" ["For if I am
famous and well known it is because he interested himself in my
works"; Stanza 150, p. 551). Set alongside that, Foster's remark that
"Dante's moral orientation is not wholly lost on Santillana" seems
grudging, and much of a piece with his view of the "congenital
inability" of these fifteenth-century poets "to approximate [Dante's]
poetic vision".[2]

The claim that these poets were not as good as Dante need not
detain us: few poets are. The assertion that they differed from
Dante, while obviously true, does not tell us how or why they did
so. Foster himself has twice addressed these problems. In 1964 he
noted that the Spaniards imitated "only those elements of Dante
which were common to their own poetic repertory". Not being
"creative geniuses of the highest order", they could not yet
"assimilate fully the influences and new directions which they
were attempting to make their own".[3] In one way this describes,
perceptively, a normal pattern of target-oriented cultural
transmission; in another it leaves the problem where it was. Major
creative geniuses, it is implied, would have written more like
Dante (though they might, at that, have written more like

---

1   D. W. Foster, "The Misunderstanding of Dante", p. 339 and passim; T. □ J. □ Bou-
     det, Comte de Puymaigre (1873), cited by C. R. Post, "The Sources of Juan
     de Mena", *Romanic Review*, 3 (1912), 223–79 (p. 224); C. R. Post, *Medieval
     Spanish Allegory* (Cambridge, Mass., Harvard University Press, 1915), p.
     218, and "The Sources of Juan de Mena", p. 224; R. Lapesa, *La obra literaria
     del Marqués de Santillana*, p. 130. Compare M. Morreale, "Apuntes biblio-
     gráficos para el estudio del tema 'Dante en España' hasta el siglo XVII",
     Estratto dagli Annali del corso di lingue straniere della Università di Bari, 8 (1967),
     cited by M. Á. Pérez Priego, "De Dante a Juan de Mena", p. 151: "ningún otro
     tema ha causado tantas desilusiones, al percatarse los eruditos de la 'medio-
     cridad' e 'insuficiencia' de los imitadores de Dante, y de la 'incomprensión'
     de sus admiradores."
2   D. W. Foster, "The Misunderstanding of Dante", pp. 343 and 346.
3   D. W. Foster, "The Misunderstanding of Dante", pp. 346–47 and *passim*.

themselves). But in their absence the gulf between Dante and the Spaniards remained in place, with no other explanation that Foster is able to provide. Returning to the topic in 1971, he offered a more specific analysis of contrasting poetic traditions. In Italy the *dolce stil nuovo* had realized in Dante's *Commedia* "a brilliant fusion of the religious and secular visions of love". In France and Spain the two visions are brought together only through "an unabashed accommodation of religious language". As a result Spanish poets, largely indifferent to "Dante's grand design", take him as "little more than an *auctor*—a bookish authority" who lends himself to mere name-dropping and surface mimicry.[1] These judgements are relevant, but still too sweeping.

Peter Russell too argues that Dante was valued more as a legal and theological *auctoritas*, a source of *sententiae*, than as a great poet.[2] Even among the Catalans we find these priorities reflected, as in the rubric of Andreu Febrer's translation: "Comença la Comèdia de Dant Allighieri, de Florença, en la qual tracta de la pena e punició dels vicis, de la purgació e penitència d'aquells, e dels mèrits e premis de virtut" ["Here begins the *Comedy* of Dante Alighieri of Florence, where he treats of the penalty and punishment of vices, of their purgation and penance, and of the just deserts and rewards of virtue"].[3] Yet, while we might grant that this way of seeing his authority did determine and even limit the uses made of Dante, we should still be rash to conclude that it trivialized them. Authority, however superficially acknowledged, was not a superficial matter for fifteenth-century writers. Again, Foster's initial comparison between Spain and Italy calls for a degree of finer shading. In Castile, certainly, it is hard to point to any systematic "fusion of the religious and secular visions of love" prior to the emergence of the sentimental romance in the mid-to-late fifteenth century. In that development Dantean elements and examples did play some part.[4] Yet even the sentimental romances

1   D. W. Foster, *The Marqués de Santillana* (New York, Twayne, 1971), pp. 99 and 155.
2   P. E. Russell, *Temas de "La Celestina"*, p. 231.
3   Dant Alighieri, *Divina Comèdia*, i, 50. All translations from Spanish are my own.
4   See G. P. Andrachuk, "A Further Look at Italian Influences in the *Siervo libre de Amor*", *Journal of Hispanic Philology*, 6 (1981), 45–56 (p. 46); M. Scordilis Brownlee, *The Severed World: Ovid's "Heroides" and the "Novela sentimental"* (Princeton, Princeton University Press, 1990), pp. 12 and 90–93; A. D. Deyer-

remain narrower in focus than Dante's writings, and are not as a
rule particularly like them. As for Dante's own fusion of profane
and sacred love, that is perhaps best seen as one element in his
larger synthesis of personal and public, secular and spiritual
discourses. In that perspective we might very well want to conclude
with Erich Auerbach that nowhere—not even in Italy—does Dante
find successors capable of carrying forward the wholeness of his
vision.[1]

That poets in Castile did not do what Dante importantly did
may often be true, though we should always remember that their
notions of what mattered most in Dante might differ from ours,
and yet be no less pertinent or coherent. We should be altogether
more cautious, though, in asserting that they were incapable of
understanding him. That would carry the unspoken and gratuitous
premise that we ourselves fully understand what an understanding
of Dante is and is not. What we can more modestly affirm is that
their achievement of understanding and re-creation was limited in
ways and for reasons which we have some hope of clarifying. We
shall find that easier if we can detach our notions of Dantean
influence from the idea that poets who responded to it were
somehow under an obligation to be as like Dante as they could—
a view which would involve both a paradox and an assumption of
anxiety (as the vogue-term has it).

The approach to questions of influence adopted here is different.
It would regard these derivative Castilian texts as outcomes of the
inherent semantic productivity of the *Commedia*—of its capacity,
that is to say, for giving rise to newly meaningful expressions. I
have tried elsewhere to show how the semantic productivity of
linguistic expressions and the productivity in terms of influence of
literary texts may usefully be treated as parallel phenomena.[2]
There would appear in either case to be two possible patterns at
work. One of them would begin with an urgently experienced
"need to mean", to which there then presents itself a pre-existing
expression, apt and convincing in its testimony to a related meaning;

  mond, *Tradiciones y puntos de vista en la ficción sentimental* (Mexico, Universidad Nacional Autónoma de México, 1993), pp. 60–61.
1   E. Auerbach, *Lenguaje literario y público en la baja latinidad y en la Edad Media*
    (Barcelona, Seix Barral, 1969 [1st (German) edition, 1957]), p. 305.
2   N. G. Round, "Towards a Typology of Quixotisms", in *Cervantes and the
    Modernists: The Question of Influence*, edited by E. Williamson (London,
    Tamesis, 1994), pp. 9–28.

this is then *appropriated* for present purposes. In the other model the expression is first registered as present and current within a given language or culture, and thus as being *available* for meanings not previously associated with it; indeed, these need not even be especially close to the meaning which it originally bore. The distinction in this sense between "Dante appropriated" and "Dante available" is likely to prove useful to us.

Initially we might well feel that it was on the appropriation of Dante that critical attention ought to focus. Appropriation, thus defined, is something intentional; it tends to draw on well-made and central aspects of its source texts. With mere availability none of that will necessarily be the case. Yet to call it "mere" availability is to take far too much for granted. It would be pointless to downgrade or reproach those authors who opt to use Dante in this latter fashion. They are simply following out a normal semantic and literary process, often of considerable cultural interest and capable of being embodied in work of real literary consequence. In any case, the two modes of influence are almost certain in practice to occur together, with one or the other predominating, rather than in some notionally "pure" form. That certainly happens in the poem with which the rest of this essay will be mainly concerned: the *Infierno de los enamorados* of the future Marquis of Santillana, Íñigo López de Mendoza (1398–1458).

The very first Castilian poets to take an interest in Dante had belonged to the generation before Íñigo López, but his own involvement was of a notably more systematic kind. He made it his business to own the Italian text of the *Commedia*, as well as commentaries thereon. Still more remarkably, he had asked his friend and literary mentor, Enrique de Villena, to make him a translation of the poem. At some time in 1427–28, ostensibly as light relief from composing a commentary on the *Aeneid*, Villena had obliged. If, as seems virtually certain, this translation is the version in MS 10186 of the Biblioteca Nacional in Madrid, then it was a hasty piece of work.[1] Written in prose, with syntax and

---

1   See J. A. Pascual, *La traducción de la "Divina Commedia"*; also J. A. Pascual and R. Santiago Lacuesta, "La primera traducción castellana de la *Divina Commedia*: argumentos para la identificación de su autor", in *Serta philologica F. Lázaro Carreter natalem diem sexagesimum celebranti dicata*, 2 vols (Madrid, Cátedra, 1983), II, 391–402 (p. 392 for circumstances of composition). On MS BN 10186 and its place in Íñigo López's library see M. Schiff, *La Bibliothèque du marquis de Santillane* (Paris, Bouillon, 1905), pp. 275–303.

word-order manifestly calqued on its original, it displays much ill-assimilated Italian-based lexis, many of Villena's typically heavy-handed Latinisms and a generous crop of outright errors. The text is copied, with many erasures and revisions, in the marginal spaces of a fourteenth-century Italian manuscript of the *Commedia* in its original language. We know that Santillana was the owner because there are annotations in his own hand; these include several corrections of the translated version.[1]

Why Villena should have presented it to him in this rough state is less clear—especially since in his *Aeneid* commentary he cites several Dantean passages in forms which differ from the translation here. Pascual and Lacuesta suggest, credibly enough, that the work may have been farmed out to some collaborator to get it done on time. Such a need for haste would cast some doubt on Torres Alcalá's view that Íñigo López wanted the translation for the benefit of other readers of Dante, being himself well able to read the original. It is true that he knew enough Italian to check out certain errors. It is even true that he was responsive to the musical qualities of Italian verse, as well as to its lofty themes and ingenious invention. But our main direct evidence for that dates from some twenty years on, when he wrote his *Prohemio e carta* for Pedro of Portugal.[2] Of the young Íñigo López, in or around the year 1428, we might form a rather different picture. Eager to work his way through Dante's poem but wanting the support, half practical, half moral, of a comprehensive Castilian crib, he presses his literary guru to supply one, in spite of other occupation, and launches on his reading, confident that he can at least "know what Dante says"—in which, eventually, he finds himself at various points in error. His is a way of reading which we, with our sharper notions of what it is to know languages, would not encourage in our students. But to judge from the *Infierno de los enamorados* (composed,

1   For the style of the translation see J. A. Pascual, *La traducción de la "Divina Commedia"*, pp. 67–205 (conclusions on pp. 204–05); also A. Torres Alcalá, *Don Enrique de Villena: un mago al dintel del Renacimiento* (Madrid, Porrúa Turanzas, 1983), pp. 110–13.

2   See Marqués de Santillana [Íñigo López de Mendoza], "Prohemio e carta qu'el Marqués de Santillana enbió al Condestable de Portugal", in his *Poesías completas*, edited by M. Á. Pérez Priego, 2 vols (Madrid, Alhambra, 1983–91), ii, 236; A. Torres Alcalá, *Don Enrique de Villena*, p. 113; contrast J.□A.□Pascual and R. Santiago Lacuesta, "La primera traducción castellana", p. 402.

probably, between 1428 and Villena's death in 1434) it did Íñigo López little harm.

The *Hell of Lovers* consists of 68 (in some versions 67) eight-line stanzas and a four-line *envoi*, in octosyllabic verse: 548 (or 540) lines in all.[1] Along with the *Triunphete de Amor* and the *Sueño*, it forms part of a group of relatively short allegorical pieces on amatory themes. It is widely agreed that the much shorter *Triunphete* was written first, and there is a growing consensus that the *Sueño* was the last to be composed. In thematic terms, however, either of these two might logically precede the *Infierno*, since both tell the story of a man falling in love, while the other poem is about how he gets out again. And although there is no continuity between the narratives, there is in either case a strong sense that we are dealing with a companion-piece to the *Infierno*. The *Triunphete* is linked with that poem through the Italian reference of both titles: a mini-Petrarchan item, and a miniaturized Dante. The *Sueño*, of just 540 lines, parallels the *Infierno* in its length. Alan Deyermond's notion that the sequence *Triunphete–Infierno* was composed first (and in that order), but that the *Sueño* was produced later to give a more mature and balanced pairing, would make good sense.[2] But our present concern is with the *Infierno,* and with what Íñigo López does with Dante. Most of all, it is with his appropriation of elements from Dante's infernal Circle of the Lustful in order to show why lovers ought to turn away from love.

---

1   All references here are to the critical text established by M. Á. Pérez Priego (Marqués de Santillana, *Poesías completas*, I, 225–58) and reproduced in *Cancionero de Estúñiga*, edited by N. Salvador Miguel (Madrid, Alhambra, 1987), pp. 201–33. Also well worth consulting is Marqués de Santillana, *Comedieta de Ponza, sonetos, serranillas y otras obras*, edited by R. Rohland de Langbehn (Barcelona, Crítica, 1997), whose careful textual editing (pp. 75–98 and 265–68) is supplemented by many detailed notes on the parallels with Dante (pp. 312–20). Rohland de Langbehn believes that the *Infierno* underwent final revisions in the 1450s, when Íñigo López presented a copy of his poems to Gómez Manrique (pp. lxxx–lxxxi and 312).

2   A. D. Deyermond, "Santillana's Love-allegories: Structure, Relation and Message", in *Studies in Honor of Bruce W. Wardropper*, edited by D. Fox, H. Sieber and R. Ter Horst (Newark, Del., Juan de la Cuesta, 1989), pp. 75–90 (pp. 86–87); and see pp. 75–77 for relations between the three poems, as interpreted by C. R. Post, *Medieval Spanish Allegory*, p. 212, R. Lapesa, *La obra literaria del Marqués de Santillana*, pp. 111–13 and R. Langbehn-Rohland, "Problemas de texto y problemas constructivos en algunos poemas de Santillana: la *Visión*, el *Infierno de los enamorados*, el *Sueño*", *Filología*, 17–18 (1976–77), 414–31 (p. 430).

There is, as it happens, more of Dante in the poem than that. The narrator wanders at the outset in a wild wood, is attacked by a monstrous creature symbolizing lust (in this case a wild boar), is rescued by a supernatural guide (not Virgil here but Hippolytus), and enters the "fearsome castle" of the lovers' inferno (very like the Dantean City of Dis), pausing to read the inscription over the gate. Some details here—such as the simile of the ranging hawk (Stanza 9), which may come from *Purgatorio*, xix. 61–64—were simply available for use in giving the poem's main events their setting and status. Other elements are more essential to what Íñigo López's poem is doing. But the core of his indebtedness to Dante has to do with the dissuasive thrust which this inferno-in-little shares with *Inferno* v: the turning-aside of lovers from love through being made witness in quite specific ways to the suffering which love brings.

At first sight nothing in medieval culture could appear more commonplace. In the most influential of medieval literary traditions concerning love, suffering is diagnostically what the lover does: in Patrick Gallagher's phrase "the more he loves, the more he suffers."[1] That suffering may stem from desire unattainable, or merely from desire unassuaged; in either context we are left with the paradox of suffering itself being identified and pursued as a good. Further, a great many lovers were deemed due to suffer in another sense: as sinners under divine judgement. That condemnation of earthly love could operate at various levels of insight. At its crudest it could rest its case on the fact that lust and various related matters were forbidden. More reflective treatments stress how sexual transgression brings other misdeeds in its train, as confirmed in many *exempla* and in much day-to-day experience. The most searching accounts of all are those which find lovers at fault because of their aberrant notions of the good—their failure to identify and seek out that heavenly balance between *res* and *desiderium* which Peter Abelard had hymned in his enforced tranquillity. Thus for Aquinas *luxuria* is characterized as submergence and disorder of the reason; and Dante follows in this line when he describes the lustful as those "che la ragion sommettono al talento" ["who subject reason to desire"; *Inferno*, v. 39].[2] That

1   P. Gallagher, *The Life and Works of Garci Sánchez de Badajoz* (London, Tamesis, 1968), p. 285.
2   Translated portions of the *Commedia* are from Dante, *The Divine Comedy*, translated by J. D. Sinclair (London, Oxford University Press, 1971). Compare

submission, it could be argued, was its own punishment: the suffering which lovers perversely embraced was, if unrepented, their fate for ever.

Not even that argument, though, could wholly close off other authoritative ways of thinking about love, some of which still offered lovers plausible defences for their commitment to desire. Medieval science and medicine, for example, saw love as a sickness, rooted in temperament and planetary influences.[1] Appealing to such deterministic schemes was a common defensive move, though not, as it happens, prominent in Dante. The case is very different with that poetic tradition which presented the lover's desire and suffering as the outcome and expression of a personal fatality. That claim was bound to resonate in the work of a poet who was himself engaged in reinterpreting his own lover's progress as a spiritual destiny. Nor could any totalizing account of human life and its last ends (such as the *Commedia* aspires to be) ignore the fact that the generative impulse acted out in physical passion was integral to the continuance of the created world. And this fact seemed closely related to the love of God as creator. Their closeness, indeed, was inescapably attested by language itself: it was no accident that the term *amor* and others like it extended so amply across both domains. Divine charity and the act of natural love, the philosophers acknowledged, were of the same *species specialissima*.[2]

For some readers then (like the Catalan translator quoted above) and for some readers now, what matters about Dante is the comprehensive arraying of a system of rules, defining how all these matters, and all these persons, fare under the judgements of

T. McDermott, *St Thomas Aquinas, Summa Theologiae: A Concise Translation* (London, Eyre and Spottiswoode, 1989), pp. 432–43 (*Secunda Secundae*, q.□155); also*The Oxford Book of Medieval Latin Verse*, edited by F. J. E. Raby (Oxford, Clarendon Press, 1959), p. 244, no. 169 (Peter Abelard, "Saturday at Vespers").

1 See the views cited by K. Whinnom in his edition of Diego de San Pedro, *Obras completas*, II: *Cárcel de Amor* (Madrid, Castalia, 1985), pp. 13–16; also the summary and refutation of deterministic arguments in Books III and IV of Alfonso Martínez de Toledo, *Arcipreste de Talavera o Corbacho*, edited by E.□M. Gerli (Madrid, Cátedra, 1979).

2 William of Auxerre, *Summa*, I, ii, tr. 1, cap. 6, quoted by P. Rousselot, "Pour l'Histoire du problème de l'amour au Moyen Age", in *Beiträge zur Geschichte der Philosophie und Theologie des Mittelalters*, 6, vi (1908), p. 92. Compare Peter of Poitiers, *Sententiae*: "Diligere aequivoce dicitur de naturali dilectione et de caritate" (P. Rousselot, "Pour l'Histoire du problème de l'amour", p. 91).

God. Others have found more interest in the equivalences and distinctions which have to be built into any such overview—the way in which the sin itself is identified with the sinner's burden of punishment: the contrast between love as a once-for-all captivity and love as a stage in spiritual liberation. The former reading gives us a Dante within the traditions of sermon and confession manual; the latter, a Dante after the pattern of Aquinas. But neither fully covers his achievement as a poet. More than the assurance of an authority which overrides contradictions, more even than the intellectual rigour which can chart and handle them, that achievement involves the capacity to imagine and project them as realities, unattenuated by their rejection at the level of doctrine.

That this happens in Canto v of *Inferno* is hardly news. Yet it may be worth looking briefly at how it comes to happen. The parley with Minos at the entrance to the Second Circle need not detain us here. Once admitted, Dante observes how the souls of the lustful are blown about by ceaseless winds; he learns the nature of their sin, and has several of them pointed out to him by Virgil—all this in lines 25–69. In the second half of the canto he speaks with Francesca da Rimini. His pity for her grows as she tells her tale; as she nears its end, with Paolo her lover beside her wordlessly weeping, Dante faints away. There is a structural pattern here which recurs time and again in the *Commedia*, alternating Dante as witness to the fate of souls and Dante in dialogue with a soul so fated; objective exemplarity and human involvement; static spectacle and dynamic relationship; alienation and immersion. The pattern is basic to the depth and narrative authority of the poem and to that capacity for meaning to which later writers paid the tribute of imitation. But the local effect to which it works here needs to be explored further.

Its primary didactic impact is, of course, to show the punishment of lust, both through what the lovers suffer in themselves and through the torment decreed for them. In terms of intellectual analysis, the episode balances two definitions: what their passion is, and what it seems to them to be. Theologically it is *luxuria*: reason subjugated to desire, or (as examples like Dido's suicide and Semiramis's incest show) desire subverting the moral law. Paolo and Francesca, by contrast, define it as *amor*. Yet Francesca's own narrative glosses that term in ways which underwrite the lovers' condemnation. This is love as fateful external compulsion:

"Amor, ch' al cor gentil ratto s'apprende" ["Love, which is quickly kindled in the gentle heart"; *Inferno*, v. 100], "Amor, ch' a nullo amato amar perdona" ["Love, which absolves no one beloved from loving"; 103], love that "condusse noi ad una morte" ["brought us to one death"; 106]. That impression is elaborated in cultural reference—"di Lancialotto come amor lo strinse" ["of Lancelot, how love constrained him"; 128]—and in remembered experience—"sanza alcun sospetto" ["no misgiving"; 129], "solo un punto fu" ["but one point alone it was"; 132], "Galeotto fu 'l libro" ["A Galeotto was the book"; 137]. The self-exculpatory note is sounded clearly enough to create a sense that Francesca protests rather too much. Her absolutist bonding to the past, whether to pleasure that "ancor non m'abbandona" ["does not leave me yet"; 105], or to pain—"e 'l modo ancor m'offende" ["and the manner afflicts me still"; 102]—carries an element of rather chilling automatism. Paolo is engrafted in it for ever—"questi, che mai da me non fia diviso" ["he who never shall be parted from me"; 135]—yet not once in all these lines does she call him by his name. Both definitions of what is going on, then, expose reasons for the damnation of this pair. Intellectually Dante must acknowledge those reasons, whether as witness of the lovers' torment or as the compassionate inter-locutor of their experience. Emotionally, though, when Paolo's cries break in upon this second perspective, returning the poet (and the reader) to the role of witness, Dante finds the clash between sympathy and objective insight too painful to be borne. His fainting fit, however, is transparently a touch of human weakness; we have to recall that he has not been on his spiritual journey for very long. The inescapable truth, for him and his readers as for Paolo and Francesca, is that reason has to prevail over passion.

Or so, at least, one powerful tradition would have us read Dante—and as a paraphrase of what Dante might have believed about these matters it might not be wide of the mark. As a reading of the poem which he wrote it clearly falls short. Both the theological definition of *luxuria* and the sinners' definition of *amor* represent them as surrendering rational choice, and if that is enough to condemn them they must stand condemned. But a poem devised to vindicate that heavy-handed proposition need not have gone about it in this way. It could have avoided questions with which Dante engages to the point of perplexity and even of distress. As to whether that surrender of choice is a willing act—and therefore culpable—he would clearly have to answer that it is. Yet the evidence offered for that view is largely indirect. First, Dante simply assumes that it must be so; secondly, several of the exemplary figures break other laws to which their moral assent can legitimately be taken for granted; finally, there are the suspect nuances of Francesca's story, previously detailed. The evidence against an entirely willing culpability, even when due allowance has been made for those nuances, is far more direct: to the lovers it does not feel like a voluntary surrender. Perhaps they are wrong about that. But to understand how they are wrong we need to know more about the compulsion which they experience (or believe they experience). And here, just where the didactic intention would demand clear and simple answers, Dante seems bent on making the answers complex.

The first clue, obviously, is the nature of the lovers' punishment, the primary image of their sin, further elaborated in various subsidiary images. They are driven to and fro by winds, like flocks of birds—starlings, cranes, doves—in an arbitrary, rootless vitality. Sometimes the force that drives them is described in wholly negative terms. It is a wind of Hell: "l'aura nera" ["the black air"; *Inferno*, v. 51], "l'aere maligno" ["the malignant air"; 86]. But when Paolo and Francesca alight like doves "per l'aere, dal voler portate" (84), are they "borne through the air *by desire*", that is, by their own desire, voluntarily? Or are they "borne along by the wind *of desire*", that is, by an impersonal, external force? The ambiguity hangs on a breath. And what of "quello amor che i mena" (78), by whose power Virgil advises Dante to call the pair of them down? Is "that love which leads them on" their own profane love—an odd invocation for Dante's guide to propose? Or is it the divine love which ordains their punishment—an even odder basis for an appeal to the lovers themselves? For a moment we glimpse the possible notion of a love divinely ordained *as compulsive desire*—a deeply problematic concept. Prudently Dante falls back on a negative variant of the "divine love" option: "s'altri nol niega" ["if One forbids it not"; 81]. Yet it still seems to be conceded that what impels them is something called *amor*, even though this is also the name of the power under which they are condemned. The nomenclature is not perverse: the witness of language itself was seen as confirming that a link existed.

Yet the link is not being set out here in the obvious didactic fashion, with supernatural love ordaining natural and unambiguously marking off those forms of the natural not endorsed by its ordinance. Rather, Dante predicates a complex, unseizable relationship, well illustrated by his comparison of the condemned souls in their flight with flocks of starlings in winter. Sexual desire, divinely instituted as part of the natural order, was a force for generation and renewal, the animal counterpart of the natural fertility of land and crops. The image of seed scattered on the land has, as it were, a visual echo in that of birds wheeling in flocks against the sky. But as every medieval farmer knew, starlings were no help to the processes of natural fertility. Though themselves *in* nature, they were despoilers of grain. Nor is the "freddo tempo" ["the cold season"; *Inferno*, v. 41] the season of harvest. Desire thus imaged is somehow made to seem sterile, even perverse; yet it is still implicated in the natural order.

It is also—and very evidently—implicated in the cultural world of Dante's poem. What first evokes his pity is Virgil's mention of "le donne antiche e' cavalieri" ["the knights and ladies of old times"; *Inferno*, v. 71], the protagonists of classical and chivalric legend. His reading of Paolo and Francesca's experience is defined by the motifs of love poetry. Both he and they can recognize and share its specific terminology: "dolci pensier" ["sweet thoughts"; 113], the "doloroso passo" ["the woeful pass"; 114], the "tempo d'i dolci sospiri" ["the time of your sweet sighing"; 118]. The Lancelot and Galleot references are quite literally "taken as read". And the uniquely authoritative Virgil is no less implicated with the notion of love as overmastering desire. The Dido of *Aeneid* IV, it is true, has her place among the warning *exempla* because of her suicide (and, less convincingly, her infidelity to her first husband's ashes). The two Italian lovers themselves are part of the "schiera ov' è Dido" ["the troop where Dido is"; 85]. Yet missing from the poem here is that other Dido, whom Dante could not possibly have forgotten because it is in the Underworld that Aeneas in Book VI meets her again: silent, downcast, enigmatic, unmoved by his torrent of self-reproach and self-justification, and gliding away at last to join her first love among the shades.[1] But

---

1   Virgil, *Aeneid*, VI. 450–75.

when Francesca adds, after the famous lines on the pain of recalling happiness in time of sorrow, "e ciò sa 'l tuo dottore" ["and this thy teacher knows"; 123], it is surely this image of the Virgilian lovers that she has in mind. "Dottore" or not, Virgil too knows the potency of desire and loss.

Lastly, as so often in medieval writing about love, the implications extend to religion itself. They do so most obviously through the overlapping of language. Dante calls Francesca's sufferings "i tuoi martíri" (*Inferno*, v. 116; translated by Sinclair as "thy torments", but with clear overtones of "martyrdom"); the grief which they evoke in him is "tristo e pio" (117). "Pio", of course, might mean no more than "compassionate", were it not that Virgil, of all people, is standing by; as it is, the idea of a compassion rooted in sacred duty is inescapably evoked. We should not perhaps press such points: these lines are, of their nature, tenuous, ambiguous. We can scarcely know whether the doves to which Paolo and Francesca are compared (82) hint at a somehow surviving innocence, or whether they are merely Venus's doves. Always we must remind ourselves that these lovers, though in the uppermost circle of the damned, are still damned. Yet they seem able to respond to Dante's pity, and would, they tell him, pray for him if God would only hear them (91–92).

Prayer in an "if only" mode may seem a slight enough thing. But it is one more sign that Dante's sympathy is no mere matter of his being emotionally implicated with the lovers—an aesthetically appealing frailty which the stern logic of his poem has to deny. Rather, he writes into his account a sense of being implicated with them and with their experience of desire, naturally, culturally, linguistically and even religiously. He draws his readers too into that same state of being implicated—a paradoxical state because in the last of these contexts the *amor* which is postulated here still stands condemned. We can get around this if we want to. We can decode all the religious items as "accommodated" rhetorical uses. We can assign these, along with all the other involvements, to the natural order, against which we can then assert the primacy of a supernatural justice. But that would be to brush aside the notion that the God who ordains this justice is himself implicated in the natural. It is not a notion which Dante was disposed to brush aside: that is why the *Commedia* has three *cantiche*, not one. For the moment the fullness of that vision is not accessible. But the poet keeps better faith with it by presenting the torments that are sought and found by desire as unbearable paradox, rather than as a too glibly imagined equity.

Íñigo López's poem is in both scale and scope far smaller than the *Commedia*. That cannot be a matter for reproach, but it does have one unavoidable consequence. There is here no grand overarching design in whose light we might expect to reinterpret and extend the poem's given and immediate meanings. Any such enlargement of meaning will have to come from assumed frames of reference somewhere beyond the poem itself. Two such frames, fairly obviously, are taken for granted here. One is the set of assumptions made in the kind of writing about love to which we refer in a general way as "courtly". In Íñigo López's Castile these were enjoying a renewed currency in what Roger Boase calls "the troubadour revival".[1] The other frame is a relatively unanalysed moral asceticism, whose precepts and examples derive from Christian and classical ethical teaching. Elements broadly parallel to these two frames are, of course, part of the internal synthesis which governs Dante's poem. But this lesser derivative has no such governing synthesis. Conflict between its external frames of reference has to be dealt with locally within the poem; otherwise it must stand as contradiction. To an extent, then, a poem such as the *Infierno de los enamorados* was bound to be both more conventional and more prone to contradiction than its great original. But these things are the conditions of its making, not the marks of its inadequacy. They do not mean that in appropriating Dantean structures and motifs it trivializes Dante.

Certainly the theme of the suffering associated with love, though self-limited, was far from trivial. Its treatment at this length—roughly that of three Dantean cantos—still seems economical rather than inflated, especially given its episodic storyline. The poet tells how Fortune led him into a wild region, inhabited by terrifying beasts and monsters, where he was compelled to pass the night; next day he was attacked by a prodigious wild boar. The narrative line of these preliminaries is interrupted now and then by elaborate stanza-length similes, and by items of self-commentary: an invocation to the Muses, a declared

---

1   R. Boase, *The Troubadour Revival: A Study of Social Change and Traditionalism in Late Medieval Spain* (London, Routledge and Kegan Paul, 1978); see especially pp. 89 and 142–45 for the active collaboration in this area between Íñigo López and Enrique de Villena.

preference for plain truth over poetic elaboration, a pledge to keep description brief, a doubt as to whether the monstrous boar can be described at all. Even so, this opening section is over by Stanza 18. In Stanzas 19 to 41 a new character appears: a handsome young hunter, coming to the poet's rescue. Their dialogue establishes that this courteous stranger does not share the narrator's allegiance to love. He is in fact Hippolytus, permitted by the gods (along with others who have died for chastity's sake) to enjoy for all eternity the innocent delights of the chase. "How good it would be," Hippolytus urges, "if you were to follow in my way!":

> por ver en qué trabajades
> e la gloria qu'esperades
> en vuestra postrimería.
> (*Infierno de los enamorados*, 40)

[to see what it is that you strive for, and what glory you may expect in the end.]

Suppressing his fears and still protesting his commitment to love, the narrator follows him to the place where lovers are tormented.

From Stanza 42 to the end, the Lovers' Hell itself is the focus of attention: first, eleven stanzas of approach and general description; then the spectacle of various doomed lovers in their torment; finally a dialogue between the narrator and the Galician troubadour Macías. The latter speaks a version of Francesca's "Nessun maggior dolore" ["There is no greater pain than to recall the happy time in misery"; 121] and warns that his is the kind of punishment a lover may expect. The poet offers a prayer for him and turns away, to find that his guide, Hippolytus, has vanished. He himself is borne off—"bien como Ganimedes / al çielo fue arrebatado" ["as Ganymede was borne away to heaven"; Stanza 68]—, presumably back to his former life. But he is cured of love.

This order of business seems typical of a medium-length late medieval allegory, the kind of pattern which A. C. Spearing, for example, finds characteristic of many English poems of that period.[1] One episode opens out discursively from another, with little overtly governing architecture. The introductory matter (the wild wood and Hippolytus) is over half as long again (41 stanzas) as the

---

1   A. C. Spearing, *Criticism and Medieval Poetry* (London, Arnold, 1964), p. 24.

Infierno proper (a mere 25 or perhaps 27, depending on where one marks off the conclusion). Differing structural analyses seem almost equally valid. Alan Deyermond identifies six episodes; Regula Langbehn-Rohland sees the preliminaries as ending with Hippolytus's long speech at Stanza 36, then a bridge passage of dialogue, and finally the main motif.[1] It would also be possible to propose a more strictly bipartite scheme, as follows:

> A. *Outer allegory*:
> (i) approach and terrors (Stanzas 1–18)
> (ii) exemplary figure: Hippolytus (Stanzas 19–36)
> (iii) dialogue with Hippolytus (Stanzas 37–41)
> B. *Inner allegory*:
> (i) approach and terrors (Stanzas 42–52)
> (ii) exemplary figures: various (Stanzas 53–58)
> (iii) dialogue with Macías (Stanzas 59–66)
> *Conclusion*:
> the poet cured (Stanzas 67–79).

This would suggest a fuller and more purposive appropriation of Dantean structures than might at first be apparent. The central borrowing, of course, is that alternation of witness and involvement, *exemplum* and dialogue, which in canto after canto builds up the depth and complexity of Dante's vision. Here it is applied to a single topic in direct reminiscence of a single canto. But here, as in the *Commedia*, the episode thus structured is inserted into the larger story, itself allegorical, of the poet's progress from distressful confusion towards enlightenment and calm. Not only does a vestigial fragment of that story—B(i) in this scheme—serve as an immediate prologue to the particular vision of judgement; it is also elaborated at the beginning—A(i)–(iii) here—as an outer dimension of the allegory. Here once again the Dantean borrowings are plain to see: the night spent asleep in the wild, the attack by a wild beast at dawn, the supernatural rescuer who becomes a guide. There is thus a double parallel with *Inferno* v: not just in its own right but in the context created by *Inferno* i–ii.

Between the inner and the outer allegories there is also an obviously parallel array of didactic functions. This too goes back to Dante. At both these levels, in Íñigo López's poem as in the

---

1   A. D. Deyermond, "Santillana's Love-allegories", pp. 83–84; R. Langbehn-Rohland, "Problemas de texto", pp. 420–21.

Commedia, the poet is first instructed by the sheer force of what he sees, by terrors that constrain the will. Next comes the encounter with one or more exemplary figures, awakening and challenging the cultural memory. Finally, involvement in dialogue with such a figure engages the understanding; one recalls, relevantly, the dialectical basis of much medieval education. The accepted psychological theory of the time, of course, saw these three—will, memory, intellect—as the three faculties of the soul.[1] In making his response to the way in which such thinking had shaped Dante's poetic construction, Íñigo López also identified Dante's priorities as his own. For it was not at all obligatory that the three *potencias* should be ranged in this purposive, ascending hierarchy. The Archpriest of Hita, for example, had offered quite a different scheme with good understanding informing good will and the memory of God's law. Íñigo López's preference marks an important cultural shift towards a heightened intellectualism. In this he clearly had other mentors—Enrique de Villena for one. But Dante was unmistakably a model.

There is evidence of this in the elaboration of the outer allegory (as also in the introductory phase of the visit to the Lovers' Hell itself). Time and again, invocation and self-commentary dwell on the sheer difficulty of getting the rhetoric right:

> e yo non pinto ni gloso
> silogismos de poetas,
> mas siguiendo líneas rectas,
> fablaré non infintoso;
>> (*Infierno de los enamorados*, 2)

[and I do not present or gloss complex poetic arguments, but I will speak unambiguously, following straight lines;]

> fablar inmenso
> va contra las conclusiones;
>> (*Infierno de los enamorados*, 6)

[to speak disproportionately can vitiate one's conclusions;]

---

1   See Arcipreste de Hita [Juan Ruiz], *Libro de Buen Amor*, edited by G.□B.□Gybbon-Monypenny (Madrid, Castalia, 1988), pp. 104–11, especially p. 105 and references there to St Augustine, *De Trinitate*; also J. A. Chapman, "Juan Ruiz's Learned Sermon", in *"Libro de Buen Amor" Studies*, edited by G.□B.□Gybbon-Monypenny (London, Tamesis, 1970), pp. 29–51.

¿Quién es que metrificando
en coplas nin distinçiones,
en prosas nin consonando
tales diformes visiones,
sin multitud de renglones,
el su fecho dezir puede?
(*Infierno de los enamorados*, 13)

[Who can present the fact of such bizarre visions in rhythmic
poetry or subtle argument, in narrative or rhyme, without going
on at great length?]

Señor, al caso presente
tú me influye poesía,
por que narre sin falsía
lo que vi discretamente.
(*Infierno de los enamorados*, 52)

[Lord, inspire me with poetry to meet this present case, so that
I may tell truthfully what I saw with understanding.]

One senses that the poet's need for enlightenment takes a
double form: he needs to learn how not to be a slave to love, and
how to be a different kind of poet. Indeed the two went together:
both aspirations were directed towards new forms of seriousness.
To go on for ever within the conventions of the revived fashion for
courtly love rhetoric—an inexhaustible game with an indefensibly
contradictory moral basis—predicated a kind of poetry which
Íñigo López could handle with ease, but which by the 1430s no
longer satisfied him. The awareness of love as problematic not just
in itself but beyond itself demanded a new range of expressive
resource. He found it in Dante. The theme of deliverance from the
power of desire—figured allegorically in Hippolytus's killing of
the boar and fictionally in the story's end—is matched by the
theme of liberation into a less restricted poetic idiom, which the
Infierno as a whole embodies.

Again this achievement has its limits. As Julian Weiss observes,
"Dante is able to resolve his predicament in a much more radical
way than Santillana: he does not reject [...] his earlier poetry [...]:
he simply reinterprets it."[1] The Dante of the *Commedia* reinterprets

---

1   J. Weiss, *The Poet's Art: Literary Theory in Castile c.1400–60* (Oxford, Society
for the Study of Medieval Languages and Literature, 1990), p. 168.

his previous work—indeed, rewrites his own life—in a new and greatly extended array of meanings. Íñigo López achieves a convincing palinode (a thing not unknown within the traditions of courtly verse) and a new poetic manner. Underlying the relative modesty of these feats there is an evident contrast in quality of mind, at the level, at least, of abstract conceptual thought. Set beside Dante's moral theology, Íñigo López's formulations of what is wrong with love look simplistic. "El que por Venus se guía / venga penar su pecado" runs the inscription over Hell-gate ["He who takes Venus as his guide, let him come here to suffer for his sin"; Stanza 47]; "digas que fui condenado / por seguir d'Amor sus vías" is Macías's farewell word ["say that I was damned for following the ways of Love"; Stanza 64]. And the poet himself concludes: "ni sé tal que no se aparte, / si non es loco provado" ["and I know of no one who would not leave off loving, unless stark mad"; Stanza 69]. Hippolytus's warning, already quoted, is no more informative than these. It all amounts to little more than the *a priori* assertion that lovers are liable to come to a bad end.

Yet we should not confuse this conventionality of ideas with an incapacity to grasp in an imaginative way what the Dantean mode made it possible to express. The theme of desire and fate is quite differently focused, of course. Íñigo López concentrates less on the inwardness of the lovers' experience and more on the change in one man's attitude towards that theme. He prefers diachronic narrative example to synchronic psychological insight. There is even evidence that this was the way in which he himself read Dante: one of his main reasons for admiring Italian poets was, precisely, their use of "fermosas e peregrinas istorias" ["rare and beautiful stories"].[1] But if in our own time we read Dante with an opposite preference, that is not a reason for seeing Íñigo López's response as obtuse. In fact his handling of the "love and fortune" topic has subtleties of its own.

At the outset the poet describes himself as carried off into the wilderness by "La Fortuna que no çessa, / siguiendo el curso fadado" ["Fortune who never ceases to follow her fated course"; Stanza 1]. His free will has been wholly taken away. Again in Stanza 7, "ventura, / contra razón e mesura, / me levó do non quería" ["luck, against reason and restraint, carried me where I

1   "Prohemio e carta", in *Poesías completas*, II, 236.

had no wish to go"]. He is like a wind-tossed ship whose "muchos movimientos" ["many motions"; Stanza 8] may be those of his own thought, but also recall the technical term for the shifts of the planets in their courses. And since the wild place into which he is thus transported is in fact the place of his own unbridled lusts (the wild boar), we are led to suppose that he sees his enslavement to desire as brought about by uncontrollable fate. It is the old error of the Dantean lovers, and it is swiftly called in question by the encounter with Hippolytus. Now we hear the narrator assert something new: Fortune has brought him here, still against his will, in order to challenge his commitment to love, so that he will believe "que amar es desesperança" ["that loving is despair"; Stanza 38]. But in this, he insists,

> es bien engañada,
> si piensa por tal razón
> que yo fiziesse morada
> do non es mi entinçion,
> ca de cuerpo e coraçón
> me soy dado por sirviente
> a quien dixe que non siente
> mi cuidado e perdiçión.
> (*Infierno de los enamorados*, 39)

[she is greatly deceived, if she thinks that for such a reason I would settle contrary to my intent, for I have given myself over, body and soul, to serve one who, as I have said, feels nothing for my sorrow or for my ruin.]

This is to admit, unwittingly, two things: first that what binds him to love is not fate at all but his own stubborn intention—he confirms this again in Stanza 41, in speaking of "Amor, a quien me soy dado" ["Love, to whom I have given myself"]—; and secondly that love is despair after all. In this light other passages begin to look less simplistic. The grim warning to lovers inscribed above the gate, if read (as it probably should be) with the Dantean "Abandon every hope" as its subtext, confirms this central equation of *amar* with *desesperança*. And the testimony of Macías, whose "espantable/[...] fecho abominable" ["fearful (...) abominable plight"; Stanza 65] so sways the poet at the end, is very precisely an utterance of despair. Compared with much that is in Dante, these effects are still somehow rough-hewn. But they are not negligible, and they are very far from inept.

The kinship with Dante is still more recognizable in the way in which Íñigo López exploits disparate knowledges to achieve a coherent poetic effect. The most developed example involves the figure of Hippolytus. When the narrator courteously wishes the still unnamed stranger the same "plazer e buen galardón" ["pleasure and good reward"; Stanza 27] from the lady whom he loves as Jason received from his lady, anyone alert to the mytho-logical background, and remembering the later marital history of Jason and Medea, might have felt doubtful whether that was such a good thing. Íñigo López, who at about this date was getting to know Seneca's *Tragedies*, almost certainly did remember this; Íñigo López as narrator-protagonist does not.[1] He has forgotten—in a piece of negligence which typifies the condition of the lover—what it is his business to know. Worse still, it soon transpires that he is speaking to the grandson of King Aegeus of Athens, who in his dotage had been rather discreditably enamoured of Medea. So his obsession with love has led him into a piece of gross dis-courtesy—a breach of those very conventions of courtly behaviour which count for so much in this part of the poem. This in its turn brings in a second variety of knowledge: the training appropriate for a gentleman and a courtier. In the encounter with Hippolytus this knowledge is both taken for granted—as Íñigo López could expect his intended readership to take it—and subjected to revision in a way which could well have surprised them.

For Hippolytus turns out to have all the attributes of courtly perfection save one. He is handsome, dressed in high fashion "a guisa d'ombr' entendido" ["like a man of good understanding"; Stanza 20]—an equation which fashionable elites are all too apt to make, but in this case true. He is a bold and skilful huntsman. He anticipates the narrator's courtesy, sweeping off his most un-classical hat; he ignores the gaffe over Medea. He responds to the other's naïve curiosity as to why he is not a lover by gently instructing him in the rules of politeness; he thinks carefully before speaking. One important factor in the narrator's agreeing to go with him to see the Lovers' Hell is a sense that it would be churlish

---

1   For translations of Seneca's *Medea* likely to have been known to Íñigo López see N. G. Round, "Las traducciones medievales, catalanas y castellanas de las *Tragedias* de Séneca", *Anuario de Estudios Medievales*, 9 (1974–79), 187–227 (pp. 190–93). The story of Medea and Aegeus was available to him in Ovid, *Metamorphoses*, VII. 402ff.

to refuse a request from someone like this. Yet this paragon of courtliness has no time for love: "vista por mí su falsía, / me guardé de ser burlado" ["once I had seen its falsehood, I took good care not to be deceived"; Stanza 28]. In conventional courtly terms this is blasphemy, and in some of our texts the narrator actually uses the word *blasfemar* (Stanza 29) to describe it.[1] Yet the narrator is the one who repeatedly fails the tests of courtly behaviour, found wanting not only in civility but also in courage. As they near the Lovers' Hell, his feelings are those of a cowardly soldier at a siege—a disgraceful comparison, made worse by the fact that he lets those feelings show. And if Hippolytus's reproof is at first kindly in tone—"ardimiento non fallesca" ["let not your courage fail you"; Stanza 45]—he is soon telling him to set aside "toda vil covardía" ["all base cowardice"; Stanza 46]. "Vil" was the mark of the *villano*; the abject status of the slave to love could not be put in harsher terms. Notionally this kind of revision of values and its allegorical framing still lay within the poetic range of courtly tradition and of French modes of allegory. But the means of achieving it here, through an interaction of knowledges, brings us back to Dante as the precedent which mattered.

The poem's most decisively Dantean aspect, however, is still the clear appropriation of elements from *Inferno* v in its depiction of the erotic Hell proper. Here too, paradoxically, the differences from Dante are most in evidence. But to experience these primarily as disappointments (as Lapesa and others tend to do) is to miss the creative working of Dante's influence in this lesser poet. The array of exemplary figures, for example, certainly differs from his. Dante had named and briefly characterized eight guilty lovers. Íñigo López, after an apparent disclaimer of his Dantean model—"Non vimos al can Çervero, / a Minus nin a Plutón" ["We did not see the dog Cerberus or Minos or Pluto"; Stanza 53]—, lists twenty-eight persons whom he did see. They include all those named by Dante except Cleopatra and Tristan; the others come mainly from Ovid's *Heroides*. But the whole series amounts to little more than a catalogue: it would be hard nowadays—certainly harder than with the equivalent passage in the *Commedia*—to read these lines

---

1   See also Stanza 29 here: "¿Qu'es aquesto que vos faze/tan sueltamente d'amor/blasfemar, e así vos plaze?" The *Cancionero de Estúñiga* version, however, reads: "tan rotamente de amor/dezir esto que uos plaze", stressing, less boldly, Hippolytus's freedom to speak as he pleases about love (p. 214).

as poetry. In its day, though, such a commingling of authorities was a wholly valid mode of amplification. The more schematic the form of such lists, the more searchingly their content could challenge the memory, at least in that minority of readers who knew their Ovid, and that still tinier elite who knew their Dante. The esoteric reading—of Dante among others—which this restatement and amplification of his material implies has few attractions now. The poetry seems bleached of its emotional poignancy, its power reduced to a worn-down intellectual strenuousness. Yet to Íñigo López, whose version of the *Commedia* came from that paladin of the esoteric intellect, Enrique de Villena, it would not have seemed out of place to read Dante like that—which is not to say that he read him ineptly.

The treatment of Paolo and Francesca in this part of the poem certainly involves a simplification along the lines which all this implies:

> e la dona de Ravena,
> de que fabla el florentino,
> vimos con su amante digno
> de ser en tal pena puesto.
> (*Infierno de los enamorados*, 55)

[and we saw the lady from Ravenna, of whom the Florentine tells, along with her lover, deserving of such punishment.]

For Íñigo López these lovers, however appealing their history, were quite certainly guilty as charged, and their place among the damned was well deserved. Yet the further dimension which Dante brings to their portrayal was not lost on Íñigo López, and is not lost from his poem. It is, as we shall see, redeployed and re-created there, through distinctive though perhaps oblique poetic means. There is simplification too over the punishment of the lovers. Their torment by buffeting winds, whose symbolic rightness Dante so richly exploits, is altered beyond recognition. In the Spanish poem each sinner bears on the left breast a deep wound, from which issue flames. The Dantean equation between passion and punishment is still made, but in very conventional terms: the fire in the heart and the fire of eternal torment. It is not very close to anything elsewhere in Dante, not even to the punishment of heretics, condemned to lie in fiery coffins. Post's reference to "vague memories of the Ledge of Luxury in the *Purgatorio*" may be on the right track, however.[1] The penitent lustful there are certainly subjected to fire. It does not issue from their bodies, but a phrase in *Purgatorio* xxv—"nel seno / al grande ardore" ["in the heart of the great burning"; 121–22]—might have prompted Íñigo López's rather differently focused collocation of "breast / heart" and "fire". He had in any case some reason for looking to that section of the *Commedia*. His own dialogue with the damned was not going to involve Paolo and Francesca, here reduced to the ranks of merely illustrative *exempla*. Instead, as Dante does in *Purgatorio* xxvi with Guido Guinizzelli and Arnaut Daniel, he converses with a fellow poet.

The full name of Macías the Lover ("Macías el Enamorado") is one of many things about him which we do not know.[2] The language of several surviving poems (and of the refrains in several more) suggests that he was a Galician. The little that remains of his output seems to reflect the older traditions of Gallego-Portuguese love lyric, though his bold and at times blasphemous use of religious motifs brings him closer to his own time. He probably flourished just after 1400 and must in any case have died before Íñigo López wrote his poem. Legends describe (in various forms) a death at the hands of a jealous husband, a martyrdom for love. Macías, it seemed, had lived as reality much of the role-play which loomed so large in courtly literature. Or so it came to appear to later poets, for whom he was, in Otis Green's phrase, "hero, idol, martyr and saint". If a single recent figure was needed to focus the picture of what fate lay in store for lovers, Macías was a natural choice for Íñigo López here, as he was for Juan de Mena in the 1440s. In the longer cast-lists of similar poems by Juan de Andújar in the mid-century and Garci Sánchez de Badajoz many years later, Macías retains his place.[3] Another Galician, Juan Rodríguez del Padrón,

---

1 C. R. Post, *Medieval Spanish Allegory*, p. 84; compare *Purgatorio*, xxv. 112–25.

2 P. Gallagher, *The Life and Works of Garci Sánchez*, pp. 197–98, summarizes much of the material; useful details may be gleaned from N. Salvador Miguel, *La poesía cancioneril*, pp. 159, 178–79, 182 and 292; see also O. H. Green, *The Literary Mind of Medieval and Renaissance Spain* (Lexington, University Press of Kentucky, 1970), pp. 42–43 and 219.

3 For Mena's vision of Macías among the lovers in the Circle of Venus see Juan de Mena, *Laberinto de Fortuna, Poesías menores*, edited by M. Á. Pérez Priego (Madrid, Editora Nacional, 1976), pp. 98–100 (*Laberinto*, Stanzas 105–08); for Macías as the sole modern presence in the Lovers' Hell of Juan de Andújar's "Como procede Fortuna" see *Cancionero de Estúñiga*, p. 165; for his role as the

who was to fuse Macías's courtly extremism with Dantean elements
in the first of the Spanish sentimental romances, once wrote that he
would be willing, temporarily, to die "solo por uer a Macías / e de
amor me partir" ["only to see Macías, and to take my leave of
love"].[1] A rather late source offers another possible reason why
Íñigo López should have imitated this tradition by featuring
Macías here: he had served, it appears, in the household of Íñigo
López's Dantean mentor, Enrique de Villena.[2]

Verbal as well as structural echoes confirm the Dantean background of the Macías episode. The narrator addresses the doomed
lovers as "ánimas affanadas" ["wearied souls"; Stanza 59]—precisely the "anime affannate" of Dante (*Inferno*, v. 80). The much praised
rendering of the "Nessun maggior dolore" passage reveals Íñigo
López as working similarly close to the text:

> La mayor cuita que haver
> puede ningún amador
> es membrarse del plazer
> en el tiempo del dolor.
> (*Infierno de los enamorados*, 63)

[The greatest grief any lover can have is to remember pleasure in
the time of grief.]

The reference is narrowed, of course, to the *lover's* worst affliction.
But Íñigo López may well owe something more to a poem of
Macías's own.[3] Taking as its refrain Christ's cry of desolation from
the Cross—"Deus meus elli ely / E lama zabatany"—,[4] this brief
lover's complaint begins "Pues me falleçio ventura / en el tiempo

---

first of the tormented lovers in Garci Sánchez de Badajoz's "Caminando en
las honduras" see P. Gallagher, *The Life and Works of Garci Sánchez*, p. 98.

1   *Cancionero de Estúñiga*, p. 272. See B. F. Weissberger, "Authority Figures in
    Siervo libre de Amor and *Grisel y Mirabella*", in *Homenaje a Stephen Gilman* =
    Revista de Estudios Hispánicos, 9 (1982), 255–62 (pp. 256–58); also C. Martínez
    Barbeito, *Macías el enamorado y Juan Rodríguez del Padrón* (Santiago de
    Compostela, Bibliófilos Gallegos, 1951).

2   The statement appears in Hernán Núñez's commentary (1499) on Mena's
    Laberinto (edited by M. Á. Pérez Priego), p. 98.

3   *El Cancionero de Palacio*, edited by F. Vendrell de Millás (Barcelona, Consejo
    Superior de Investigaciones Científicas, 1945), p. 312 (no. 247).

4   Mark 15. 34: "Eloi, Eloi, lamma sabacthani? Which is, being interpreted, My
    God, my God, why hast thou forsaken me?"

de plazer" ["Since my luck left me in the time of pleasure"] and ends by declaring that anyone who knows of his sorrow will weep with him: "quanto mas si bien supiesse / el gran ben qu' eu perdi" ["the more so if they understand the great good I have lost"]. The kinship between what Francesca was saying and what Macías was saying could hardly be overlooked. Yet Íñigo López presents that common element in a manner which differs significantly from Dante.

Here is no humanly recalled evocation of the lovers' experience of loss, but instead a lucid intellectual analysis of Macías's suffering. That suffering goes beyond the fire, whether construed as desire or as the punishment for desire. Such things are pure pain. But there is more at work:

> E con la pena del fuego
> tristemente lamentavan,
> pero que tornavan luego
> e muy manso razonavan.
> (*Infierno de los enamorados*, 58)

[And they complained in their distress of the pain caused by the fire, but would then turn aside and talk quietly together.]

It is when Íñigo López enquires into the substance of that quiet speech that he learns of the loss that is worse than all:

> E sabe que nos tractamos
> de los bienes que perdimos
> e del gozo que passamos,
> mientra en el mundo bivimos,
> fasta tanto que venimos
> arder en aquesta llama,
> do non se curan de fama
> ni de las glorias que hovimos.
> (*Infierno de los enamorados*, 63)

[Know that we are talking about the good things we have lost, and the joy that we had while we lived in the world, before we came to burn in this fire, where reputation and the glory that we once enjoyed are of no account.]

The lovers' sorrow embraces everything that they have forfeited: their *gozo* (their satisfaction as lovers), their *glorias* (perhaps that

too, but much else besides), their *fama* or good name and all their
other lost *bienes*. Once the poet grasps the scale of this "espantable
[…] fecho abominable" ["fearful (…) abominable plight"; Stanza
65], his cure is assured. His "llaga incurable" ["incurable wound";
Stanza 65] is no longer love; it is his own reaction to the enormities
wrought by love. That reaction, essentially, is one of pity and
terror. And here another departure from Dante becomes relevant.
Francesca identifies herself as soon as she begins to speak; Macías
does not reveal his name until the very end of his lament. Up to that
point readers would have been aware of a nameless Spaniard,
reduced to terminal despair through his enslavement to love. Now
this abstract exemplar was suddenly named as the poet and the
lover whom they knew. The effect achieved in the *Commedia*
through Francesca's poignant narrative is here accomplished by
the Macías legend, operating from outside the poem: the exemplar-
ily condemned lover is invested with a tragic human substance.

Other elements work in the same sense. The overtones of elegy
and epitaph in Macías's naming of himself deepen its pathos:

> digas que fui condenado
> por seguir d'Amor sus vías;
> e finalmente Maçías
> en España fui llamado.
> (*Infierno de los enamorados*, 64)

[tell them that I was damned for following the ways of Love, and
lastly that in Spain I was called Macías.]

The narrator does more than pity him: he calls him "brother".
This from the heir of the Mendozas, addressing a provincial squire,
dead in perhaps disreputable circumstances, was courtesy indeed.
It was in many ways matched by Íñigo López's recorded treatment
of other poets of lesser birth—the royal secretary Juan de Mena, or
the converted Jewish clothier Antón de Montoro.[1] In the *Infierno* it

---

1   On his dealings with Mena see R. Lapesa, *La obra literaria del Marqués de
    Santillana*, pp. 265–71. In the poetic exchanges between them (Santillana,
    Poesías completas, II, 300–11) Íñigo López addresses him as "poeta de Mena"
    (p. 304), as "omne que sabe" (p. 305) and—with yet greater courtesy—as his
    "buen amigo" (p. 301). According to Hernán Núñez he paid the costs of
    Mena's monument in the church of Torrelaguna: see Juan de Mena, *Laberinto
    de Fortuna*, edited by M. Kerkhof (Madrid, Castalia, 1995), p. 11. On Montoro,
    whose plea to Íñigo López for money evoked a respectful request for a poem

testified to an enlightened civility, marking out the Íñigo López who had rejected love as no less the perfect courtier than the chaste Hippolytus of the outer allegory. But it also bore witness to the fact that the poet—albeit through behaviour which he had been led to renounce—was himself implicated in the attitudes which had brought about Macías's damnation. Along with the pity and the terror there goes an element of fellow feeling.

It goes so far indeed as to hint, in theologically anomalous terms, that Macías might not actually be damned after all. At an earlier point the poet had addressed him as one in Limbo: "en este limbo e miseria" ["in this Limbo and wretchedness"; Stanza 60]. Here he remits his case to God, "como el soberano/sólo puede reparar/en tales fechos" ["since the sovereign ruler alone can remedy such a case"; Stanza 66]. To this Macías replies: "Dios te guarde,/el qual te quiera guiar" ["God keep you and grant you his guidance"; Stanza 66]. Such an exchange would surely be out of place in Hell. It may be that Íñigo López was merely recalling, none too opportunely, the dialogue between Dante and the poets in Purgatory. It may be that he sought to link the exemplary secular civility of a non-amorous courtliness with the obligations of Christian charity. But one cannot mistake the impulse to render rather more to Macías by way of solidarity than any objective view of his case would allow.

Perhaps, indeed, objective views are not really in place here. One major contrast with Dante—initially unpromising—certainly points to that. In the *Commedia* the speaking part falls to a woman; her lover, Paolo, has nothing of his own to say. But Macías (like every other character who speaks in any of the "erotic Hells" composed in Spain) is a man. He too, though, has a companion:

> por ver de qué tractavan
> mi passo me fui llegando
> a dos, que vi razonando,
> que nuestra lengua fablavan.
> (*Infierno de los enamorados*, 58)

[to discover what they were talking about, I drew closer to two of them, whom I saw speaking together in our language.]

of his own, see R. Lapesa, *La obra literaria del Marqués de Santillana*, pp. 273–74.

With whom, then, is Macías talking in Castilian? With his lady? Possibly so, but this is never stated. And why in that case should the narrator ignore her in all that he says? It seems an odd limit to set to courtesy. We might, then, venture another guess: that the mysterious Other is a vision of Íñigo López as he will end if he dies still in thrall to love. Once he has made his renunciation, this figure of an imperilled self quietly vanishes from the poem. Such an explanation comes to seem more plausible when we note that Íñigo López—no doubt prompted by Virgil's disappearance in *Purgatorio* xxx—instigates a rather similar effect at the end of his *Infierno*. When the narrator turns from Macías to Hippolytus once more, Hippolytus is no longer there. He has not, like Dante's Virgil, passed his pupil to another guide; there is no Beatrice in this poem. The meaning of the disappearance, rather, is that Hippolytus is no longer needed: his lesson of chaste courtesy has now been fully internalized and the poet will follow in his way from now onwards.

By quite other means, then, Íñigo López does find room in his poem for that sense of being implicated with the condemned lovers which is so potent in Dante. That being so, it is hard to go on seeing the poem as a defective response to the *Commedia*, crude and limited in its vision, and shallow in its human feeling. Its miniature scale notwithstanding, the *Infierno de los enamorados* remains an impressive appropriation of Dantean matter. And it is governed by a formidable poetic craft. We may well find that the human fictions and feelings in Dante are imaginatively realized in ways with which our twentieth-century sensibilities can more readily connect. But if we dismiss Íñigo López's preferred method of deploying cultural counters of fixed and known value—of filling out, as it were, an initial act of "appropriation" with an arraying of "available" uses—we will go very badly astray. For not only does that method work locally within the poem to the kinds of effect which have been explored here. It was also the way of most medieval poetry—not least, in many of its aspects, of Dante's own.

LANDMARKS IN THE FORTUNES OF DANTE IN THE FLORENTINE QUATTROCENTO

Corinna Salvadori

Florence, of course, was Dante's native city, but in January 1302 he had been forced into exile, on a false charge of barratry and a true charge of hostility to Charles of Anjou and Pope Boniface VIII, as well as for causing a breach of the peace; since he did not present himself to answer the charges his goods were confiscated, and in March of the same year he was condemned to death. Thereafter, for close on twenty years—he died in 1321—he was to wander from court to court, mostly dependent on the goodwill of others, and thus experiencing

> come sa di sale
> lo pane altrui, e come è duro calle
> lo scendere e 'l salir per l'altrui scale.
> (*Paradiso*, XVII. 58–60)

[how salty tastes the bread of others, and how hard it is to go down and climb again the stairs of others.][1]

Dante's most searing comment on his exile is to be found in *Convivio*, I. 3. 4:

> Poi che fu piacere delli cittadini della bellissima e famosissima figlia di Roma, Fiorenza, di gittarmi fuori del suo dolce seno— nel quale nato e nutrito fui in fino al colmo della vita mia, e nel quale, con buona pace di quella, desidero con tutto lo core di riposare l'animo stancato e terminare lo tempo che m'è dato—, per le parti quasi tutte alle quali questa lingua si stende, peregri-

---

1   All English translations in this essay are my own unless indicated otherwise. For a full biography of Dante see G. Petrocchi, *Vita di Dante* (Bari, Laterza, 1983); for the same author's compact version see *Enc. dant.*, VI, 3–53.

no, quasi mendicando, sono andato, mostrando contra mia voglia la piaga della fortuna, che suole ingiustamente al piagato molte volte essere imputata. Veramente io sono stato legno sanza vela e sanza governo, portato a diversi porti e foci e liti dal vento secco che vapora la dolorosa povertade.

[From the time when the citizens of Rome's most beautiful and famous daughter, Florence, saw fit to cast me away from her sweet bosom—where I was born and nourished until my full maturity, and where, with her gracious consent, I desire with all my heart to rest my weary mind and complete my allotted span—I have made my way through almost all the regions to which this language extends, a homeless wanderer, reduced almost to beggary, and showing against my will the wound inflicted by fortune, which is very often imputed unjustly to the one afflicted. I have indeed been a ship lacking sail and rudder, carried to various ports and river mouths and shores by the parching wind raised by painful poverty.][1]

Yet despite this, and despite the enraged condemnations of Florence in the *Commedia*, the abundance of Florentines among the damned and their paucity in Heaven, no one can deny that Florence is the epicentre of the work, and that the intensity of Dante's *saeva indignatio* is outstripped only by the depth of his love for his native city. Indeed, in several places in the *Commedia* "pare che si glorii di essere fiorentino" ["he seems to take pride in being a Florentine"], as Cristoforo Landino put it in 1481.[2] As proof of this one could cite, as Landino does, the idealistic eulogy of ancient Florence in *Paradiso* XV and XVI. But one may also mention the incident in *Inferno* XIV where Dante accompanies an affirmation of love with an unequivocal gesture of affection, restoring to the anonymous Florentine suicide, in violation of a law of Hell, the twigs that represent the parts severed from his body:

> Poi che la carità del natio loco
> mi strinse, raunai le fronde sparte
> e rende'le a colui, ch'era già fioco.
> (*Inferno*, XIV. 1–3)

1   Translations of passages from *Convivio* are by Christopher Ryan and are taken from Dante, *The Banquet* (Saratoga, Anma Libri, 1989). Here, p. 18.
2   See "Proemio al commento dantesco: apologia nella quale si difende Dante e Florenzia", in C. Landino, *Scritti politici e teorici*, edited by R. Cardini, 2 vols (Rome, Bulzoni, 1974), I, 103–05.

[Because the love of my native place seized me, I gathered the scattered twigs and gave them back to him, who was now hoarse.]

If such was Dante's attitude to Florence, what was, one may ask, the Florentines' attitude to Dante, a century or so after his exile, in that crucial period when Humanism flourished and Florence was reaching its political and cultural apogee?

There is no doubt that Dante aroused strong emotions among his fellow citizens, whether they accepted him or rejected him. On the one hand, it was abundantly clear to most that he belonged to Florence and was "poeta nostro fiorentino". More importantly, he came to be used, by some, as a prop to Florentine ideology, becoming the outstanding symbol of *florentina libertas*, even though his damnation of Brutus, whom the Humanists saw as a defender of republican liberty against tyranny, caused much controversy (giving rise to many ingenious justifications).[1] Moreover, he came to be seen as a champion of the *volgare illustre fiorentino*, in which he had chosen to write his greatest works of poetry and philosophy. Not everybody, however, saw him in that light. At the end of the Trecento leading Florentine intellectuals rejected the vernacular as a cultural language, and moreover considered Dante to have failed the test of *latinitas*. This was to create a dilemma, for Dante's greatness was beyond dispute—but how could one reconcile it with the view that to be a great poet one had to write in Latin? Inevitably Petrarch was dragged into the argument (the Petrarch of the Latin works, not the *Rime*), but while all the evidence showed Petrarch to be the greater writer, the fact remained—which most could accept though none could explain—that Dante's stature was gigantic. The less extreme Humanists, including Coluccio Salutati (1331–1406), who admired Dante as a kindred spirit, sided with one of Dante's earliest commentators, Benvenuto da Imola, who, asserting Dante's greatness and superiority over all, had claimed that whereas Petrarch was the "maior orator" Dante was the "maior poeta".[2] Dante himself, who had used the phrase "poete volgari" in *Vita nuova*, xxv. 4, would of course have recognized that the term *poeta* implied superiority. Had he not

---

1   It is interesting to record that as recently as August 1993 the matter of the damnation of Brutus was used to make a political point in a letter published in *The Observer*.

2   *Enc. dant.*, i, 595.

implicitly styled himself *poeta* in *Inferno* IV, by putting himself on
a par with the greatest poets of antiquity, when, accompanied by
Virgil, *poeta* of the *Aeneid*, he is greeted by four outstanding
classical poets and accepted into their exclusive circle, "sí ch'io fui
sesto tra cotanto senno" ["so that I became the sixth among such
minds"; line 102]? Leonardo Bruni (?1370–1444) and, much later,
Cristoforo Landino (1425–98) would have had no doubt that Dante
should be so styled. Indeed, Bruni ultimately reached the conclusion
that one is a *poeta* for the style and content of one's work, not for
one's choice of language,[1] a position that is in fact quite close to the
view expressed by Dante himself in *Vita nuova*, XXV. 4 ("dire per
rima in volgare tanto è quanto dire per versi in latino, secondo
alcuna proporzione" ["rhyming in the vernacular is equivalent to
using metrical forms in Latin, observing due proportion"]).[2] The
Platonist Landino, for his part, proclaimed to the Signoria (in 1481)
that Dante was a "poeta" who had been moved by "divino furore".[3]

Whatever may be said about the Humanists' reservations
concerning Dante's linguistic skills, by the end of the Trecento he
was all but a cult figure in Florence, and what had won him the
veneration of his native city was above all his civic commitment.[4]
This was of course the period of Civic Humanism, synonymous
with Coluccio Salutati, the greatest Humanist of the time. Although
his own formation initially owed more to Petrarch and Boccaccio
than to Dante, in due course his enthusiasm for the latter was to
grow beyond measure, and his was to become an influential voice.
It was difficult for Florentines at the time to accept that Boccaccio,
only a few decades earlier, could have written a "biography" of
Dante which mentioned many nonsensical and irrelevant events
of his life but made no reference to his exile. What is more,
Boccaccio had stated that Dante's purpose in writing had been
didactic, and also that he had written with a view to "a sé perpetua

1   L. Bruni, *Le vite di Dante e del Petrarca*, edited by A. Lanza (Rome, Archivio
     Guido Izzi, 1987), pp. 47–49.
2   See Dante Alighieri, *Vita nuova*, edited by J. Petrie and J. Salmons (Dublin,
     UCD Foundation for Italian Studies, 1994), p. 104.
3   This conviction of Landino's underlies his entire "Proemio al commento
     dantesco", which includes a specific section on "furore divino": see
     C. □Landino *Scritti politici e teorici*, I, 95–174.
4   Some of the information in this and the next two paragraphs is an expansion
     of points to be found in E. Bigi, "Dante e la cultura fiorentina del
     Quattrocento", in his *Forme e significati nella "Divina Commedia"* (Bologna,
     Cappelli, 1981), pp. 145–72.

gloria apparecchiare" ["securing for himself everlasting glory"].[1]
But for someone like Filippo Villani, writing in about 1381–82,[2]
Dante's work arose from a deep sense of ethical and civic mission.
For men like Salutati and Villani, who were public servants and
not secluded in ivory towers, Dante was a poet-citizen, whom they
praised not only for his religious, scientific and stylistic
achievements, but also for his service as a citizen, for which he had
paid the highest of prices in terms of personal suffering. We should
not forget that this was the period too of the war against the
Visconti of Milan, when Florentines felt it necessary to proclaim all
aspects of their city's supremacy, most notably her cultural
achievements. In 1396, when the war against the Visconti was at its
most intense, the Florentine Signoria decided to place memorial
plaques in the cathedral to the greatest representatives of Florence's
cultural tradition, and among these it included Dante.[3]

Possibly in the following year, a political pamphlet of major
importance in this cultural battle saw the light of day. Cino
Rinuccini had been provoked by the Milanese Antonio Loschi's
Invectiva in Florentinos to praise, in his *Risponsiva*, "il teologo Dante
degli Alighieri" above all poets, both Greek and Latin, for his
marvellous inventions and the subtlety of his genius. The text of
the *Risponsiva* has come down to us in a vernacular rendering, in
which the translator may have intervened, but its language is
certainly very strong, Loschi being called "demente" ["insane"]
and addressed as "garullo e protervo" ["stupid and arrogant"].[4]
Salutati had also praised Dante in an *Invectiva* against Loschi,
which he reworked between 1397 and 1403; and in a letter datable

1   Quoted by E. Bigi, "Dante e la cultura fiorentina", p. 165, from Boccaccio's
     Trattatello in laude di Dante, edited by P. G. Ricci, in G. Boccaccio, *Tutte le
     opere*, edited by V. Branca, 10 vols (Milan, Mondadori, 1967–92), III, 437–538.
2   Quoted by E. Bigi, "Dante e la cultura fiorentina", p. 146. For Villani's life
     of Dante see *Le vite di Dante, Petrarca, Boccaccio scritte fino al secolo XVI*, edited
     by A. Solerti (Milan, Vallardi, 1904), pp. 82ff.
3   E. Bigi, "Dante e la cultura fiorentina", p. 147.
4   Rinuccini's *Risponsiva* may be read in *Invectiva Lini Colucii Salutati in
     Antonium Luschum Vicentinum*, edited by D. Moreni (Florence, Magheri,
     1826), pp. 199–250; the passages quoted here are on pp. 228–29, 208, 209. He
     also wrote an *Invettiva* against "cierti caluniatori di Dante"; this, like the
     Risponsiva, has come down to us "ridotta di gramatica [Latin] in vulgare"
     and may be read in Giovanni da Prato, *Il paradiso degli Alberti*, edited by
     A. Wesselofsky, 3 vols (Bologna, Commissione per i Testi di Lingua, 1867),
     I, 303–16.

to 1399 he points to the rhetorical mastery and profound scientific, historical and religious knowledge to be found in Dante's work, in which any limitations are due solely to Dante's use of the vernacular. Although these texts seem to belong to the arena of political rather than literary conflict, to us they reveal a debate in which politics and literature are closely intertwined and cultural supremacy is politically crucial. Salutati sees Dante as expressing his own political ideals, and as another staunch upholder of *florentina libertas*.[1]

What these works also reveal is that there were strong dissenting voices in this very heated debate, and that these grew louder in the early Quattrocento. Humanists of the generation following Salutati's are referred to by Rinuccini as "litteratissimi",[2] a term which, given the tone of the *Risponsiva*, can only be pejorative, alluding to their perceived preciosity and affectation. In other words, Humanists of the new generation were more extreme than those who had taught them, still more exclusive in their unqualified worship of classical culture, and correspondingly less enamoured of the local tradition. This literary avant-garde was led by Niccolò Niccoli (1364–1437), an important but elusive Florentine whose views—in particular his scorn for Dante and the achievements of the Tuscan Trecento—we infer mainly from what Leonardo Bruni has him say in his two dialogues dedicated to Pier Paolo Vergerio, *Dialogi ad Petrum Paulum Histrum*, the first of which is datable to 1401.[3] This work, a key document in the *querelle* between ancients and moderns, has been viewed as the manifesto of the new literary movement, and reveals a polarization of the two positions.[4] Interestingly, Bruni admits to sharing the views of Niccoli, one of the speakers in the dialogues, who in the first dialogue expounds and strongly defends an extremist position in favour of classical culture. Such a stance perforce implies a rejection of the local, Florentine culture, for to praise it could be seen as undermining the greatness of antiquity. Members of Niccoli's generation saw themselves as bringing light after centuries of darkness, with no

1   See evidence in E. Garin, "Dante nel Rinascimento", *Rinascimento*, 18, vii (1967), 3–28 (p. 10).

2   See C. Rinuccini, *Invettiva*, pp. 306, 310.

3   See L. Bruni Aretino, "Ad Petrum Paulum Histrum Dialogus", in *Prosatori latini del Quattrocento*, edited by E. Garin (Milan–Naples, Ricciardi, 1952), pp. 44–99.

4   C. Dionisotti, "Dante nel Quattrocento", in *Atti del Congresso internazionale di studi danteschi: 20–27 aprile 1965* (Florence, Sansoni, 1966), pp. 333–78 (p. 345).

one having preceded them or held a lantern for them; and Niccoli is the spokesman of those who believed that Dante was a poet fit only for the uneducated, for carders, cobblers and bakers.[1] But puzzlingly Bruni has Niccoli retreat from his position in the second dialogue, referring to it as a ruse to draw out the indignation of Salutati, who could not fail to recognize it as such ("ut dissimulationem meam non intelligeret"). This statement follows a strong eulogy of Dante, in which Niccoli claims to have committed the *Commedia* to memory in his youth and to be still able to recite it. Surely, he argues, this would not have been possible without singular affection on his part ("sine singulari quadam affectione").[2] We cannot tell for sure whether Niccoli ever did change the views he expresses in the first dialogue, nor indeed whether he actually held them so strongly in the first place, since we have nothing in his own hand to testify to this. It may also be that Bruni had not originally planned to write a second dialogue, but only did so when a major change in his own position necessitated a formal recantation of the first. Hans Baron has cogently argued that "there exists a difference of intent and texture between Bruni's two dialogues", and he thus attributes the second to a date later than 1401.[3]

Bruni believed that Florence's cultural greatness was a contributory factor in her strengthening position in the peninsula, and in the *Laudatio Florentinae Urbis*, in which he celebrates the political triumph of Florence on the death of Giangaleazzo Visconti in 1402, he bases his claim for Florence's cultural pre-eminence on Florentine achievements in both the vernacular and the revival of classical studies, concluding that the whole of Italy looks up to Florence as a model of linguistic purity and refinement, for that city alone can boast of citizens "who in this popular and common tongue have shown all other men to be mere infants".[4] The fact that Dante had written in the vernacular was no longer to be excused

---

1   This variation on the scathing list is in the second dialogue ("lanistae, sutores atque proxenetae, homines qui nunquam litteras viderunt"): see L.☐Bruni, "Ad Petrum Paulum Histrum", p. 84. See also p. 70, where Dante is excluded from the ranks of the learned ("a concilio litteratorum") and cast as the poet of carders, bakers and such like ("lanariis, pistoribus atque eiusmodi turbae").
2   L. Bruni, "Ad Petrum Paulum Histrum", pp. 82–85.
3   H. Baron, *The Crisis of the Early Italian Renaissance* (Princeton, Princeton University Press, 1966), pp. 226–44.
4   H. Baron, *The Crisis of the Early Italian Renaissance*, p. 288.

or forgiven; it was now to be praised. But the Dante controversy in Florence was never a straightforward matter and always involved more than simply literature or language. Niccoli, whose assiduous collecting and copying of manuscripts enabled him to build up an outstanding library, which after his death became the nucleus of the public library that Cosimo de' Medici established at San Marco, was a staunch Medici supporter. This is an indication that he may indeed have belonged to the anti-Dante camp, for in Florence, which as in Dante's time was a *città partita*, it was the republican, anti-Medici party which championed Dante, and the rivalry between the parties at times erupted into violence with Dante as the pretext. We know that this is so from an event in which Francesco Filelfo, a Humanist from the Marche, gained notoriety, and which might have been reported in the tabloids, had they existed, under the headline HUMANIST KNIFED IN DANTE BRAWL. Filelfo, whose stay in Florence from 1429 to 1434 was, to say the least, tempestuous, had been commissioned to read Dante in public in S. Maria del Fiore on feast days during the academic year 1431–32, but his lectures were seen as an indication that he was taking sides and opposing the Medici faction, and this led to his being knifed and having to flee the city with his face permanently scarred. Filelfo had in fact written an invective against Cosimo de' Medici and was actually exploiting the situation. He seems to have been deliberately provocative and polemical, taunting the opposing faction, which was led by Niccoli and Carlo Marsuppini. This is how the readings caused a disturbance of the peace (there is always more to Dante than meets the eye!). The dispute also had its humorous side: Filelfo's opponents temporarily (and literally) deprived him of his chair, and an ordinance had to be passed to ensure better teaching conditions and the allocation of "unam cathedram transportandam et collocandam in ecclesia Sanctae Mariae del Fiore seu alibi, ut eidem domino Francisco placuerit, pro lectura Dantis" ["a chair to be taken and placed in the church of Santa Maria del Fiore or elsewhere, as it pleased the same lord Francesco, for the purpose of reading Dante"]. The incidents, which reveal acrimonious and petty academic rivalry, the manipulation of students to create public disorder and the way in which political tensions will find any pretext to explode,[1] make

---

1   See E. Garin, "Dante nel Rinascimento", pp. 13–14; also Giuseppe Zippel, *Niccolò Niccoli: contributo alla storia dell'umanismo* [sic] (Florence, Bocca,

Dante's outburst in *Purgatorio*, VI. 115—"Vieni a veder la gente quanto s'ama!" ["Come and see just how people love one another!"]—and his unequivocal condemnation, in *Paradiso*, VI. 97–108, of both Guelphs and Ghibellines, emblematic of any pair of opposing sides in civil strife, all too apt.

Although there was undoubtedly dissension, by the 1430s the pendulum was again swinging decisively in Dante's favour. Two important works bear witness to this. The first is Matteo Palmieri's *Della vita civile*, a treatise in dialogue form written, between 1431 and 1438, deliberately in the vernacular in order to defend Dante's own use of it; Palmieri's language, not suprisingly, has strong echoes of the *Commedia*. As the title indicates, it deals with the education and formation of the citizen, examining the relationship between private and public interest, and extolling total commitment to the public good. Palmieri sees Dante as the greatest vernacular writer on whom one could draw for civic teaching, and praises him in no uncertain terms:

> Il primo et sopra a ogni altro degnissimo è il nostro Dante poeta [...]. In nelle cose grandi sempre si monstra sublime et alto; nelle piccole è diligente dipintore della vera proprietà; lui si truova lieto, rimesso, jocondo et grave; ora con abondanza, altra volta con brevità mirabile, et non solo di poetica virtú, ma spesso oratore, philosopho et theologo si conosce excellente. Sa lodare, confortare, consolare, et è copioso di tante lode che è meglio tacerne che dirne poco.[1]

> [The supreme and most worthy of all is our poet Dante (...). He is sublime and lofty in all matters of great importance, and in lesser ones he portrays accurately what is appropriate. One finds him to be joyous, meek, blithe and serious, sometimes copiously so and at other times with wonderful concision. His excellence is recognized not only in his poetic achievement but also in his qualities as an orator, a philosopher and a theologian. He can praise, fortify and console, and he deserves so much praise that it is better to remain silent than to speak of it inadequately.]

1890) and *Il Filelfo a Firenze (1429–1434)* (Rome, 1899), reprinted in his *Storia e cultura del Rinascimento italiano*, edited by Gianni Zippel (Padua, Antenore, 1979), pp. 215–53. See also P. G. Ricci, "Filelfo, Francesco", in *Enc. dant.*, II, 871–72.

1   M. Palmieri, *Della vita civile*, edited by G. Belloni (Florence, Sansoni, 1982), pp. 5–6.

Of the many ways in which Dante showed commitment to the public good, Palmieri makes much of the fact that he fought at Campaldino: "In quella battaglia Dante, quanto piú fortemente poté, s'aoperò" ["Dante fought in that battle as vigorously as he could"].[1]

Dante was to remain a major influence on Palmieri, who two decades later wrote the *Città di vita*, on the origin and fate of the human soul, a Dantesque work in a hundred *capitoli* divided into three books, each *capitolo* consisting of precisely fifty tercets of *terza rima* plus one line. It is as full of theological and philosophical digressions as it is devoid of poetry, but historically it is an important document of the development of Neoplatonism. It is also evidence of the extent to which Dante was imitated in the Quattrocento and has been aptly described by Gino Belloni Peressutti as a "fantastico prodotto della eterogenea cultura di un ambiente omogeneo, il piú grande omaggio della Firenze medicea a Dante" ["marvellous product of the heterogeneous culture of a homogeneous milieu, the greatest homage paid by the Florence of the Medici to Dante"].[2]

At about the time of *Della vita civile*, in the 1430s, Bruni wrote, also in the vernacular, an exceptional biography of Dante, *Vita di Dante*, followed by a life of Petrarch with a comparison of the two poets. It is the type of text that Lorenzo de' Medici must have had in mind when he said that theorizing on the vernacular would of itself never convince anyone of its greatness; its greatness would have to be proved by the degree of excellence achieved by those using the *volgare illustre fiorentino*.[3] Superior to Boccaccio's meandering biography, Bruni's *Vita* is beautifully sparse and taut, cutting out all that in Boccaccio is anecdotal and trivial, like the story of the pre-natal dream of Dante's mother, or that of the women of Verona who remarked that Dante's bushy hair and beard were so very black because of the fires of Hell. Bruni's is also a biography that reveals as much of its author as of its subject, being emblematic of Bruni's own values, such as commitment to

1   M. Palmieri, *Della vita civile*, p. 208.
2   See G. Belloni Peressutti, "Palmieri, Matteo (1406–1475)", in *Dizionario critico della letteratura italiana*, 3 vols (Turin, UTET, 1973), II, 149–54 (p. 152).
3   Lorenzo writes on the *volgare* in the introduction to his *Comento de' miei sonetti*; the section specifically on language may be read in L. de' Medici, *Selected Writings*, edited by C. Salvadori (Dublin, UCD Foundation for Italian Studies, 1992), pp. 117–20.

family, city and learning. Bruni has little time for sentimentality and is dismissive of Boccaccio's poetic sighs and tears and misogynous bachelor views, against which he hits back hard in defence of marriage:

> L'uomo è animale civile, secondo piace a tutti i filosofi: la prima congiunzione, della quale multiplicata nasce la città, è marito e moglie; né cosa può esser perfetta dove questo non sia, e solo questo amore è naturale, legittimo e permesso.[1]

> [Man is a social animal, as all the philosophers agree; the first relationship, which is then multiplied and gives rise to the city, is that between husband and wife; and there can be no perfection without it, and only this love is natural, lawful and permitted.]

Bruni never mentions Beatrice (or for that matter Laura in his life of Petrarch). He rehabilitates the much maligned Gemma Donati, and extols Dante as a man who did not fear to fight for his country:

> Virtuosamente si trovò a combattere per la patria in questa battaglia: e vorrei che il Boccaccio nostro di questa virtú piú tosto avesse fatto menzione che dell'amore di nove anni e di simili leggerezze, che per lui si raccontano di tanto uomo. Ma che giova a dire? La lingua pur va dove il dente duole, ed a cui piace il bere, sempre ragiona di vini.[2]

> [He fought valorously for his native land in this battle, and I wish our Boccaccio had mentioned this military prowess rather than the love of a nine-year-old and similar trifles, which he is responsible for spreading about so great a man. But what is the point of saying this? Our tongue seeks out the aching tooth, and the man who fancies his drink always talks of wines.]

When comparing the lives of Dante and Petrarch, Bruni comments that Petrarch had had a "vita tranquilla e soave ed onorata ed in grandissima bonaccia l'opere sue compose" ["a serene, peaceful and honoured life, and it was in this fair weather that he wrote his works"],[3] echoing Boccaccio's sentiment that, given the difficult circumstances in which Dante had written, he deserved not one but two laurel crowns, for other laureates had done their writing

1   L. Bruni, *Le vite*, p. 35.
2   L. Bruni, *Le vite*, p. 34.
3   L. Bruni, *Le vite*, pp. 62–63.

in sylvan peace (a very clear thrust at Petrarch).[1] Petrarch, Bruni implies, may have been the wiser man ("saggio e prudente"); Dante had made enemies and had had to write while hounded by exile and poverty ("da esilio e da povertà incalzato"). Petrarch is undoubtedly superior in both knowledge of the classics and skill in the writing of Latin, but Dante in his "opera [...] principale vantaggia ogni opera del Petrarca" ["major work surpasses every work of Petrarch's"].[2] That Dante wrote in the vernacular is no longer a stumbling-block. Greek having now entered the Humanists' sphere of knowledge and somewhat undermined the superiority of Latin, Bruni is able to state that one can be a *poeta* in *volgare* just as much as in Greek or Latin.

Bruni's *Vita* reflects an ideology that was characteristic of the Civic Humanism of the time, and while one may see it as being a propaganda piece in support of the traditions and ideals of Florence, one has to recognize that these are close to Dante's own ideals.[3] It is an exceptionally valuable biography and very different from earlier ones, because it "results from genuine research [and] also shows discernment in its use of sources".[4] Bruni drew on documents and even on letters of Dante no longer known to us, describing Dante's handwriting with Humanist sensitivity: "Fu ancora scrittore perfetto, ed era la lettera sua magra e lunga e molto corretta, secondo io ho veduto in alcune epistole di sua mano propria scritte" ["His handwriting was perfect, and his letters were slender, long and very accurate, as I myself have had occasion to note in some epistles written in his own hand"].[5] He saw more than we have been privileged to see, and by the middle of the next century his work had come to be accepted as the standard life of Dante. The Lucchese scholar Alessandro Vellutello, whose Dante commentary was printed in Venice in 1544, and who had read several other lives of Dante, says of it:

> Volendo fondarci su la verità, siamo costretti attenerci a quello
> che ne scrisse esso Aretino [Bruni], il quale, non come poeta, ma

1 See G. Tanturli, "Il disprezzo per Dante dal Petrarca al Bruni", *Rinascimento*, 25 (1985), 199–219 (p. 212), and G. Boccaccio, *Trattatello in laude di Dante*.
2 L. Bruni, *Le vite*, pp. 63, 62, 65.
3 G. Resta, "Dante nel Quattrocento", in *Dante nel pensiero e nella esegesi dei secoli xiv e xv*, by various authors (Florence, Olschki, 1975), pp. 71–92 (p. 89).
4 R. Weiss, *The Spread of Italian Humanism* (London, Hutchinson, 1964), p. 62.
5 L. Bruni, *Le vite*, p. 45.

da vero istorico per molti scontri che ne abbiamo, sappiamo averla con somma fede e diligenza scritta.[1]

[As we want to rely on the truth, we are obliged to accept what Bruni himself wrote, because he wrote it not as a poet but as a true historian, with the greatest honesty and accuracy, as is well proven.]

One of the biographies seen by Vellutello was that of Giannozzo Manetti, the politically powerful intellectual who delivered the oration at Leonardo Bruni's funeral. We might wonder what need there was for another life of Dante in the 1440s, so soon after Bruni's, especially as Manetti has no new information to offer. One major difference is that Manetti wrote his biography in Latin, for the Humanist cultural elite which regarded Bruni's life in the vernacular as not entirely acceptable. But although the main thrust is the same—Dante is praised as the embodiment of Florentine literary prestige—, Manetti reflects a different ideology. His portrait of Dante is a blend of Bruni and Boccaccio, with rather more of the latter than the former. He occasionally embroiders on Boccaccio's already dubious and unascertainable information, for example on the relationship with Gemma Donati.[2] But the main point to note is that Dante emerges from Manetti's text primarily as a writer, dedicated to the values of the "contemplative" life. His political activities are passed over as a weakness attributable to "natura nostrarum rerum fragilis atque caduca" ["the frail and transient nature of human affairs"],[3] for by Manetti's time the Civic Humanism which had made Dante so acceptable to Salutati and Bruni was on the wane, as was indeed republican Florence. Although, when Manetti discusses Dante in relation to Petrarch,

1   *Le vite*, edited by A. Solerti, p. 203.
2   *Le vite*, edited by A. Solerti, p. 121. The prize for writing the most creatively fictional account of Dante's life must go to Filelfo's son Giovanni Mario, whose totally unreliable *Vita Dantis*, written in Latin in the 1460s, served merely to proliferate what Passerini calls "spropositi madornali": G.□L.□Passerini, *Le vite di Dante scritte da G. e F. Villani, Boccaccio, Leonardo Aretino, G.□Manetti*(Florence, Sansoni, 1917), p. xlii. G. Resta, "Dante nel Quattrocento", p. 89, is kinder than most to the younger Filelfo, attributing to him the rhetorical intention of *amplificatio* and the desire to create not an accurate portrait of Dante but an ideal one.
3   Quoted by C. A. Madrignani, "Di alcune biografie umanistiche di Dante e Petrarca", *Belfagor*, 18 (1963), 29–48 (p. 44). His analysis of Manetti's biography is particularly helpful.

he expresses a preference for the former over the latter because Dante was supreme as an exponent of both the active and the contemplative dimensions,[1] ultimately the Dante who emerges from Manetti's life is the Dante who brought glory to poetry, after almost nine centuries of obscurity, and was a theologically committed poet, whose poem Manetti calls more divine than human, possibly echoing Dante's own "poema sacro/al quale ha posto mano e cielo e terra" ["sacred poem/to which both Heaven and earth have set their hand"; *Paradiso*, xxv. 1–2], and anticipating the Platonist "furor divino" which Landino would regard as the main inspiration of Dante's poetry.[2]

Someone not generally mentioned in Dante surveys of this period, although he is of interest, is Antonino Pierozzi (St Antoninus), the Dominican friar who became Archbishop of Florence in 1446. In his Latin chronicles, written between 1440 and 1459, he mentions Dante several times.[3] Contrary to what is sometimes implied, Antoninus did not adopt a doctrinaire stance against Humanism, and, having himself been exiled from his native Florence, he sees Dante as inextricably tied to the values of Civic Humanism; he thus praises him as an upholder of liberty and republican values who was exiled because of partisan envy. Later in his chronicles, however, Antoninus considers Dante's errors. Dante does not have a *limbo puerorum*, and he places the "antiquos sapientes, philosophos, poetas, rhetores infideles, ut Democritum […] et alios" ["ancient pagan sages, philosophers, poets and orators, such as Democritus (…) and others"] among the souls of Limbo, in the Elysian fields. One cannot excuse this, Antoninus argues, by claiming that it is poetic fiction, for the text is in the vernacular and public readings of it are well attended. Because its rhythm is sweet and its words elegant, one is easily beguiled and may not be able to distinguish between fiction and truth, and so

---

1   *Le vite*, edited by A. Solerti, p. 110. The text of Manetti's *Vita*, with an Italian translation, occupies pp. 108–51. The next two references are to pp. 144 and 147.

2   See above, p. 46 n. 3.

3   For an assessment of St Antoninus and Humanism see E. Sanesi, "Sant' Antonino e l'umanesimo", *La Rinascita*, 3 (1940), 105–16. See also P. G. Ricci, "Antonino da Firenze, santo", in *Enc. dant.*, I, 308–09. The comment on Dante's exile is in *Chronicorum tertia pars* (Lyons, 1586), tit. xx, par. 14, 15; the comments on Dante's errors are more easily read in *Le vite*, edited by A. Solerti, pp. 152–53, where the text is that of Nüremberg, 1484.

may come to believe that matters in the next life, contrary to Church teaching, are indeed as Dante says (XXI. 5). This, of course, reveals how widely Dante was known, how strong an impact his poetry made and how he was regarded as a sage, with no proper distinction being made between doctrinal truth and what might be termed "poetic fiction". Furthermore, Antoninus censures Dante for condemning Pope Celestine V for his pusillanimity—and in his mind there is no doubt about the identity of "l'ombra di colui/che fece per viltade il gran rifiuto" ["the shade of him who, out of cowardice, made the great refusal"; *Inferno*, III. 59–60]—, whereas the Church had exalted him for his humility. He also finds fault, incidentally, with *Monarchia* III, where it is stated that the Emperor's power derives directly from God. But *Monarchia* was in Latin and so less likely to do much harm.

Antoninus was not to know that less than twenty years later, in 1468, *Monarchia* would become available in the vernacular. But by then the cultural climate in Florence was that of Medici-inspired Neoplatonism. The translator of *Monarchia* was none other than the great Plato scholar Marsilio Ficino, the person more closely identified than anyone else with Renaissance Neoplatonism. Although *Monarchia* had been famous in European courts, at least in the first half of the Quattrocento, the Florentines had on the whole ignored it, together with Dante's other minor works. Boccaccio had mentioned the Church's ban;[1] Bruni and Manetti had been dismissive of the work. Bruni had written: "In latino scrisse in prosa ed in verso. In prosa un libro chiamato *Monarchia*, il quale è scritto a modo disadorno, senza niuna gentilezza di dire" ["He wrote both prose and verse in Latin; a prose work was entitled *Monarchia*, and it is written in a plain manner with no refinement of expression"].[2] Why then did Ficino, in the midst of his great work on Plato, take time to translate Dante's treatise? The immediate stimulus may well have been, as he states in the "Prohemio",[3] a request by two friends (Bernardo Neri and Antonio Manetti), but a more sophisticated suggestion has been put forward

---

1   Boccaccio mentions this both in the *Trattatello in laude di Dante* (par. 16) and in *Della origine, vita, studi e costumi di Dante Alighieri e delle opere composte da lui* (par. 25); both passages are in *Le vite*, edited by A. Solerti, pp. 61–62.

2   L. Bruni, *Le vite*, p. 52.

3   The dedicatory letter, which Ficino calls "Prohemio", may be read in P. Shaw, "La versione ficiniana della *Monarchia*", *Studi danteschi*, 51 (1974–75), pp. 327–28.

by Cesare Vasoli, who believes that Ficino may have undertaken
the translation as a result of political turbulence which led to the
conflict between Pope Paul II and Piero the Gouty (head of the
Medici household between 1464 and 1469, and father of Lorenzo
the Magnificent).[1] The time was ripe for a political theory based on
"reductio ad unum", leadership by a single ruler, and the clear
affirmation of the full independence of civil authority from religious
authority, with civil authority, to quote Ficino, deriving directly
from God "senza mezzo del papa" ["with no pope in the way"]. To
such an extent did *Monarchia* become identified with Florence, and
in particular with the Medici circle, that when it was first printed—
in 1559, not (predictably) in post-Tridentine Italy but in Basel—its
editor stated that it was not really by Dante but by a perceptive and
learned man ("acutissimi et doctissimi viri") who was a friend of
Poliziano's.[2] In his own "political" writings Ficino expounds
theories very close to Dante's and, by selecting judiciously, finds
in Dante a kindred spirit. He believed that the ruler should be a
"vir civilis" who lives as a private citizen, but is chosen by God to
lead others and to create an earthly harmony similar to celestial
harmony, and that this will bring about a "renovatio", a renewal,
and an "aetas aurea", a golden age. It is, of course, not difficult to
put a name to that "vir civilis": he was none other than Lorenzo de'
Medici.

The preface to Ficino's vernacular rendering of *Monarchia*
begins eloquently: "Dante Alighieri, per patria celeste, per
abitazione fiorentino, di stirpe angelico, in professione filosofo
poetico" ["Dante Alighieri, whose fatherland was Heaven, was by
dwelling a Florentine, by race angelic, by profession a poetical
philosopher"]. Gone is the warrior at Campaldino, and in his stead
we have a Dante who spoke in spirit (for he knew no Greek) with
Plato and filled his works with "molte sentenzie platoniche [...] e
per tale ornamento massime illustrò tanto la città fiorentina, che
cosí bene Firenze di Dante come Dante di Firenze si può dire"
["many Platonic concepts (...) and for this distinction he rendered
illustrious the city of Florence, so that Florence may be said to be

---

1   For this and other background information to this section see C. Vasoli,
     "Note sul volgarizzamento ficiniano della *Monarchia*", in *Umanesimo e
     Rinascimento a Firenze e Venezia*, by various authors (Florence, Olschki,
     1983), 451–74 (pp. 467–70).
2   C. Vasoli, "Note sul volgarizzamento ficiniano della *Monarchia*", p. 469.

Dante's just as Dante may be said to be Florence's"].[1] The twain would not be parted—or so the Florentines liked to think. There was trouble afoot, however, more specifically abroad; but before we consider it we should briefly glance at one of the men who had requested the translation of *Monarchia*, the Florentine architect, mathematician and writer Antonio Manetti (1423–97).

Dante studies have always reflected the interests of the age of his readers, and it is thus apt that in fifteenth-century Florence, where remarkable progress was being made in mathematical studies, someone should apply that science to a feature of the *Commedia* that had not previously been studied. Manetti established the study of Dante's cosmography. The complex material of his calculations on the location and size of Hell—which he had only gathered together in a disorganized fashion by the time of his death, though by then his work had been used and acknowledged by Landino—was made accessible to the general reader by his friend Girolamo Benivieni, who produced the highly technical data in dialogue form (the first *monografia dantesca*, it might be said).[2] A first dialogue features Manetti as an interlocutor and contains solely Manetti's material. The second is imagined as having taken place after Manetti's death, and in it Benivieni expands some of Manetti's points and voices doubts about others. Dante, like the good storyteller he is, provides enough detailed information on the layout of Hell to enable the reader to draw a map, and this lends conviction to the notion that the journey was real and not a vision. We know from *Inferno* XI that a complex moral order underlies the organization of Hell and that this is expressed in certain physical features, scientifically thought out. The descriptions, however, lack the kind of accuracy that would make them acceptable, so to speak, to the Ordnance Survey, but this is deliberate. There is sufficient information to give Hell a semblance of reality and thus to arouse strong emotions in the reader, but not enough to render it commonplace. Since each circle is narrower than its predecessor, are the lustful, for instance, necessarily more numerous than the traitors? This is the sort of question Dante presumably did not intend us to ask, for it might betray the spirit of the work; but that did not deter Manetti. Although he fails in his

1   See above, p. 57 n. 3.
2   *Prefatione di Hieronymo Benivieni, Dialogo di Antonio Manetti cittadino fiorentino circa il sito, forma et misura dello Inferno di Dante Alighieri poeta excellentissimo*, edited by N. Zingarelli (Città di Castello, Lapi, 1897).

endeavour, mainly because his reading is too literal and the data are too approximate for his sophisticated calculations, he is eminently successful in graphically establishing Dante's order. He himself recognizes part of the problem. The *alla* and the *braccio*, while standard linear measures, varied from city to city ("L'alle sono diverse secondo la diversità dei paesi dove elle si usano"), and when Dante describes Antheus he does not specify "quale e' s'intenda" ["which he meant"].[1] Yet Manetti is very precise about the meaning of the word *braccio*:

> N'ho facto pruova e truovo che egli è a puncto la terza parte, piglando [*sic*] pel braccio quello che proprio in ello huomo si dice braccio, che è da quello luogho ove elli esce dalla spalla insino alla ghangheratura [*sic*] della mano.[2]

> [I have tested this and I find that it is precisely one third, taking arm to mean exactly what is meant by a man's arm, that is from the point it comes out of the shoulder to the articulation of the hand.]

Taking as his base the common man ("uomo comune"), who is three arms ("tre braccia") tall—generally eight heads and a little more—, he calculates that a "gigante comune" (but are Dante's giants common ones?) is fourteen and two-thirds times ("quattordici volte et due terzi") the average man. On this basis Lucifer's height works out as 1,936 *braccia*. Since the *braccio* was slightly more than half a metre, should we conclude that Lucifer's height is rather more than a kilometre? To consider this eventuality nullifies the impact made on us by "la creatura ch'ebbe il bel sembiante" ["the creature whose countenance was once so fair"; *Inferno*, xxxiv. 18] and seems to make nonsense of it all, though not everyone might take this view.

Manetti's interpretations were upheld by Florentine academicians of the following century, who, when they came under scathing attack by Vellutello for upholding them, grew so angry that they asked Galileo Galilei to defend Manetti. Galileo did so in two public lectures to the Florentine Academy, at the end of 1587 and the beginning of 1588, probably acceding to the request in the hope of obtaining the university chair of mathematics. He provided

1   *Prefatione di Hieronymo Benivieni, Dialogo di Antonio Manetti*, p. 69.
2   *Prefatione di Hieronymo Benivieni, Dialogo di Antonio Manetti*, p. 71, which also contains the remaining passages quoted in this paragraph.

no critical evaluation of Dante, however, and regrettably his illustrations are not available to us. He argued that Manetti correctly interprets what Dante writes about the shape and size of Hell, and by thus confuting Vellutello's objections he confirmed the Florentine academicians in their chauvinism.[1]

One more point needs to be made about Manetti. In the century that more than any other was that of Dante's *florentinitas* it was a cause of great regret to his fellow citizens that his remains should lie in what they considered foreign soil, in Ravenna. Efforts had periodically been made to bring them back: in 1430 the Signoria had asked the Lord of Ravenna, Ostasio da Polenta, for their return, and Cosimo de' Medici had also tried to obtain them, sending Benedetto Dei as his envoy. When Lorenzo became head of the Medici household in 1469, Manetti appealed to him to renew the effort to have Dante brought back home, and it seems that Bernardo Bembo, father of Pietro, while ambassador to Florence from 1470 to 1480, having developed a love of Florentine culture and especially of Dante, promised Lorenzo that he would try and have the remains sent to Florence. Later, while *podestà* of Ravenna, he kept his promise but failed to achieve what he had undertaken. We nonetheless owe it to him that in 1483 Dante's remains were moved to a special chapel in the church of S. Francesco in Ravenna. All this was done at Bembo's own expense.[2] It evoked the Florentines' gratitude and was publicly acclaimed by Landino, who in his commentary on *Inferno*, XXVII. 38 had written, "È giudicio d'ogni savio e litterato uomo, che el Popolo Fiorentino doverebbe ridurlo nella patria, et onorarlo di sepoltura degna di tal poeta" ["It is the opinion of every man of wisdom and letters that the people of Florence should bring him back home and should honour him with a tomb worthy of such a poet"]; and to Bernardo Bembo he wrote a letter thanking him for the restoration of Dante's sepulchre in Ravenna and expressing regret for not having known of it when writing his commentary, as he would have wished to immortalize the deed.[3] Efforts to bring back Dante's remains were to continue into the next century. In 1515

---

1   For further details see M. Barbi, *Della fortuna di Dante nel secolo* XVI (Pisa, Nistri, 1890), pp. 142–44.

2   I. Del Lungo, *Florentia: uomini e cose del '400* (Florence, Barbera, 1897), pp. 450–57.

3   I. Del Lungo, *Florentia*, p. 453; see also G. Resta, "Bembo, Bernardo", in *Enc. dant.*, I, 566–67. Landino's commentary is quoted from Dante Alighieri, *La*

Manetti's friend Benivieni wrote a letter for Lucrezia, daughter of
Lorenzo de' Medici, to copy and to send to her brother, Pope Leo Ⅹ,
to remind him of Bernardo Bembo's unsuccessful efforts and
exhort him to have the remains moved to Florence. The Medici
Academy was to send an appeal to the Pope in 1519 for the same
reason, and that petition was signed by two hundred leading
citizens, including Michelangelo, who offered to design a worthy
tomb free of charge.[1] The Florentines also tried to induce the
Alighieri family to return to Florence, but nothing came of that
either. In 1495 Dante Ⅲ declined an invitation to return and regain
his ancestor's possessions, "avendo egli a Verona da poter vivere
signorilmente" ["as in Verona he had the means to live in lordly
manner"].[2]

But let us return to Ficino and his circle. The most famous
devotee of Neoplatonism—he all but made it a state religion—was
Lorenzo de' Medici. What is more, throughout his tragically brief
lifetime he was the strongest and most famous supporter of the
volgare illustre fiorentino. He wrote on the vernacular with an
emotion equalled only by Dante's, finding in their common tongue
all that was essential for a language, namely that it be "comunicabile
e universale [...], copiosa e abondante" ["accessible to all and
universal (...), rich and varied"], that it have sweetness and
harmony ("dolcezza e armonia") and that it be capable of expressing
subtle and deep reasoning. He believed that the Florentine language
was only in its adolescence and that it would grow and conquer,
hand in hand with the "Florentine empire" ("fiorentino imperio")
to which it intrinsically belonged. Like Dante, he strongly believed
that he was right to write in the language "nella quale io sono nato
e nutrito" ["into which I was born and nurtured"].[3]

comedia cum comment. *Christopheri Landini, cum figuris ligneis* (Venice, Petro
Cremonese dito Veronese, 1491).

1   The facts and the relevant documents may be read in P. O. Kristeller, *Studies
in Renaissance Thought and Letters* (Rome, Storia e Letteratura, 1956), pp. 328–
36.

2   This information, cited by M. Barbi, *Della fortuna di Dante*, p. 82, comes from
Vellutello and may be read in *Le vite*, edited by A. Solerti, p. 209: "Messer
Dante terzo, come per un decreto fatto a Firenze l'anno 1495, nel consiglio
da gli Ottanta, la copia del quale tratta da l'originale abbiamo appresso di
noi, fu invitato a repatriare con offerta di restituirli tutto quello che de' suoi
antichi si poteva, il che era da la maggior parte de le facoltà in fuori; e per
questo avendo egli a Verona da poter vivere signorilmente, non si curò di
accettar l'invito."

3   See above, p. 52 n. 3.

Lorenzo was the instigator of the publication, in 1481, of the monumental vernacular commentary on the *Commedia* by Cristoforo Landino, the Humanist who had guided Lorenzo's own studies. It was written with enormous speed—in less than a year—but was the result of a lifetime of Dante studies, as Landino himself tells us and as is proven by class notes of one of Landino's students discovered quite recently.[1] The launch was an extraordinary event, heralding the publication not as a private achievement but as a collective one: a special copy of the work was presented to the Signoria by Landino, who also delivered an oration, in which he expressed the wish that Dante be "dopo lungo essilio restituito nella sua patria e riconosciuto nella sua lingua" ["after a long exile restored to his fatherland and recognized in his own language"].[2] There was also a procession to the Baptistery—Dante's own "bel San Giovanni"—, where the volume was exhibited for the Florentines to view. This solemn yet spectacular event marks the climax of Dante studies in the Italian Renaissance, and it took place, appropriately, where it was felt Dante rightly belonged: in Florence. Twelve hundred copies of Landino's work were printed by Niccolò della Magna. It was the first illustrated *Commedia* ever printed, with copper engravings based on drawings by Botticelli, which introduced a new technique in printing. It became the Quattrocento text most often reprinted, and presumably most read, in the following century,[3] dominating the market until 1544, when Vellutello's commentary appeared. Landino's labours were rewarded by the gift of a tower at Borgo di Collina, in the Casentino, though Michele Barbi was wryly to comment, "dono non cosí splendido [...] dacché solo per ridurla abitabile dové il Landino spendere piú di 250 scudi" ["not really such a splendid gift (...) since, just to make it habitable, Landino had to spend more than 250 *scudi*"].[4]

The commentary proper is preceded by a lengthy introductory section, where Landino first explains the need for his work and then provides an apologia defending Dante and Florence from false calumny. Here he illustrates the Florentines' supremacy in all things: "in dottrina, in eloquentia, in musica, in pittura e scultura,

1   See R. Cardini, "Landino e Dante", *Rinascimento*, 30 (1990), 175–90 (p. 180).

2   C. Landino, *Scritti politici e teorici*, I, 172.

3   R. Cardini, "Landino e Dante", p. 178.

4   M. Barbi, *Della fortuna di Dante*, p. 154.

in ius civile" ["in learning, in eloquence, in music, in painting and sculpture, in civil law"] and finally in trade ("mercatura"), recognizing trade as vital to the survival of a city-state, as long as it is practised with dignity ["purché sia esercitata con dignità"]— we could still stand over that![1] The defence of Florence is followed by a life of Dante, which is mainly a compendium of earlier ones.[2] It presents Dante as both contemplative poet and active citizen, and states that he was loved by the people because he strove to achieve peace and liberty in their community:

> Né gli mancò l'animo né le forze nella disciplina militare perché spesse volte si trovò in guerra e nella pericolosissima battaglia di Campaldino virilmente combattendo, [...] onore a sé e utile alla patria partorí.[3]

> [Neither did he lack the courage or the strength for military prowess, as he was often involved in wars and he fought valorously in the very dangerous battle of Campaldino, (...) bringing glory upon himself and benefit to his fatherland.]

Dante's love for Beatrice is interpreted in Neoplatonist terms. Earthly beauty arouses human love, which is an aspect of divine love, and through this experience man can reach divine contemplation ("con queste bellezze terrene c'inalziamo alle divine").[4] In the lengthy piece which follows this, on "Che cosa sia poesia e poeta e della origine sua divina e antichissima" ["The meaning of poetry and poet, and on their divine and very ancient origin"], Landino presents a more "contemplative" Dante and writes of "divino furore", a gift of the Muses that seizes the poet and without which the poet's labours would be in vain. Next comes a flowery letter (in both Latin and *volgare*), allegedly from Florence to Dante but written by Ficino, which clearly conveys the message that Dante, through Landino's commentary, has finally returned in apotheosis to his native city. Emilio Bigi has identified two basic themes in what both Ficino and Landino write: on the one hand the claim that Dante enhanced the political and literary prestige of Medicean Florence, and on the other the insistence on

---

1   C. Landino, *Scritti politici e teorici*, I, 125.
2   C. Landino, *Scritti politici e teorici*, I, 135.
3   C. Landino, *Scritti politici e teorici*, I, 132.
4   C. Landino, *Scritti politici e teorici*, I, 132.

the contemplative, Platonist and Neoplatonist aspects of his poetry.[1] Provided one recognizes that this is but one part of Dante's philosophy, it is probably true that he can be read as a (Renaissance) Neoplatonist *avant la lettre*. Did he himself, after all, not gloss his own poetry in language similar to theirs? Consider, for instance, "Sono chiusi li nostri occhi intellettuali, mentre che l'anima è legata e incarcerata per li organi del nostro corpo" ["The eyes of our intellect are closed while our soul is bound and imprisoned by the organs of our body"; *Convivio*, II. 4. 17]; or, "La sua bellezza ha podestade in rinnovare natura in coloro che la mirano: ch'è miracolosa cosa. [...] dico che ella è aiutatrice della fede nostra" ["Her beauty has the power to renew nature in those who gaze on her—which is something miraculous. (...) I declare that she helps our faith"; *Convivio*, III. 8. 20]. Landino's prefatory section ends with a version of Manetti's work on the "sito, forma e misura dello 'nferno e statura de' giganti e di Lucifero" ["location, shape and measure of Hell, and the size of the giants and of Lucifer"], which has led Cardini to praise Landino's critical acumen in incorporating Manetti's research into his commentary well before Manetti may have finished it.[2] Despite his Neoplatonist "idealism", Landino was sensitive to the sheer corporeal quality of Dante's text, to its realism, and Manetti, as we have seen, had tried to give this mathematical expression. Seeing the *Commedia* as an interaction of mathematical science ("matematica disciplina") and great imagination ("alta fantasia"), Landino opens this section of his introduction with the statement: "Benché questo poeta in ogni cosa sia maraviglioso, nientedimeno non posso sanza sommo stupore considerare la sua nuova né mai da alcuno altro escogitata invenzione" ["Although this poet is a marvel in all matters, nevertheless I cannot consider this new and previously unheard of invention of his without the greatest amazement"].[3] What we do not know is whether in the points where Landino diverges from what we accept as Manetti's work (as attributed to the latter and published by his friend Bienivieni) he deliberately expressed a different viewpoint or whether it was Manetti who subsequently changed his mind. While one may sympathize with Vellutello, who was to write in derisory fashion of both Manetti's and

1   E. Bigi, "Dante e la cultura fiorentina", p. 161.
2   C. Landino, *Scritti politici e teorici*, II, 222–23.
3   C. Landino, *Scritti politici e teorici*, I, 155.

Landino's efforts in this area and dismiss them as "avendo il cieco preso per sua guida l'orbo" ["the blind having taken the unseeing as his guide"], one must nonetheless recognize the importance of such pioneering work.[1]

Landino, who was possibly the most authoritative Humanist of the time, treated the *Commedia* as a classic, on a par with the *Aeneid*, and in order to reflect the cultural and political ideology of Laurentian Florence he wrote a completely new commentary on it, much of which, however, he based on earlier commentators, in the belief that those commentators, having lived closer to Dante's own time, had a better understanding of the poem. Even from a superficial acquaintance with his writings we may concur with Cardini's assessment of Landino as the greatest critic of Italian literature in the fifteenth century.[2] His influence was to last for centuries; many later commentators were to copy his glosses (mostly without acknowledgment) and a good number of his interpretations of Dante's text are still valid today. The work cannot, however, be called a critical edition of the *Commedia*, as Landino seems fairly insensitive to textual matters; Gennai has drawn attention to the fact that there are even occasional discrepancies between the text of the *Commedia* to which the commentary is appended and the text as Landino quotes it in smaller print in the commentary.[3] An element that gives liveliness to Landino's text and deserves much more attention than it has hitherto received is, as Cardini pointed out,[4] the topic of language. Landino writes on points of language with a degree of aggressivity which, as we shall see, may be due in part to the fact that he felt provoked. He is certainly very sensitive to linguistic variants, and his changes shed an interesting light on the development of the *volgare fiorentino* from Dante's time to his own. He may exaggerate the linguistic continuity between past and present, but at least Dante's language is scrutinized for the first time. The commentary contains a wealth of digressions on both stylistic and contextual

---

1   M. Barbi, *Della fortuna di Dante*, p. 134.
2   R. Cardini, "Landino e Dante", p. 181.
3   S. Gennai, "Cristoforo Landino commentatore di Dante", in *Atti del Convegno di studi su aspetti e problemi della critica dantesca*, by various authors (Rome, De Luca, 1967), pp. 115–24 (p. 122). This is an informative article but without references.
4   R. Cardini, "Landino e Dante", p. 184.

points, and possibly its greatest fault is that sometimes these are prolix and only tenuously linked with the actual text. He displays a vast and eclectic culture, and draws liberally on the classics. He hardly alludes, though, to Dante's minor works (he refers only twice to the *Convivio* and once to *Monarchia*).[1] His highly original allegorical interpretation reflects Neoplatonist positions, but it is not at variance with certain fundamental doctrines of Dante's. Critics have accused Landino of interpreting everything allegorically, but one can find several instances where he accepts a more literal sense, rejecting interpretations that he considers inappropriate.[2] His glosses are at times very perceptive, as for instance in connection with the expression "a frusto a frusto", used of the begging Romeo (a figure with whom the exiled Dante is often identified) in *Paradiso* VI. 141. In this connection Landino writes: "frusto in latino significa pezzo; adunque dinota el mendicare dove non è dato pane intero ma in pezzi" ["*frusto* in Latin means piece; therefore it implies begging where bread is not given whole but in pieces"], suggesting that help is indeed given, but grudgingly and stintingly, with every morsel having to be begged for.

Why was the publication of Landino's commentary a major civic event and from where did the initiative come that led to its conception? Dionisotti has argued that in view of its strongly nationalistic dedication it must have been a response to outside provocation,[3] for although the Florentines may have liked to think otherwise, Dante was not in fact their exclusive property. The *Commedia* had been published many times before. In 1472 it had been printed in no less than three places (Foligno, Mantua and possibly Venice), and in 1477–78 there had been five more printings (two in Venice, two in Naples, one in Milan). The 1477 Venice edition was the first printed edition to include a commentary and thus to raise the *Commedia* to the status of a "classical" text (since only the classics had been considered worthy of commentary). Recognizing the *florentinitas* of Dante's language, that edition introduced Boccaccio's life of Dante, which precedes the comment-ary proper, with the statement, "Qui comincia la vita e ' costumi

---

1   S. Gennai, "Cristoforo Landino", p. 122.
2   C. Landino, *Scritti politici e teorici*, II, 106
3   "L'usurpazione straniera d'un'opera come la *Commedia* colpiva Firenze dal vivo" (C. Dionisotti, "Dante nel Quattrocento", p. 372).

dello excellente Poeta vulgari Dante Alighieri, honore e gloria dell'idioma Fiorentino" ["Here begin the life and ways of that most excellent vernacular poet, Dante Alighieri, the honour and glory of the Florentine tongue"].[1] The commentary itself was that by Jacopo della Lana, though curiously it was attributed to Benvenuto da Imola, for the presumable reason that his was a more prestigious name and more acceptable to Humanists. His own commentary, however, was in Latin, and this edition of the *Commedia* was meant to appeal to a wider audience. The editor of the 1478 Milan edition was Martino Paolo Nibia from Novara, known to Humanists as Nidobeato, and this edition had contributed greatly to the spread of Dante's work outside Tuscany. Nidobeato too had chosen to include the commentary by Jacopo della Lana and, attributing it correctly, had justified his choice by saying that it was the best of the eight commentaries available and moreover written in the Bolognese vernacular ("in bononiensi lingua"), which, he claimed, was the most important vernacular in Italy, given the city's achievements and its strategic position at the heart of the country ("urbs ita in umbilico Italiae posita").[2] In Florence the linguistic controversies concerned themselves with the relative merits of *volgare* and Latin, but it had apparently not occurred to anyone that a challenge to the superiority of the Florentine vernacular might come from another *volgare*! Landino, though, meets this challenge head on. He tells the Signoria, "Affermo aver liberato el nostro cittadino dalla barbarie di molti esterni idiomi" ["I maintain that I have freed our citizen from the uncouthness of many foreign tongues"], proudly proclaiming that Dante was

> riconosciuto né romagnuolo essere [*pace* Jacopo della Lana] né lombardo [*pace* Nidobeato] né degli idiomi di quegli che l'hanno comentato, ma mero fiorentino. La quale lingua quanto tutte l'altre italiche avanzi manifesto testimonio ne sia che nessuno nel quale apparisca o ingegno o dottrina né versi scrisse mai né prosa che non si sforzassi usare el fiorentino idioma.[3]
>
> [recognized to be neither Romagnol nor Lombard nor of the languages of those who have written commentaries on him, but

---

1   E. Bigi, "Dante e la cultura fiorentina", pp. 171–72.
2   Nidobeato's preface is conveniently accessible in C. Landino, *Scritti politici e teorici*, II, 104–05.
3   C. Landino, *Scritti politici e teorici*, I, 102.

simply a Florentine, which language is clearly shown to be superior to all the other languages of Italy by the fact that anyone of genius and learning who has written either verse or prose has striven to do so in the Florentine idiom.]

With this Landino and the Florentines believed that the matter of linguistic supremacy had been settled once and for all. But it was not to be so.

The year 1502 saw the publication by Aldus in Venice of an edition of the *Commedia* curiously entitled *Le terze rime di Dante*. It was edited by Pietro Bembo, son of Bernardo, the former Venetian ambassador to Florence who had worked so tirelessly for the return of Dante's remains to his native city.[1] That edition was completely different from any of its predecessors. Stark, with no commentary, no preface, no appendix and no abbreviations, it made liberal use of punctuation and regular use of apostrophes and accents. Its simplicity was epoch-making. Moreover, the editor had ignored the *vulgata*, the standard text which Landino had used, and instead published a version taken from a manuscript belonging to his father, which in turn was based on codices belonging to Boccaccio and Petrarch. What emerges from this is a Dante in pre-Humanist linguistic garb, much closer to the original genuine Dante, and definitely lacking the linguistic veneer of the Florentine Quattrocento. The rock to which all the Humanists— extremists and moderates—had clung in all the stormy controversies was Dante's *florentinitas*. At the beginning of the Cinquecento they had to face the grim reality that Dante belonged elsewhere, and perhaps even with greater authority. The Florentine Giunti edition in 1506 came all too late. Printed from Milan to Naples, Dante had now become the poet of all Italy, and Gian Giorgio Trissino, not long after the publication of Bembo's edition, was to strike a final blow to the Florentines' sense of supremacy. To what was in essence the language of Dante and substantially the *volgare illustre fiorentino* he gave a new name: he and generations after him were to call it *italiano*.

---

1   For some of the information in this paragraph see C. Dionisotti, "Bembo, Pietro", in *Enc. dant.*, I, 567–68.

ARIOSTO ON DANTE:
TOO DIVINE AND FLORENTINE

Eric G. Haywood

In 1481, amid great fanfare, the launch took place in Florence of a new edition of Dante's *Commedia*. It contained a commentary by the classical scholar and Medici protégé Cristoforo Landino, and in its title it proudly proclaimed the Florentine origin of both poet and commentator: *Comento di Christophoro Landino fiorentino sopra la Comedia di Danthe Alighieri poeta fiorentino* [*Commentary by the Florentine Cristoforo Landino upon the Comedy of the Florentine Poet Danthe Alighieri*].[1] In the oration which Landino delivered on that occasion, he boasted of how he was doing his patriotic duty ("debitore alla mia patria") by returning Dante to his native city after long years of exile ("dopo lungo essilio restituito nella sua patria") and by granting him that recognition in his own native language ("riconosciuto nella sua lingua"). Moreover, he invited the rulers of Florence, to whom the commentary was being presented, to take pride in the divinity of Dante's mind: "Voi [...]

---

1   From the time of the earliest printed edition of the *Commedia* it had become the established practice to refer to its author in the title as being Florentine. What is new about Landino's commentary is the dual Florentine claim ("Landino fiorentino", "Dante fiorentino") and the appropriation of Dante, as it were, by Landino, through the mention of the commentary first and of the poem only second, as though to make it quite clear that this work emanates from Florence and that that is where Dante belongs. A catalogue of the early editions of the *Commedia* may be found in G. Mambelli, *Gli annali delle edizioni dantesche* (Bologna, Zanichelli, 1931). The edition of Landino's commentary from which I quote—except for the proem—was published in 1491 in Venice by Petro Cremonese dito Veronese; the proem I quote from C. Landino, *Scritti critici e teorici*, edited by R. Cardini, 2 vols (Rome, Bulzoni, 1974), I, 97–164. All translations of Landino are my own. On Landino's aim to "rivendicare la 'fiorentinità' di Dante" see E. Bigi, "La tradizione esegetica della *Commedia* nel Cinquecento", in his *Forme e significati nella "Divina commedia"* (Bologna, Cappelli, 1981), pp. 173–209.

illustrissimi Signori nostri, riconoscendo in questo nostro volume la divinità dello ingegno di Dante [...] congratulerete alla vostra splendidissima patria alla quale el sommo Dio tanto dono abbi conceduto" ["You (...) our most illustrious Lords, recognizing in this our volume the divinity of Dante's mind (...) will rejoice that God Almighty granted such a gift to your most glorious father-land"].[1] There had been other printed editions of the *Commedia*, and in 1478 the Milanese publisher Nidobeato had sought to turn the poem's fame to the advantage of other cities and regimes, but never before had Dante been marketed in such an avowedly partisan and chauvinistic manner.[2] And never before had the stakes been so high: Dante was being given the kind of recognition which hitherto had been granted only to writers of antiquity, and Landino's was intended to be *the* authorized version of the *Commedia*.[3] Never, moreover, had the times been so propitious for

---

1   The oration was delivered before the Signoria of Florence on 30 August 1481. I quote from the following version: C. Landino, "Orazione dedicatoria del commento dantesco", in R. Cardini, *La critica del Landino* (Florence, Sansoni, 1973), pp. 372–82 (pp. 378, 379, 379, 381).

2   "L'edizione del Nidobeato fu, nel 1478, tale suggello da sgannare, allora, ogni uomo: da Milano, con eloquenza umanistica, la *Commedia* veniva offerta in lettura ai principi": C. Dionisotti, "Dante nel Quattrocento", *Atti del Congresso internazionale di studi danteschi: 20–27 aprile 1965* (Florence, Sansoni, 1966), pp. 333–78 (p. 371). The Nidobeato edition contained Jacopo della Lana's commentary, and justifying his choice of commentary the publisher wrote: "Materna eadem et bononiensi lingua superare est visus, cum sit illa urbs ita in umbilico Italie posita ut assiduo commertio non tersa solum vocabula sed provintiis omnibus etiam communia habeat, nec minore gratia dignitateque sit in Italia bononiensis sermo quam laconicus olim in Grecia fuit" (quoted by Dionisotti, p. 371). It was this, according to Dionisotti, that acted as a stimulus for Landino's commentary, which "non poté [...] sorgere in quel momento e modo, con un impegno e intento nazionalistico cosí scoperto se non per improvviso e prepotente stimolo polemico [...]. L'usurpazione straniera d'un'opera come la *Commedia* colpiva Firenze nel vivo" (p. 372). For more on Landino, and other early editions of the *Commedia*, see C. Salvadori, "Landmarks in the Fortunes of Dante in the Florentine Quattrocento", in the present volume, pp. 43–69. On the political allegiance of Landino and whether or not he may really be said to be a Medici partisan, see below, p. 81 n. 1.

3   "[...] col Landino, ed è avvenimento significativo ed importante, per la prima volta la *Commedia* attinge un livello di alta cultura 'universitaria' ed insieme laica, e si stacca dal suo consueto 'pubblico' borghese per elevarsi ad *auctoritas* consacrata da un 'corso' nello Studio fiorentino, tenuto da uno degli intellettuali di professione piú in vista del tempo": G. Resta, "Dante nel Quattrocento", in *Dante nel pensiero e nella esegesi dei secoli* xiv *e* xv: *atti del*

such a launch. The market responded positively to it, as we might say today, and Landino's edition was shortly to establish itself as a best seller, becoming in due course the Quattrocento text most often reprinted in the Cinquecento.[1] As a result, "for over fifty years, in an age which was now dominated by the printed book, the vast majority of those who read the *Commedia* were also readers of Cristoforo Landino's commentary."[2]

It would be impossible thereafter for anyone to ignore what Landino had done. When Bembo published the *Commedia* with the Aldine Press, in 1502 and again in 1515, he reacted to Landino's extravagant claims and ponderous glosses by offering the reader no more than Dante's bare text, under the simple title *Le terze rime di Dante* and *Lo 'nferno e 'l Purgatorio e 'l Paradiso di Dante Alaghieri* (though admittedly Dante is referred to, in the 1515 dedication to Vittoria Colonna, as "the divine poet" ["il divino poeta"]).[3] And when in 1555 Lodovico Dolce brought out the edition whose popularity was soon to eclipse Landino's, he set the seal for all times on Dante's divinity, by transferring to the work itself the adjective which Landino had so successfully attached to its author, and thus giving it the title by which it is still known today, the DIVINE *Comedy*.[4]

III *Congresso nazionale di studi danteschi, Melfi 27/9–2/10/1970* (Florence, Olschki, 1975), pp. 71–91 (p. 81).

1   "Fu questo il libro quattrocentesco piú ristampato nel Cinquecento, e di conseguenza il libro umanistico presumibilmente piú letto nell'epoca successiva": R. Cardini, "Landino e Dante", *Schifanoia*, 15–16 (1995), 99–109 (p. 101). Cardini's article had already appeared in *Rinascimento*, 30 (1990), 175–90.

2   "Per oltre cinquant' anni, in età ormai dominata dal libro a stampa, i lettori della *Commedia* furono anche in assoluta maggioranza lettori del commento di Cristoforo Landino" (C. Dionisotti, "Dante nel Quattrocento", p. 374).

3   "[…] la prestigieuse édition aldine de 1502 […] établie par Pietro Bembo et réalisée par le grand imprimeur et humaniste vénitien Aldo Manuzio, constitue en fait une critique implicite contre l'hégémonie landinienne jusqu'à elle absolue": S. Fabrizio-Costa and F. La Brasca, "De l'âge des auteurs à celui des polygraphes: les commentaires de la *Divine Comédie* de C. Landino (1481) et A. Vellutello (1544)", in *Les Commentaires et la naissance de la critique littéraire (France et Italie, xvème–xvième siècles): actes du Colloque International, Paris VIII, 19–21 mai 1988,* edited by M. Plaisance and G.☐Mathieu-Castellani (Paris, Université de Paris VIII, 1990), pp. 175–93 (p. 176). Quite how polemical Bembo's and the publisher's decision was is evident if one bears in mind that it had become the accepted practice to refer to Dante as "fiorentino" (see above, p. 71 n. 1).

4   See D. Parker, *Commentary and Ideology: Dante in the Renaissance* (Durham, NC–London, Duke University Press, 1993), p. 153.

Since nothing has survived of Ariosto's library, we cannot be absolutely certain whether it was indeed Landino's edition of the *Commedia* which he owned and read, but even to the most casual reader it must be "manifestissimo"—to use Rajna's word—that he knew the work extremely well, and that it constitutes, by *contaminatio*, an essential ingredient of his own poem.[1] Who could possibly fail to notice, for instance, the Dante allusions in Astolfo's journey to the other world?[2] It is only fairly recently though that we have come to know just how extensive Ariosto's debt to Dante was. The first scholar to study the matter, a century or so ago, while asserting that Ariosto clearly knew "the *Divine Comedy* almost by heart", could only detect an "unconscious (or at most only half-conscious) verbal imitation" of Dante's poem in *Orlando furioso*,[3] and some thirty years later another scholar still spoke of "diverse, uneven [...] and slightly haphazard [...] reminiscences of Dante".[4] Following the thorough and learned investigations of Segre, Blasucci and Ossola (dating from the 1960s and 1970s), however, we may now claim not only that Ariosto's knowledge of Dante was extensive, but that he systematically used the *Commedia*—as a "mine of stylistic and narrative forms" ("miniera di istituzioni stilistico-narrative"; Blasucci), a "linguistic repertory" ("repertorio linguistico"), a model for a "technique" ("tecnica"; Segre)—, to the point where *Orlando furioso* is replete with Dante borrowings. According to Segre, these tend to come in clusters, following what he calls a "law of viscosity" ("legge di vischiosità"), and most of them (61.6%) are drawn from *Inferno*, with fewer (25.4%) from *Purgatorio* and fewer still (12.6%) from *Paradiso*. According to Ossola, they can be classified as belonging to three types: "dantismi di repertorio, stereotipati dalla tradizione canterina" ["standard Dantisms, stereotyped by the storytelling tradition"], "paradigmi di rima danteschi di eletta rarità per innalzamento di tono (in

1   P. Rajna, *Le fonti dell'"Orlando furioso"*, edited by F. Mazzoni (Florence, Sansoni, 1975), p. 545. On Ariosto's library see C. Segre, "La biblioteca dell'Ariosto", in his *Esperienze ariostesche* (Pisa, Nistri–Lischi, 1966), pp. 45–50.

2   Astolfo's journey is narrated in Cantos xxxiv and xxxv of *Orlando furioso*.

3   L. O. Kuhns, "Some Verbal Resemblances in the *Orlando furioso* and the *Divina commedia*", *Modern Language Notes*, 10 (1895), 340–47 (pp. 341–42).

4   "Réminiscences dantesques [...] un peu au hasard [...] diverses et inégales": H. Hauvette, "Réminiscences dantesques dans le *Roland furieux*", in *Mélanges de linguistique et de littérature offerts à M. Alfred Jeanroy*, by various authors (Paris, Droz, 1928), pp. 299–306 (p. 301).

contesti celebrativi)" ["rare and select Dantean rhyme paradigms used for raising the tone (in gratulatory contexts)"] and borrowings in which is evident an "opera di desublimazione" ("degradazione / rimotivazione semantica") ["process of desublimation" ("semantic debasement / remotivation")].[1] What is more, it has emerged that the number of borrowings from Dante in the third and final redaction of *Orlando furioso* (1532) is quite considerably higher than in the first and second redactions (1516 and 1521). In other words, Ariosto chose, deliberately and provocatively, to pay no heed to the strictures contained in the *Prose della volgar lingua*: even as Bembo was seeking to ostracize Dante from the world of polite

1   C. Segre, "Un repertorio linguistico e stilistico dell'Ariosto: la *Commedia*", in his *Esperienze ariostesche*, pp. 51–83; L. Blasucci, "Ancora sulla *Commedia* come fonte linguistica e stilistica del *Furioso*", *Giornale storico della letteratura italiana*, 85 (1968), 188–231; C. Ossola, "Dantismi metrici nel *Furioso*", in *Ludovico Ariosto: lingua, stile e tradizione: atti del Congresso organizzato dai Comuni di Reggio Emilia e Ferrara, 12–16 ott. 1974*, edited by C. Segre (Milan, Feltrinelli, 1976), pp. 65–94. These studies have rendered obsolete the Positivist catalogue of Dante "reminiscences" established at the beginning of the century by G. Maruffi, *La "Divina commedia" considerata quale fonte dell'"Orlando furioso" e della "Gerusalemme liberata"* (Naples, Pierro, 1903), who concluded that, although Ariosto owed a lot to Dante, his attitude towards him was like that of "que' figli che finiscono col manifestare un'indole tutta propria, diversa assai dall'indole de' genitori, a cui in fondo non resta altra gloria che d'averli messi al mondo" (p. 63). Later studies have, on the whole, simply offered variations on the Segre–Blasucci–Ossola theme. A-J. Mariani, "Rassegna della presenza della *Commedia* nella poesia cavalleresca dell'Ariosto", *Critica letteraria*, 9 (1981), 569–600, is a list of yet more Dante borrowings and, by the author's own admission, little more than a footnote to the studies of Blasucci and Segre (she does not mention Ossola). S. Vazzana, "Postille sulla presenza di Dante in Ariosto", *L'Alighieri*, 28, i (1987), 22–43, lists and discusses more Dantisms in Ariosto, to show how Dante "illuminates" Ariosto and Ariosto emulates and transforms Dante, whom he prizes above all for his "suprema attenzione alla natura e all'uomo" (in particular as manifested in *Inferno*). R. D'Alfonso, "Ricezione dantesca nell'*Orlando furioso* (XXXIII. 127, XXXV. 21. 4)", *Schifanoia*, 4 (1987), 53–71, illustrates the "tecnica diminutiva" used by Ariosto in his parody of Dante, whereby he undermines the entire purpose and credibility of the *Commedia* and renders void medieval and Humanist philosophies of history. On whether it is correct to say that Ariosto "parodies" Dante see below. See too M. Beer, *Romanzi di cavalleria: il "Furioso" e il romanzo italiano del primo Cinquecento* (Rome, Bulzoni, 1987), especially pp. 41–50, and E. Kanduth, "Bemerkungen zu Dante-Reminiszenzen im *Orlando furioso*", in *Studien zu Dante und zu anderen Themen der romanischen Literaturen*, edited by K. Lichem and H. J. Simon (Graz, Universitäts-Buchdruckerei Styria, 1971), pp. 59–70.

letters, Ariosto was proclaiming him to be a model well worthy of imitation.[1]

Paradoxical though it may seem (and it is no doubt that which misled some into talking of "unconscious verbal imitation" and "slightly haphazard reminiscences"), the most characteristic feature of Ariosto's debt to Dante, of "come lavorava l'Ariosto" ["how Ariosto worked"], is said to be the fact that "he never quotes Dante" ("non cita mai Dante").[2] He never quotes the *Commedia* word for word, that is, but always re-works it "in proprio, secondo i canoni del suo gusto rinascimentale" ["in his own way, following the rules and taste of the Renaissance"].[3] In so doing, he appears to want deliberately to change not just the words but also the mood created by Dante, and since he achieves this, more often than not, by a lowering of the tone, it would seem logical to conclude, as many have done, that Ariosto's main intent, in rewriting the *Commedia* (for that is what he does), was to parody Dante. Certainly "parody" is the word which most readily falls from the pen of critics as they try to explain the wherefore of Ariosto's *modus operandi* in relation to Dante. Rajna, for instance, while warning that it would be "the most pompous nonsense" ("la più solenne delle corbellerie") to assert that Ariosto had sought to ridicule Dante, nonetheless claimed that the story of Lydia (in Canto XXXIV of *Orlando furioso*) was "a clear and simple parody" ("una parodia bella e buona") of Francesca's.[4] More recently Ascoli has written of Ariosto's "extensive parody" of the *Commedia* in *Orlando furioso*, which he describes as an attempt to "mock", "trivialize" and "misrepresent" Dante,[5] while Ossola has claimed that the "ideological result" ("résultat idéologique") of Ariosto's imitation

1   On Bembo's attitude to Dante see, among others, C. Grayson, "Dante and the Renaissance", in *Italian Studies Presented to E. R. Vincent*, edited by C.□P.□Brand and others (Cambridge, Heffer, 1962), pp. 57–75, and A. Vallone, *L'interpretazione di Dante nel Cinquecento: studi e ricerche*, second edition (Florence, Olschki, 1969).

2   C. Segre, "Un repertorio linguistico", p. 51. The main concern of critics in assessing Ariosto's debt to Dante has been to establish, precisely, "come lavorava l'Ariosto"—an expression initially coined by G. Contini, "Come lavorava l'Ariosto", in his *Esercizî di lettura* [1947] (Turin, Einaudi, 1974), pp. 232–41.

3   C. Segre, "Un repertorio linguistico", p. 80.

4   P. Rajna, *Le fonti dell'"Orlando furioso"*, p. 537. On the story of Lydia and on how it may be said to be a parody of Francesca's see below.

5   A. R. Ascoli, *Ariosto's Bitter Harmony: Crisis and Evasion in the Italian Renaissance* (Princeton, Princeton University Press, 1987), pp. 287, 300.

of Dante in Astolfo's journey—which yet another critic has labelled the poem's "most sustained parody of Dante"—is to provide a "parodic echo of the sublime" ("écho parodique du sublime").[1] The effect, and intent, of such parodying, these critics would agree, is to "demolish" the authority of Ariosto's source,[2] and by extension the authority of any text, even his own. That would seem a fair enough observation, but others have argued that it is insufficient or incorrect to think of Ariosto's relationship to Dante in terms of parody. One American critic prefers to view the question in psychological rather than literary terms, of "anxiety" rather than "parody": "Ariosto's authorial anxiety about Dante's pervasive influence" and "his doubts about his ability to shake off that influence and write a poem that is truly his own".[3] And an Italian critic has lately posed the question in more political terms, seeing Astolfo's journey to the moon not as a parody of Dante but as an act of homage, which however expresses Ariosto's realization of the "unbridgeable gap" ("distanza incolmabile") separating Dante's world from his own and seeks to contrast their respective "ethics of literary creation" ("etiche della creazione letteraria"): Dante's vision of poetry as a heroic search for truth, and Ariosto's notion of poetry as a compromise with political and social exigencies.[4]

Whereas it is plainly not incorrect to think of Ariosto's relationship to Dante in terms of parody (or "respectful parody", as it were, since Ariosto's decision to try and undermine Dante's stature is also a way of acknowledging it), it is not particularly helpful or enlightening to do so, given that that is the nature of Ariosto's relationship to all his models. *Tra omaggio e parodia* [*Between Homage and Parody*] is the title of a recent book on Ariosto's debt to Petrarch,[5] but it is a title which could well

---

1   C. Ossola, "Métaphore et inventaire de la folie dans la littérature italienne du xvième siècle", in *Folie et déraison à la Renaissance*, by various authors (Brussels, Editions de l'Université de Bruxelles, 1976), pp. 171–96 (pp. 186–87); P. A. Parker, *Inescapable Romance: Studies in the Poetics of a Mode* (Princeton, Princeton University Press, 1979), p. 45.

2   "[...] azione demolitrice delle *auctoritates* tipica del rapporto di Ariosto con le sue fonti": M. C. Cabani, *Fra omaggio e parodia: Petrarca e petrarchismo nel "Furioso"* (Pisa, Nistri–Lischi, 1990), p. 281.

3   M. Johnson-Haddad, "Gelosia: Ariosto Reads Dante", *Stanford Italian Review*, 11 (1992), 187–201.

4   M. Scalabrini, "Il cigno senz' ali: l'idea di Dante nell'*Orlando furioso*", *Schede umanistiche* (1994, ii), 67–78.

5   See n. 2 on this page.

describe his dealings with almost any other writer, be it Virgil, Boccaccio, Boiardo, or indeed Dante. The "anxiety" of the psycho- logical interpretation does not have all that much to commend it either, given the universality of its application; it possibly says more about the act of literary creation in general than about the particular nature of Ariosto's relationship to Dante. Therefore, if there is anything unique about that relationship—which on the face of it there would appear to be, since the high point of *Orlando furioso* is set within a framework (Astolfo's journey to the other world) which is unmistakably of Dantean inspiration—,[1] it makes more sense, I contend, to follow the "political" line of argument suggested by the last of the above-mentioned critics, and that is the line I now propose to take. In doing so, it is also my intention to fill a gap in the history of the transmission of the *Commedia* during the Renaissance. Curiously, none of the scholars, all of them great, who have written on Dante in the Renaissance has actually included Ariosto in his survey, and yet without Ariosto that survey is bound to be incomplete, for *Orlando furioso*, which deliberately calls attention to the intertextual nature of its "istoria" and thereby challenges the reader to reflect on the nature of literature, especially literature as imitation, is just as much a work of literary criticism as it is a work of literature. The *fortuna* of the *Commedia* in the Renaissance is inextricably bound up with the *fortuna* of *Orlando furioso*.[2]

1   It was for long traditional to view *Orlando furioso* as a typical "romance" poem, without closure or sense of direction, and consisting therefore of a succession of anecdotes none of which was more important than any other. It is now more fashionable (and I would subscribe to this view) to see the poem as an epic poem with a clear sense of purpose and direction, and therefore containing episodes of great significance for an overall under- standing of that sense. Because it is as a result of Astolfo's journey that Orlando is cured of his "romantic" fantasies and allowed to fulfil his epic destiny, which in turn will pave the way for Ruggiero to meet his own destiny, and since one of the major themes of the poem, if not *the* major theme, is the meaning of literature (that is, how we read and interpret what we read), which is what St John reveals to Astolfo on the moon, it makes good sense to view Astolfo's journey as the high point, or at least one of the highest points, of the poem.

2   On Dante in the Renaissance, besides the works already quoted above in n. 1 on p. 76, see E. Bigi, "Dante e la cultura fiorentina del Quattrocento", in his *Forme e significati*, pp. 145–72, as well as his "La tradizione esegetica"; also E. Garin, "Dante nel Rinascimento", *Rinascimento*, 7 (1967), 3–28. "Istoria" is the word repeatedly used by Ariosto when referring to his poem (his "story").

The *Commedia* in the Renaissance, especially the early Cinque-cento, was above all, let us remind ourselves, the *Commedia* as proposed by Cristoforo Landino, and although we may not know for certain, as has already been mentioned, whether that was the version which Ariosto owned and read, it makes good sense to assume that it was.[1] This should therefore be the obvious starting-point for anyone studying Ariosto's debt to Dante, yet few if any of those who have studied it have thought of mentioning the point, let alone taking it into account. For Ariosto, who in the frontispiece of his poem was proud to proclaim himself "nobile ferrarese" ["nobleman of Ferrara"], Dante cannot have been just any poet, or simply a Great Poet: he could not but be Dante divine and Florentine. And given that that is what Dante was, merely to read the *Commedia* was in a sense a declaration of one's political allegiance; but to imitate or parody it was definitely to take a political stance.

Anyone unconvinced by this should pay heed to what St John the Evangelist says to Astolfo on the moon in *Orlando furioso* xxxv. Astolfo has been brought to the moon—bodily, let it be said, and by public transport ("Un carro apparecchiossi, ch'era ad uso / d'andar scorrendo per quei cieli intorno: / quel già ne le montagne di Giudea / da mortali occhi Elia levato avea" ["A chariot was made ready, designed for travelling about those skies—it had once lifted Elias from mortal gaze in the mountains of Judaea"])—[2] in order to retrieve the lost wits of Orlando, for everything that has been lost on earth is to be found on the moon (Orlando's wits deserted him when he found out about his beloved's love for a good-looking good-for-nothing from the Land of the Infidel). Foremost among the lost objects on the moon is the meaning of literature. Astolfo, having retrieved the flask containing Orlando's wits from the Valley of Lost Things, is then taken by St John to view a mystery play, a "real" allegory which, he is told, shows how, after death, the names of princes (in the form of name-tags) are raised from the river of forgetfulness (that same River Lethe which is to be found in Dante's earthly paradise) by two types of bird: birds of

1   For the influence of Landino's edition on all the great writers and artists of the time see E. Bigi, "Dante e la cultura fiorentina", p.163, and A. Chastel, *Art et humanisme à Florence au temps de Laurent le Magnifique* (Paris, Presses Universitaires de France, 1982), p. 108.

2   *Of,* xxxiv. 68. The edition I quote from is L. Ariosto, *Orlando furioso,* edited by N. Zingarelli (Milan, Hoepli, 1959). All English translations are taken (with the occasional correction) from L. Ariosto, *Orlando furioso,* translated by G. Waldman (London, Oxford University Press, 1974).

prey and white swans. The birds of prey, however, which are numerous and stand for courtiers and sycophants, are unable to hold on to the names and drop them in the river, where they sink out of sight and out of mind for all eternity. Only the white swans, which are few in number and stand for true poets, can bear the names aloft and bring them to the Temple of Fame, where they will be remembered for ever more. The moral of the story—for patrons— is that princes should learn to have "good taste in poetry" ("in poesia buon gusto": xxxv. 26) so as to befriend only those writers who will bring them fame: "E gli scrittor vi fate amici, donde / non avete a temer di Lete l'onde" ["If you (...) make writers your friends you need have no fear of Lethe's waters"; xxxv. 22]. For readers, the moral of the story is that all (good) literature lies, since it was written not to tell the truth but to repay princes for their generous friendship. Therefore, reader,

> se tu vuoi che 'l ver non ti sia ascoso
> tutta al contrario l'istoria converti;
> che i Greci rotti, e che Troia vittrice,
> e che Penelopea fu meretrice.
> (*Orlando furioso*, xxxv. 27)

[if you want to know what really happened, invert the story: Greece was vanquished, Troy triumphant, and Penelope a whore.]

To the reader this message is certainly confusing. If all poetry (literature) lies, we should not believe St John, "ch'al [nostro] mondo [fu] scrittore anch' [egli]" ["(who) in (our) world (...) was a writer too"; xxxv. 28]—yet if we do not, we do! One thing, however, is clear: whether or not literature lies, and whether it is good or bad, its inspiration, and its sense, is always political. The difference between a bird of prey and a swan is not *what* they do, but *how* they do it. Both exalt their masters, only swans do it better. Swans praise, the others flatter. Both however distort the truth, for the sake of political (and financial) gain. So when Astolfo, and the reader, is advised to "invert" the story, what he is being asked is to bear in mind the political circumstances which determine the meaning of a particular text.[1]

---

1   "Nel discorso dell'evangelista [...] si riflette, sia pure in modo paradossale, una presa di coscienza del rapporto tra società e poesia, del problema della 'funzione' e della destinazione della poesia": M. Santoro, *Ariosto e il Rinascimento*, p. 260.

To any reader of the time St John must have been stating the obvious. From the earliest days of the Renaissance, the phase known to us as Civic Humanism, literature had been made to serve a cause, be it that of a party or a city, and this was particularly true of Dante's *Commedia*. "Militant literature" ("letteratura militante") is what Carlo Dionisotti called it, with particular reference to the study of Dante. In Florence rival political factions had come to blows over Dante in 1431, and in 1481, as we have seen, the launch of Landino's commentary was intended as a partisan and political affair.[1] Is it any wonder that Ariosto should turn St John into the mouthpiece of a Church militant about the just deserts of political correctness? He knew only too well that the aesthetics of writing could not be divorced from its politics (in the "gospel" according to St John, the "good taste", power and liberality of princes are all one), and he quite realized that reading was not a harmless or innocent activity (indeed, as we readers already know, the

---

1   C. Dionisotti, "Dante nel Quattrocento", p. 369 (see too above, p. 72 n. 2). Equally, Garin writes: "Ai tempi di Salutati e del Bruni, o del Filelfo e del Marsuppini, come poi a quelli del Landino e del Benivieni, la filigrana della controversia dantesca non è stilistica o linguistica, ma politica—o meglio, come sempre, il fatto culturale è indissolubilmente connesso con vicende piú gravi" ("Dante nel Rinascimento", p. 14). And more recently D. Parker stated, "Critical treatments of Dante in the Renaissance are often politically inflected" (*Commentary and Ideology*, p. 57). In connection with Landino's political allegiance, and taking up a point made by Dionisotti ("Dante nel Quattrocento", p. 373), Bigi argues that the commentary was written in the aftermath of the Pazzi conspiracy and that its aim was thus (in part) to shore up the authority of the Medici ("Dante e la cultura fiorentina", pp. 161–62). M. Martelli, "La cultura letteraria nell'età di Lorenzo", in *Lorenzo il Magnifico e il suo tempo*, edited by G. C. Garfagnini (Florence, Olschki, 1992), pp. 39–84, on the other hand, is of the opinion that Landino may have sympathized with the party of the oligarchs and written the commentary when it seemed that Lorenzo, following the Pazzi conspiracy, was politically a spent force; but he stresses that Landino never broke off relations with Lorenzo and was never openly hostile to him, nor Lorenzo to Landino. R. Cardini, "Landino e Dante", argues that although the stimulus for the commentary may have been political this did not affect the substance of Landino's interpretation of Dante: "Io credo che esso sia tutto percorso da una prepotente passione patriottica non estranea all'isolamento e all'accerchiamento politico, militare e diplomatico di Firenze nel periodo seguito alla Congiura dei Pazzi. [...] Ma anche credo però che queste circostanze e questi stimoli immediati non abbiano né determinato la sostanza dell'interpretazione landiniana di Dante, né inciso in profondità su di essa" (p. 104). It is true that the most explicitly political parts of the commentary are its proem and the oration delivered upon its presentation to the Signoria.

immediate cause of Orlando's madness was his reading and "inversion" of Medoro's poem about the consummation of the latter's and Angelica's love affair). It goes without saying, therefore, that if we seek to understand Ariosto's relationship to Dante, we need to consider the political context of that relationship, or rather, the political implications of having such a relationship.

To borrow from the *Commedia* as extensively as Ariosto did, especially in the aftermath of Bembo's criticisms, was to signal that Dante's poem was a worthy model, but so to acknowledge Dante's worthiness, and what is more, in the very language of Dante's native city, was to acquiesce to the claims of those who would call Dante their own; it was to bolster the aspirations of Florentine (and Medicean) imperialism, which Landino's commentary promoted with such undisguised fervour. "Merita adunque la nostra republica buona grazia da tutta Italia," Landino had written in the comment-ary,

> poiché in quella nacquono e' primi che l'una e l'altra eloquenzia, non solo morta ma per tanti secoli sepulta, in vita ridussono e dalle tartaree tenebre in chiara luce rivocorono.
>
> (Proem, p. 119)

> [Our republic therefore deserves the gratitude of the whole of Italy, for it was there that were born the first men who returned to life and brought from the darkness of Hell into the light of day the one and the other eloquence, which were not only dead but had lain buried for many centuries.]

If it was Ariosto's aim to write a poem for the greater glory of the Este and Ferrara (as it most certainly was), he had no choice, I contend, but to send up the political correctness of Dante the divine Florentine, even as he paid homage to Dante the poet. This is indeed a case of "omaggio e parodia" but, I would suggest, of a different sort, or to a different degree from Ariosto's attitude of homage and parody towards, say, Petrarch and Boccaccio. While similar attempts at political appropriation may have been made in connection with Petrarch and Boccaccio (I am thinking in particular of the best-selling edition of Petrarch's *Trionfi* with the commentary by Bernardo Ilicino),[1] Dante was really in a category of his own. For

---

1   On Ilicino's commentary see V. Merry, "Una nota sulla fortuna del Commento di Bernardo Ilicino ai *Trionfi* petrarcheschi", *Giornale storico della letteratura italiana*, 163 (1986), 235–46; and on its political significance see my own "'Inter urinas liber factus est': il Commento dell'Ilicino ai *Trionfi* del Petrarca",

no other modern writer had there been such public manifestations of political support, and for no other modern writer had such unambiguous claims of infallibility been advanced.

Like all politicians, or indeed writers, with totalitarian aspirations, Landino was completely lacking in a sense of humour (which in Ariosto's book must surely rate as the greatest crime); his Dante was therefore to be taken entirely seriously. God himself being a poet and the world His poem ("è Idio sommo poeta, ed è el mondo suo poema" ["God is a supreme poet, and the world is His poem"; proem, p. 142]), poets are godlike, says Landino, and their poetry is divinely inspired ("dal furore divino [procede] la facultà poetica" ["from divine fury does the poetic faculty proceed"; p. 141]); they are the prophets of God ("non piccola similitudine troverremo essere tra 'l poeta e el profeta" ["we shall find that there is no small resemblance between the poet and the prophet"; p.□142]), who, like Orpheus or Amphion, bring civilization to the world ("con la suavità de' versi gli uomini e' quali sanza leggi, sanza costumi vagando pe' propinqui monti vivevono in solitutidine, ridusse insieme e mollificando la lor dureza gli compose in vita civile" ["with the charm of his verses he gathered together all human beings, who were living without laws and in solitude, wandering in the nearby hills, and mitigating their harshness he set them to living a civil life"; p. 145]). Nothing therefore can be more useful to a state than poetry ("nessuna cosa si truova che in una libera e bene instituta republica piú utilità e ornamento seco arrechi che la eloquenzia o oratoria o poetica, purché da vera virtú e somma probità accompagnata sia" ["there is nothing to be found in a free and well-ordered republic that bears greater utility and grace than eloquence, be it oratorical or poetic, as long as it is associated with true virtue and the utmost probity"; p. 140]), and no poem, naturally, can do this better than Dante's ("tutto el suo poema niente altro [contiene] che lode di virtú" ["his entire poem contains nothing but praises of virtue"; p. 152]). Landino's Dante was thus a *poeta theologus*, and Landino's job to explain "the depth and range of his learning, and the excellence and divinity of the mind of our Tuscan and Florentine poet".[1] It must be said of course

in *Petrarca e la cultura europea*, edited by L. Rotondi Secchi Tarugi (Milan, Nuovi Orizzonti, 1997), pp. 139–59.

1   "[...] la profondità e varietà della doctrina, e excellentia e divinità dello ingegno del nostro toscano e fiorentino poeta": commentary (on *Inf.*, I. 1–21), p. 11r.

that it was not just Landino who took Dante so seriously. The *Commedia* had long been considered "a weighty philosophical poem",[1] and even Bembo, in the dedication to the 1515 Aldine edition of the *Commedia*, speaks admiringly of the depth and range of Dante's knowledge ("tali e tante scienze"). And had not Manetti gone to extraordinary lengths, just a few years before, to prove Dante's scientific *bona fides* by providing exact measurements of his other world? This, then, is the background against which we must "invert" Ariosto's rewriting of the *Commedia*—which in effect amounts to a systematic challenge to Dante's cosmos and authority, and by extension to the authority of those who patronized him. If, by "parodying" Dante, Ariosto could show him to be an idol with clay feet and limited vision, serious doubts must clearly be cast on the wisdom of those who would bask in the reflected glory of that sham divinity. If Dante, and Landino, spoke rubbish, where did that leave Florence and its rulers?

Florence, in Landino's book, was naturally enough the best place on earth, "rated most honourably among the topmost republics" ("tra le prime republiche onorificentissimamente collocata": proem, p. 103). Not only had Florence produced the best philosophers, the best writers, the best musicians, the best painters and sculptors, the best lawyers and the best merchants, but it was and always would be the saviour of Italy, the state to which all other Italian states owed their liberty. Foremost among those in Florence's debt were the Este and Ferrara:

> Né con altro essercito piú difese Nicolò da Esti marchese di Ferrara el suo principato che con mille cinquecento barbute, che cosí in quegli tempi chiamavono gl'uomini d'arme, e' quali tutti cittadini fiorentini e in gran parte nobili mandò la nostra republica in aiuto al collegato principe.
>
> (Proem, p. 112)

> [Nor did Niccolò d'Este, Marquis of Ferrara, defend his principality with any other army save fifteen hundred helmets, as the men-of-arms were called in those days, who were all Florentine citizens, for the most part noble, and had been sent by our republic to assist that ruler, who was her ally.]

---

1   "[...] un severo poema filosofico" (E. Bigi, "Dante nel Quattrocento", p. 156).

Not surprisingly, Ariosto did not share this view. For him, Florence was the city which, while the Estensi fought for Italy, was counting its money and taking Azzo VII d'Este as surety for a loan (*Orlando furioso*, III. 35), the city which could not make cloth splendid enough to clothe the gorgeous limbs of beautiful Olimpia (XI. 75), the city which, to its eternal "shame and ignominy" ("vergogna e scorno": XXVI. 45), allowed itself to be defeated by Francis I. It was, in short, a city not of noble warriors but of greedy moneylenders and merchants. For Ariosto there was only one "bella terra che siede sul fiume" ["beautiful city seated on the river"; III. 34], namely Ferrara, and only one family capable of saving Italy and restoring it to its ancient glory, the Estensi:

> I capitani e i cavallier robusti
> quindi usciran, che col ferro e col senno
> ricuperar tutti gli onor vetusti
> de l'arme invitte alla sua Italia denno:
> quindi terran lo scettro i Signor giusti,
> che come il savio Augusto e Numa fenno,
> sotto il benigno e buon governo loro
> ritorneran la prima età de l'oro.
> (*Orlando furioso*, III. 18)

[From you shall spring the captains and dauntless knights who, by their sword and wits, are to reclaim for Italy all the former honours of unvanquished arms. From you the just rulers will hold their sceptres, under whose mild and virtuous government, as under wise Augustus and Numa, the Golden Age will once again relive.]

And whereas Landino had boasted that Florence was descended from Rome and was "a true colony of Roman citizens" ("di romani cittadini vera colonia": proem, p. 105), Ferrara could go one better. Being descended from the Romans meant descending only indirectly from the Trojans, but the Estensi, through Ruggiero, were direct descendants of the Trojans: only they were "the blood deriving from ancient Troy" ("l'antiquo sangue che venne da Troia": III. 17). That Ariosto was fond of his native city is well known, and his growing pride at belonging to such a great place— or at such a great place belonging to him, perhaps—is reflected not only in the increasing "epic" seriousness of *Orlando furioso* as it evolves from the first to the third redaction, but in the very title-pages of the editions. The first edition, in 1516, was *Orlando furioso de Ludovico Ariosto da Ferrara* [*Orlando furioso by Ludovico Ariosto from Ferrara*], the second, in 1521, *Orlando furioso di Ludovico Ariosto nobile ferrarese* [*Orlando furioso by Ludovico Ariosto, Ferrarese nobleman*], and the third, in 1532, on Ariosto's explicit insistence, *Orlando furioso di messer Ludovico Ariosto nobile ferrarese* [*Orlando furioso by Master Ludovico Ariosto, Ferrarese nobleman*].[1]

The same base metal of which the Florentines, in *Orlando furioso*, are made seems to be the stuff from which St John the Evangelist is fashioned. "Blessed old man" ("Vecchio benedetto": xxxv. 30) he may be, but his is the language of usurers and money-lenders. He talks and behaves less like a mystic than a pawnbroker and blackmailer, intent on bartering his reputation for his salvation:

> Gli scrittori amo, e fo il *debito* mio,
> ch'al vostro mondo fui scrittore anch' io.
>
> E sopra tutti gli altri io feci *acquisto*
> che non mi *può* levar tempo né morte;
> e ben *convenne* al mio lodato Cristo
> *render*mi *guidardon* di sí gran sorte.
> (*Orlando furioso*, xxxv. 28–29; my italics)

[I like writers and am paying my debt, for in your world I was a writer too. / And I, above all others, acquired something which neither Time nor Death can take from me: I praised Christ and rightly earned from Him the reward of so great a good fortune.]

Writing the Gospel had been a good investment indeed! And Ariosto may have wished to intimate that writing the *Commedia* had not, after all, been such a bad investment either, since Dante

---

1   See A. Casadei, *La strategia delle varianti: le correzioni storiche del terzo "Furioso"* (Lucca, Pacini Fazzi, 1988), p. 151. In an earlier article ("L'esordio del canto xlvi del *Furioso*: strategia compositiva e varianti storico-culturali", *Italianistica*, 15 [1986], 53–91), Casadei had pointed out how Ariosto's rewriting of the beginning of the last canto of *Orlando furioso* proves that he had little regard for Florentine culture and deliberately aimed to play down its significance: "Sarà sufficiente ricordare l'esclusione dei Fiorentini (e del Machiavelli in particolare), che sono menzionati anche lungamente dal Giovio. Tuttavia Ariosto, che aveva avuto contatti anche importanti con quella città, non inserisce suoi poeti nel canto finale, e ricorda solo il fuoruscito Alamanni e l'amico Guidetti nel c. xxxvii. 8, evidentemente convinto della non-centralità della cultura fiorentina di quel periodo" (p. □90).

was now getting the "guidardon" he deserved. It has long been believed that Astolfo may be a figure of Ariosto, but no one has ever suggested that St John may possibly stand for Dante. Yet Landino's commentary would justify such an interpretation, for it says of Dante that he may have been an imitator of St John: "Imita Ioanni Evangelista el quale dormendo sopra el pecto di Christo redemptore hebbe visione delle chose celeste" ["He imitates John the Evangelist, who, sleeping in the bosom of Christ the Redeemer, had a vision of the things of Heaven"].[1] Perhaps that is why the utterances of Ariosto's St John are so confusing and his vision so earthbound and limited, and why Astolfo is so unimpressed by his speech (he reacts to it with stony silence): "Who are you, Dante-St John-Landino-pawnbroker, to lecture to us on matters divine, and what have I, Ariosto, *nobile ferrarese*, to learn from you?" Ariosto appears to be saying. No one better than St John could have incarnated Landino's ideal of *poeta theologus*, but by portraying him in the way he does, Ariosto clearly puts paid to such fancy notions.[2]

It is also Landino's conception of poetry, of Platonic fury, that Ariosto turns on its head. "Dal furore divino procede la facultà poetica" ["From divine fury does the poetic faculty proceed"], Landino had written (proem, p. 141), to which Ariosto might well have answered, "Dalla facultà poetica procede il furore" ["From the poetic faculty does fury proceed"]! This is graphically illustrated in Orlando's descent into madness. The immediate cause of Orlando's fury is not so much Angelica's infidelity as Medoro's poem about it—which, let it be said, is a reward for a favour received ("De la *commodità* che qui m'è data,/io *povero* Medor ricompensarvi,/d'altro non posso che d'ognior *lodarvi*" ["I, poor

---

1   Commentary (on *Inf.*, I. 1–21), p. 11r.
2   "Avec Landino [...] la *Commedia* devenait le réceptacle du savoir moderne et le *poeta theologus* le héros spirituel de l'humanisme florentin" (A. Chastel, *Art et humanisme*, p. 110). Bigi stresses how Landino views the *Commedia* "come un organismo altissimo e congeniale strumento espressivo di una sublime sapienza teologica" ("La tradizione esegetica", p. 175). Ariosto may of course have been reacting not only to Landino's view of Dante as *poeta theologus*, but to a long-established Humanist tradition of viewing poetry, especially ancient poetry, as theology; on this see C. Kallendorf, "From Virgil to Vida: The *Poeta Theologus* in Italian Renaissance Commentary", *Journal of the History of Ideas*, 56 (1995), 41–62, who argues that from the time of Albertino Mussato onwards "the theory of the poet as theologian became the cornerstone of Humanist poetics" (p. 45).

Medor, cannot repay you for your indulgence otherwise than by ever praising you"; XXIII. 108; my italics]), which the narrator has to "invert" ("Medoro [...]/questa sentenzia in versi avea ridotta;/che fosse culta in suo linguaggio io penso,/et era ne la nostra tale il senso" ["(Medor's) inscription was written in verse. (...) I believe it was written in his native tongue; in ours this is how it reads"; XXIII. 107]), and which Orlando tries to interpret "tutta al contrario" ("cercando invano/che non vi fosse quel che v'era scritto" ["trying in vain to make that which was written not be there"; XXIII. 111]), but which ultimately has the better of him ("Fu allora per uscir del sentimento,/sí tutto in preda del dolor si lassa" ["He was ready to go out of his mind, so complete was his surrender to grief"; XXIII. 112]). And when Orlando is finally able to verify the meaning of Medoro's poem (he is shown the bracelet which he himself gave Angelica as a token of his love, but which Angelica then passed on to a shepherd to thank him for allowing her and Medoro to consummate their love under his roof), his behaviour is described in terms which seem, playfully and dismissively, to evoke the very words Landino had used to prove the power of Orpheus's poetry:

> Per nessuna altra cagione dicono avere con la citara potuto fermare e' fiumi, muovere e' sassi, mitigare le fiere, se non perché con la suavità de' suoi versi poté reprimere l'empito e el furore di molti, e' quali nelle forze del corpo fidandosi tutti gl'altri abbattevono e conculcavono, e altri e' quali erono d'efferato ingegno o stupidi o quasi insensati condusse a vita razionale e civile.
>
> (Proem, p. 145)

> [For no other reason, do they say, was he able with his cither to stop rivers, move rocks and calm beasts, except that with the charm of his verses he managed to repress the violence and fury of many who, trusting in the strength of their body, would strike and oppress anyone else, and to lead others, who were of cruel disposition or stupid or almost brainless, to a rational and civil form of life.]

Orlando too stops rivers, moves rocks and calms beasts, but to quite different effect:

> Che rami, e ceppi, e tronchi, e sassi, e zolle
> non cessò di gittar ne le bell' onde,

fin che da sommo ad imo sí turbolle,
che non furo mai piú chiare né monde.
(*Orlando furioso*, XXIII. 131)

[Branches, stumps and boughs, stones and clods he kept hurling
into the lovely waters until he so clouded them from surface to
bottom that they were clear and pure never again.]

Furthermore, "a pugni, ad urti, a morsi, a graffi, a calci/cavalli e
buoi rompe, fracassa e strugge" ["horse and oxen (…) were shat-
tered, battered and destroyed by dint of punches, thumps and
bites, kicks and scratches"; XXIV. 7]. And all because he had had the
mischance to stumble upon a "suave" poem! One small poem—a
Petrarchan "sonnet" composed in *ottava rima*—has the power to
bring down the entire edifice of Landino's poetics (and St John's
too, as we saw). In vain had Landino sought to cast in stone the
pronouncements of Dante "driven by fury" ("spinto da furore":
proem, p. 141) and to demonstrate the efficaciousness and infallibility of poetic fury (and in vain will St John—Dante gone
gaga?—expound his "tutta al contrario" theory). To be "furioso",
Ariosto says, is to be insane, and far from being God-given "furore"
is a dangerous and destructive force (and a poem simply says what
is says, no matter what gloss you put on it).[1]

Although a poem like Medoro's may have such punch, it is as
nothing compared with the power of a few spots. When Dante the
character had reached the moon, his first question to Beatrice had
been: "Che son li segni bui/di questo corpo?" ["What are the dark
marks on this body?"],[2] to which his beloved had answered with

---

1   With reference to *Orlando furioso*, III. 1 ("Chi mi darà la voce e le parole/
     convenienti a sí nobil suggetto?/chi l'ale al verso presterà, che vole/tanto
     ch'arrivi all'alto mio concetto?/Molto maggior di quel furor che suole,/ben
     or convien che mi riscaldi il petto"), E. A. Chesney, *The Countervoyage of
     Rabelais and Ariosto* (Durham, N. C., Duke University Press, 1982), pp. 172–
     73, argues that although generally folly ("furore") in *Orlando furioso* is
     equated with unreason, Ariosto also has a conception of the notion as a
     creative force. To this one could reply that Landino can also view "furore"
     as a destructive force ("con la suavità de' suoi versi poté reprimere l'empito
     e el furore di molti"), but on the whole it is correct to say that whereas for
     Landino "furore" is something positive, for Ariosto it is something negative.
2   *Par.*, II. 49–50. Translations of the *Commedia* are taken from Dante, *The Divine
     Comedy*, translated by J. D. Sinclair (London, Oxford University Press, 1971).

a long philosophical discourse explaining how creation is infused with God's intelligence and each creature perceives it differently according to its ability to do so; but when Astolfo reaches the moon the first thing he notices is that it is "like untarnished steel" ("come un acciar che non ha macchia alcuna").[1] Thus with one stroke of the pen, or the eraser rather, Ariosto upsets Dante's entire cosmology, and by wiping out the spots he does away with the two fundamentals on which Dante's poem and his vision had rested, namely that the world *has* sense and that woman can *speak* sense. And so, in *Orlando furioso*, instead of a well-ordered universe which is the expression of a supreme intelligence, you have a chaotic one which reflects the limited understanding of the narrator: "Or *se* mi mostra la mia *carta* il vero" ["Now if my chart tells me true"], he is reduced to saying at the beginning of the last canto (XLVI. 1; my italics). Instead of a moon which moves to God's tune in a predictable manner and leads the way to transcendence, you have a moon which is as immanent as the world it reflects, and "che dei pianeti a noi più prossima *erra*" ["which of all the planets wanders closest to us"; XXXIV. 67; my italics]. And instead of a beloved who can reason ("argomentar": *Paradiso*, II. 63) and inform ("informar": line 110), and who according to Landino is the very incarnation of theology,[2] you have a lady who bewitches and befuddles, and is the very enemy of inspiration:

> Dirò d'Orlando [...];
> se da colei [...],
> che 'l poco ingegno ad or ad or mi lima,
> me ne sarà però tanto concesso,
> che mi basti a finir quanto ho promesso.
> (*Orlando furioso*, I. 2)

[I shall tell of Orlando (...) if she, who (...) even now is eroding my last fragments of sanity, leaves me yet with sufficient to complete what I have undertaken.]

---

1 *Of*, XXXIV. 70. G. Savarese, "Lo spazio dell'"impostura': il *Furioso* e la luna", in his *Il "Furioso" e la cultura del Rinascimento* (Rome, Bulzoni, 1984), pp. 71–89, shows how the rewriting of this passage in the third redaction of the poem actually highlights the fact that there are no spots on the moon (p. 78).

2 "[...] induce a parlare Beatrice, laqual habbiamo detto essere la theologia, perhò che lei parla non come phisico ma come theologo": Landino, commentary (on *Par.*, II. 112–26), p. 241r.

No longer is Beatrice in Paradise making sense of the pilgrim's doubts: she has been replaced by St John, who makes non-sense of things he little understands. Indeed the beloved is no longer in Paradise for Paradise is now in the beloved, where it "wanders" and draws the lover's body in no uncertain terms—not for Ariosto, in other words, Dante's "S'io era corpo" ["If I was body"; *Paradiso*, II. 37]:

> Per riaver l'ingegno mio m'è aviso
> che non bisogna che per l'aria io poggi
> nel cerchio de la luna, o in Paradiso;
> che 'l mio non credo che tanto alto alloggi:
> ne' bei vostri occhi, e nel sereno viso,
> nel sen d'avorio, e alabastrini poggi
> se ne va *errando*; et io con queste labbia
> lo corrò, se vi par ch'io lo riabbia.
>   (*Orlando furioso*, xxxv. 2; my italics)

[I do not imagine, however, that there is any need for me to take flight through the air to the orb of the moon or into paradise in order to recover my wits. I don't believe they inhabit those heights. Their haunts are your beautiful eyes, your radiant face, your ivory breasts, those alabastrine hillocks; and I shall sip them up with my lips if that proves the way to recover them.]

How could one not conclude that Ariosto deliberately set out to subvert every one of the most cherished tenets of Dante *poeta theologus*?

Besides the theology, it is also the geography of the *Commedia* that Ariosto puts to the test. "Io non so ben ridir com' i' v'intrai" ["I cannot rightly tell how I entered there"; *Inferno*, I. 10], Dante had said, regarding his entry into the underworld. He had not specified the "where" either, but Landino had made sure that the record was set straight: "Fingendo lui essere sceso allo 'nferno, certo è verisimile che imitando Virgilio ponga la medesima entrata; e questa è appresso al lago Averno non molto lontano da Napoli" ["Pretending he descended into Hell, it is likely indeed that, imitating Virgil, he posited the same entrance, namely beside Lake Avernus, not far from Naples"; proem, p. 156]. No doubt it suited the Florentines, in the aftermath of the war with Naples which followed the Pazzi conspiracy, to think of Hell as being close to Naples! Ariosto, though, was to have none of that, and so we learn in *Orlando furioso* that the entrance to Hell (as though Ariosto were doing a favour to the Neapolitan allies of Ferrara?) is "most certainly" in Africa, at the foot of a mountain near to "where the Nile rises—if it rises anywhere" ("ove il Nilo ha, se in alcun luogo ha, fonte": xxxiii. 126), that is, close to somewhere which may not exist (so much for Manetti's careful calculations, on which Landino had based his own!):[1]

> Quasi de la montagna alla radice
> entra sotterra una profonda grotta,
> che *certissima* porta esser si dice
> di ch'allo 'nferno vuol scendere talotta.
> (*Orlando furioso*, xxxiii. 127; my italics)

[Almost at the base of the mountain a deep cave penetrates below ground—it is said to be undoubtedly the gateway for a descent into Hell.]

Moreover, as one critic has pointed out, Ariosto's Hell, unlike Dante's, is open to the public, while at the same time being inaccessible to humans, as Astolfo will soon find out.[2] In other words, not only is Ariosto saying that the *Commedia* got it wrong, he is also suggesting (or so it would appear) that Landino wasted his time in attempting to double-guess Dante. And it had also been wasted effort on Landino's part to explain and justify Dante's unorthodox location of Purgatory in the *Commedia*. Clearly bemused by that unusual setting, Landino had wondered, in the prologue to the second *cantica*, whether Dante might not in fact have been mistaken:

> Tre cose dobbiamo in questo luogho considerare. La prima si è el purgatorio dopo questa vita. La seconda, chi son quelli che vanno al purgatorio. La terza, se è luogo alcuno certo nel quale si purghino l'anime.

---

1   Landino had patriotically—even though somehwat patronizingly—endorsed Manetti's calculations: "Ma del sito e spatio dell'inferno discripto da questo poeta spero diremo piú distinctamente quando arriveremo al basso, e con piú dimostratione che forse altro che n'habbi scripto, maxime con l'aiuto del *nostro* Antonio Manetti, el quale con suo ingegno mathematico ha investigato cose molto verisimili e *quasi* dimostrative" (commentary [on *Inf.*, iii. 1–12], p. 28v; my italics).
2   "L'inferno ariostesco, nonché essere inaccessibile ai viventi come quello di Dante, si può dire aperto al pubblico": E. Zanette, *Conversazioni sull'"Orlando furioso"* (Pisa, Nistri–Lischi, 1958), p. 277.

[We must consider three things at this point. The first is whether there is a Purgatory after this life; the second, who are those who go to Purgatory; the third, if there is a definite place in which souls purge themselves.]

But after much deliberation he had concluded, not surprisingly, that "Dante, a man of remarkable intelligence and remarkable inventiveness, found a new location, which does not in any way substantially contradict Christian belief" ("Danthe, homo di mirabile ingegno e di mirabile inventione, trovò nuovo sito, el quale niente è contra substantialmente al opinione christiana": pp. 145r–v). Neither Dante's innovation, however, nor Landino's defence of it was to impress Ariosto, who decided to set the mountain on whose summit lies the Garden of Eden not, as Dante had done, in "Australia" but in Africa, and furthermore to remove Purgatory from the slopes of that mountain and locate it instead in the north of Europe, where he made it accessible—*in* and not *after* this life— to any jet-setting (or rather, hipogryff-setting) tourist:

> Quindi Ruggier poi che di banda in banda
> vide gl'Inglesi, andò verso l'Irlanda;
>
> e vide Ibernia fabulosa, dove
> il santo vecchiarel fece la cava,
> in che tanta mercé par che si truove,
> che l'uom vi purga ogni sua colpa prava.
> (*Orlando furioso*, x. 91–92)

[(Ruggiero) at once shaped his course towards Ireland, for he had seen Englishmen from all parts. / He beheld fabled Hibernia, where the little old saint hollowed out the cave wherein such grace is—it seems—to be found, that the visitor there can cleanse himself of all his iniquity.]

Much more *à la page* than Landino, Ariosto is referring here to St Patrick's Purgatory, the famous shrine in present-day County Donegal, which for close on three centuries had been attracting pilgrims from many parts of Europe, not a few of whom had come all the way from Italy. He may not have been too convinced by the efficaciousness of that purgatory ("*par* che si truove"), but at least it was there for all to see![1]

1   On St Patrick's Purgatory see *The Medieval Pilgrimage to St Patrick's Purgatory: Lough Derg and the European Tradition*, edited by M. Haren and Y. de Pont-

Possibly Ariosto's strongest rebuke of Dante (and Landino) is to be found in the story of Lydia in Canto xxxiv of *Orlando furioso*. Advancing into Hell as far as the stench and darkness will allow, Astolfo happens upon something dangling from the roof like a corpse from the gallows. It turns out to be Lydia, daughter of the King of Lydia, who tells Astolfo that in life she was beautiful but proud, and that Alceste, a young knight from neigbouring Thrace, fell hopelessly in love with her. To be close to her, Alceste joined her father's army and in the course of time became so indispensable to the king that he ventured to ask for Lydia's hand in reward; but the king, being greedy and ambitious, flatly turned down Alceste's request, thus driving him to join forces with the King of Armenia. The King of Armenia, thanks to Alceste's help, deprived the King of Lydia in no time at all of all his possessions and so left him with no option but to throw his daughter upon the mercy of Alceste. No sooner had that victor of so many battles set eyes on his beloved, however, than he fell prey once again to her beauty, wherefore she, sensing her own victory, rebuked him in no uncertain terms for his unfaithfulness. She nevertheless promised to forgive him should he make amends for all the wrongs he has done to her father, by winning back from the King of Armenia the many territories he has conquered for him. But when Alceste had done so, Lydia and her father were simply more determined than ever to get rid of him. They sent him abroad on many perilous missions, and lest that should fail to do the trick (which it did), they set about in the meantime depriving him, by rumour and slander, of his many friends at home. Having thus finally rendered him quite harmless, Lydia was able to admit to him that she had always hated him and wished never to see him again. Overcome with grief, Alceste fell ill and died, and Lydia was then condemned, for her ingratitude, to wail in Hell for ever.

Critics have noted, as anyone is bound to do, that Lydia, the first (and only) sinner Astolfo meets in Hell, is Ariosto's reply to Dante's Francesca. She is an anti-Francesca, and she is in Hell, it has been claimed, to confute—or rather to provide "a more logical application" ("una piú logica applicazione") of—Francesca's "Amor, ch'a nullo amato amar perdona" ["Love, which absolves

farcy (Enniskillen, Clogher Historical Society, 1988), especially J-M. Picard, "The Italian Pilgrims" (pp. 169–89); also my own "'La divisa dal mondo ultima Irlanda' ossia la riscoperta umanistica dell'Irlanda", *Giornale storico della letteratura italiana*, 176 (1999), 363–87.

no one beloved from loving"; *Inferno*, v. 103].[1] Where Francesca is
punished for loving too much, Lydia is punished (in characteristic
Arioso fashion, it is said) for loving too little. Where Francesca had
been all too ready to respond to the dictates of love, Lydia was
determined to ignore the pleas of her lover. She was ungrateful,
and that is why she lingers in Hell. Yet to say that her sin is
ingratitude is no more than to state the obvious,[2] for that is the
explanation which she herself gives of her punishment:

> Lidia sono io, [...]
> al fumo eternamente condannata,
> per esser stata al fido amante mio,
> mentre io vissi, spiacevole et ingrata.
> (*Orlando furioso*, XXXIV. 11)

[I am Lydia, (...) condemned to this eternal smoke (...) for having
been unpleasant and ungrateful to my faithful suitor while I
lived.]

In truth, no one has come up with a better explanation, and very
few, for that matter, have actually sought one, Lydia being perhaps
the least studied of Ariosto's female characters. To call her story,
as has been done,[3] "a devastating pamphlet against women" is
hardly more enlightening, or correct, as there is much female
goodness throughout the poem to act as counterweight to her
wickedness. Some have simply suggested that it is wrong to read
too much into her story and give it too much importance, since Hell
cannot possibly have any particular role to play in Ariosto's poem,
where deviance is punished in all places and at all times.[4] Her case

1   G. Maruffi, *La "Divina commedia" considerata quale fonte*, pp. 48–49.
2   See M. Santoro, "Lidia o dell'ingratitudine", in his *Ariosto e il Rinascimento*,
    pp. 295–301; C. Segre, "Da uno specchio all'altro: la luna e la terra nell'*Orlando
    furioso*", in his *Fuori del mondo: i modelli nella follia e nelle immagini dell'aldilà*
    (Turin, Einaudi, 1990), pp. 103–14 (p. 104).
3   "[...] uno schiacciante pamphlet contro le donne" (E. Zanette, *Conversazioni
    sull'"Orlando furioso"*, p. 288).
4   "Punishments are meted out in a variety of ways to a number of characters
    in the *Orlando furioso*": J. A. Molinaro, "Sin and Punishment in the *Orlando
    furioso*", *Modern Language Notes*, 89 (1974), 35–46 (p. 39). C. Segre, "Da uno
    specchio all'altro", p. 104, suggests that Lydia is also an anti-Dido; and
    A. R. Ascoli, *Ariosto's Bitter Harmony* (pp. 287, 275), who calls her an "anti-
    Francesca mockingly placed in Hell for excessive chastity", sees her story as
    a lead-in to the question of wealth and avarice explored by St John.

would thus be no more than a diversion. Segre, for one, implied that it could be read as such when he asked why Astolfo did not go straight to Heaven. It is true of course that Astolfo's visit to Hell is an afterthought and his meeting with Lydia a chance encounter, but that does not render his journey dispensable (any more than anything else is dispensable in Ariosto's "erratic" world).[1] What it does is simply heighten the parodic and subversive tone of Ariosto's poem. Indeed, gone is the sense of purpose and mystery which made Dante's mission unique (or so Dante himself, and Landino, wanted to believe). But gone too is Francesca, for Ariosto's words make it quite clear that it would be illogical to expect to see anyone else in the underworld (besides, possibly, the other ungrateful women and men whom Lydia mentions):

> Poi che non parla piú Lidia infelice,
> va il Duca per saper s'altri vi stanzi;
> ma la caligine alta ch'era ultrice
> de l'opre ingrate, sí gl'ingrossa inanzi,
> ch'andare un palmo sol piú non gli lice;
> anzi a forza tornar gli conviene, anzi,
> perché la vita non gli sia intercetta
> dal fumo, i passi accelerar con fretta.
>   (*Orlando furioso*, XXXIV. 44)

[When unhappy Lydia had finished, Astolfo went on to see if anyone else were lodged here; but the dense smoke which punished ingratitude so swelled before him that it prevented him from making another step forward—indeed he had to turn back and beat a hasty retreat, if the smoke were not to be the death of him.]

And that, I would suggest, is the very point of Astolfo's journey: it takes place precisely so that Ariosto may put Lydia in and let Francesca out.

For Landino, Francesca's case is essentially one of misguided reading. Good Humanist that he is, he has some sympathy for the

---

1   C. Segre, "Da uno specchio all'altro", p. 104. M. Santoro, "La sequenza lunare nel *Furioso*: una società allo specchio", in his *Ariosto e il Rinascimento*, pp. 237–62 (pp. 239, 231), argues that Astolfo is no more than a "turista in vacanza" whose journey suddenly acquires a providential sense on the moon. To this I would reply that Astolfo, and the reader, have already been made aware by the Senapo, whose blindness Astolfo is to cure, that his journey is willed by God (see *Of*, XXXIII. 114).

fact that she sought to put into practice what she read: "Ciaschuno intende che l'exemplo facilmente commuove a fare el simile, maxime quando v'è l'auctorità di persone reputate, come era Lancilotto e Ginevra" ["Everyone understands that an example easily moves one to do the same thing, especially when there is the authority of well-known people, as were Lancelot and Guinevere"]. He strongly disapproves, however, of the frame of mind in which she approached her reading: "Chi è occupato non cerca trastullo" ["No one who is occupied seeks amusement"] and "Legger per dilecto significa esser in ocio" ["Reading for pleasure means being idle"]. But above all it is for her choice of books that he condemns her: because she wasted her time with "cavalieri erranti [...] le prodeze de quali sono piú fabulose che vere" ["knights errant (...) whose feats are more fabled than real"], she now justly misspends her eternity.[1]

Such reasoning was bound to offend Ariosto. From the very outset of *Orlando furioso* a clear distinction is made between the real world of "lofty thoughts" ("alti pensier") and the imaginary world of "my verses" ("miei versi": I. 4), and throughout the poem readers are repeatedly warned not to take their reading too seriously. They are never allowed to forget that what they have in front of them is no more than a story written on paper that can be dismissed with the merest flick of the page:

> Passi, chi vuol, tre carte o quattro, senza
> leggerne verso, e chi pur legger vuole,
> gli dia quella medesima credenza
> che si suol dare a finzioni, e a fole.
> (*Orlando furioso*, XXVIII. 3)

[Those who wish (...) may skip three or four pages without reading a line of them; those who prefer to read them must regard the story in the same light as legends and fables.]

As Ariosto saw it, reading could be no more than a delightful "amusement". Someone like Francesca therefore, who takes what she reads literally and wants the story on the page to be real, must have seemed a pretty dumb reader to him, and he has little time for dumb readers:

---

1   Commentary (on *Inf.* v), pp. 44v, 45r, 43v.

> Non bisogna
> ch'io ponga mente al vulgo sciocco e ignaro;
> a voi [...]
> che 'l lume del discorso avete chiaro,
> [...] ogni mio intento agogna
> che 'l frutto sia di mie fatiche caro.
> (*Orlando furioso*, VII. 2)

[I shall not trouble myself about the ignorant and mindless rabble. (...) To convince you, and you alone, my sharp, clear-headed listeners, is all that I wish to strive for, the only reward I seek.]

If serious reading had been Francesca's only sin, then Ariosto might just have approved of her being consigned to Hell, but what he surely could not countenance was Dante's, and Landino's, condemnation of the kind of books she liked, for if it was the destiny of anyone who read of "ladies and knights, arms and love" ("le donne, i cavalier, l'arme, gli amori": *Orlando furioso*, I. 1) to be punished for ever in the company of "ladies and knights of old times" ("le donne antiche e' cavalieri": *Inferno*, V. 71), then anyone who read *Orlando furioso* was doomed. That meant the whole court of Ferrara was destined for Hell, and so Ariosto was left with no other option, clearly, than to let Francesca out. But why should he have chosen to replace her with Lydia?

There is, I would suggest, a very good reason why Lydia is in Hell. Her story, one might say, is the manifesto of Ariosto's "sexual politics", for it is not just a story about love: it is also a story about politics. Every one of its amorous twists has a political consequence, and the political repercussions of Lydia's *ingratitudine* are just as momentous as its amorous consequences. Indeed "ingratitudine" is the sin *par excellence* of both love *and* politics, just as its opposite, *gratitudine*, or in other words faith (*fede*), loyalty (*lealtà*), is the quintessence of all amorous and political virtues. In Lydia's story, *raison d'état* and *raison de cœur* are truly one and the same thing. Her father wills and unwills what her heart wants or does not want, and laying siege to her heart is laying siege to her father's kingdom. She is in Hell, one could say, for being at once a bad lover and a bad ruler. On the moon Astolfo will learn that one cannot separate literature from politics. Here he learns that it is love which cannot be separated from politics.

The link between love and politics is made most explicit in Lydia's name. Since she is called by the name of her country, she is in a sense the embodiment of her father's kingdom and a personification of the state. Had she been Italian, her name would have been Italia, or more to the point, had she been from Ariosto's native city, it would have been Ferrara. Just as remarkable as her name is the fact that no other part of the poem lays bare the mechanics of politics in all its ugliness, selfishness and arbitrariness in quite the same "realistic" way as this story does; no other part of the poem stresses the material cost of making war (and love) quite so openly as this one does. Here we read of wanton wars waged to grab more territories, of lands granted and taken back without rhyme or reason, plundered and despoiled ("terre depredate e vote": XXXIV. 33), burdened with great ransom ("[gravate] di gran fio": XXXIV. 36), of mercenaries paid to do the bidding of whimsical generals, of devoted service repaid with indifference or ingratitude, of allies who are not to be trusted, and of that bane of every body politic, slander. And all for the sake of what? Fickle pride and ambition! For sure, we are a lot closer here to the world of the *Cinque canti* than to that of *Orlando furioso*, and it is thus no wonder that Lydia should be banned from the company of true ladies and knights ("donne e cavallier"), just as the *Cinque canti* were to be from the other forty-six.[1] Through her, it would seem, Ariosto lifts the veil and points a finger at the murky underbelly of Este grandeur, to which in life he had been exposed all too often. In her stand condemned the evil machinations of feudal politics. It is the arrogance and pettiness of princes that is the real sin for which "in Hell there is no redemption" ("nulla redenzione è ne l'inferno": XXXIV. 43), and it is for being a bad prince as well as a bad lover that Lydia is punished in Hell, or indeed for being a bad prince *because* she is a bad lover. Her story should be read as a warning to take seriously the political consequences of (princely) amorous pursuits, or at least to be aware that the amorous pursuits of princes do have political consequences.

This is something which the knights and damsels of *Orlando furioso*, just like Lydia (and the readers of the poem?), choose on the whole to ignore, preferring instead to believe that all that matters in the world, regardless of their duty, is the fancies of their heart. But such irresponsibility never goes unpunished. Orlando, as we

---

1   On the *Cinque canti*, the five cantos not included in the final version of *Orlando furioso*, see D. Quint, "Introduction", in L. Ariosto, *Cinque canti/Five Cantos*, translated by A. Sheers and D. Quint (Berkeley–London, University of California Press, 1996), pp. 1–44.

know, is rendered insane for putting himself and his beloved before his Lord and his Faith. Ruggiero all but drowns for refusing to heed the call of matrimony and progeny. Rodomonte, who will only bend to the will of his own machismo, is made to suffer the ignominy of humiliation at the hand of women. Angelica, who attempted to turn sexual allurement into a statecraft, is brought low by morganatic love and having to make the most undignified exit from the poem of any of the characters, on her back with her legs in the air (as clearly befits someone who might possibly have mistaken that position for a political stance).[1] Olimpia, who is almost as bad in this respect as Lydia, sacrificing as she does her father, brothers and many subjects to the whims of her selfish infatuation, is abandoned by the man for whom she gave up everything and is then exposed naked on a rock (*and* made to marry an Irishman!). The list could go on and on. Lydia's story is thus emblematic of all the stories of misguided love in *Orlando furioso*, and she is made the scapegoat for all those who would justify anything carried out in the name of love and live out the fantasy that love indeed "absolves no one beloved from loving" ("a nullo amato amar perdona"). There need be no other sinner in Hell. In the world of courtesies ("cortesie") and daring deeds ("audaci imprese"), Lydia's "ingratitudine" is Sin by antonomasia.[2]

One could of course argue that Lydia's story is a warning to keep love and politics separate, that she is punished precisely because she confused the two. But if we look for her opposite number in the poem, we will see that that cannot be so. If Lydia stands for all those who have failed, the (female) character who stands for those who have succeeded has to be Bradamante; and the hallmark of the latter's success is the steadfast pursuit of a love which is true, and therefore viable, both emotionally and politically. She loves only one man, Ruggiero, and her love can have only one goal, marriage—a marriage ("genus unde Estense") sanctioned by both Church and Empire. This is the real novelty of *Orlando furioso*, the real "cosa non detta in prosa mai né in rima" ["thing never before recounted in prose or rhyme"].[3] Whereas hitherto, especially in the literary tradition of Italy, love had been by definition

1 See *Of*, XXIX. 65.
2 A similar view has been expressed by E. Zanette (*Conversazioni sull'"Orlando furioso"*, p. 279).
3 *Of*, I. 2. "Genus unde Estense" is a paraphrase of *Aeneid*, I. 6 ("genus unde Latinum").

adulterous, or at the very least indifferent to marriage (one need only think of Dante's love for Beatrice, or Petrarch's for Laura), Ariosto now brings marriage into the equation. In *Orlando furioso* any love which cannot lead to matrimony is doomed to failure, and only such loves as do can be successful (which is not the same thing, of course, as saying that all married or marriageable loves are happy ones).[1] It is for this reason that Lydia truly deserves eternal punishment. Not only did she trifle with love (and therefore politics), but she thereby made light of marriage. By turning down Alceste's advances, she turned her back on the possibility of a marriage which might have brought happiness to her, and would certainly have brought stability and prosperity to the Kingdom of Lydia.

By casting into darkness all the other sterile loves of *Orlando furioso*, the fruitlessness of Lydia's "ingratitudine" allows the love of Bradamante and Ruggiero to shine all the brighter, and in so highlighting the originality of Ariosto's conception of love it points to the failings of previous (vernacular) love traditions, which had painted love as an irresistible force, had failed to take proper account of the lover's social and political responsibilities or had been misguided in the understanding of those responsibilities. Lydia's story, and by extension the poem as a whole, may be read as a condemnation of Petrarchism (the mania for which was even then being officially sanctioned by Bembo), with its obsession with literary preciosity and its preoccupation with narcissistic *états d'âme*. How wrong Petrarch was may be gauged, among others, from the scene of Orlando's downfall. As the strange course of his horse brings him to

> un rivo che parea cristallo,
> ne le cui sponde un bel pratel fioria,
> di nativo color vago e dipinto,
> e di molti e belli arbori distinto
> (*Orlando furioso*, xxiii. 100)

---

1   It should be noted that the misguided love of the poem *par excellence*, Orlando's love for Angelica, is defined (by St John) as "*incesto* amore": "Renduto ha il vostro Orlando al suo Signore / di tanti benefici iniquo merto […]. / Sí accecato l'avea l'incesto amore […]. / E Dio per questo fa ch'egli va folle" (*Of*, xxxiv. 64–65). "Incestuous" must here stand for "impure", "un-marriageable" (as it were).

[a stream which looked like crystal, on the banks of which bloomed a pleasant meadow, picked out with lovely pure colours and adorned with many beautiful trees]

he and we, as good Petrarchists, have every reason to believe that all the trees, all the rocks and every blade of grass will speak to him of his beloved. And so they do, but... in the arms of someone else— for which Petrarch had never prepared us. Moreover Petrarch's frustrated fantasizing ("Con lei foss' io da che si parte il sole, /[...]/ sol una notte, e mai non fosse l'alba!" ["Oh! to be with her from when the sun departs, (...) for just one night, and would that dawn then never be!"])[1] is no match for Medoro's jubilant gloating:

> Liete piante, verdi erbe, limpide acque
> spelunca opaca, e di fredde ombre grata,
> dove la bella Angelica che nacque
> di Galafron, da molti invano amata,
> spesso ne le mie braccia nuda giacque;
> de la commodità che qui m'è data.
> io povero Medor ricompensarvi
> d'altro non posso che d'ognior lodarvi.
> (*Orlando furioso*, XXIII. 108)

[Happy plants, verdant grass, limpid waters, dark, shadowy cave, pleasant and cool, where fair Angelica, born of Galafron, and loved in vain by many, often lay naked in my arms, I poor Medor, cannot repay you for your indulgence otherwise than by ever praising you.]

Orlando furioso is also a condemnation of Boccaccio and the wantonly erotic and self-congratulatory love of the *Decameron*. Canto XXVIII of Ariosto's poem, whose heroine is named after one of Boccaccio's characters (Fiammetta) and which has been said to be the most "Boccaccesque" part of the poem, is also presented as its most dispensable: "Lasciate questo canto, che senza esso / può star l'istoria, e non sarà men chiara" ["Skip this canto: it is not essential—my story is no less clear without it"; XXVIII. 2]. In other words, *Orlando furioso* has no need of the *Decameron*. It has little time either for the unreal social refinements of Platonic love, with its aspiration to shed all earthly attachments. Not for Ariosto, that is, a kiss which is a "conjoining of souls" ("congiungimento

---

1   *RVF*, 22. The edition I quote from is F. Petrarca, *Il canzoniere*, edited by N.☐Vianello (Milan, Bietti, 1966). The translation is my own.

d'anima"), as Castiglione's *Libro del cortegiano* (IV. 64) was shortly to put it:[1]

> Non cosí strettamente edera preme
> pianta ove intorno abbarbicata s'abbia,
> come si stringon li dui amanti insieme,
> cogliendo de lo spirto in su le labbia
> suave fior, qual non produce seme
> indo o Sabeo ne l'odorata sabbia:
> del gran piacer ch'avean, lor dicer tocca;
> che spesso avean piú d'una lingua in bocca.
>
> (*Orlando furioso*, VII. 28)

[Ivy never clung so tightly to the stem round which it was entwined as did the two lovers cling to each other, drawing from each other's lips the spirit of flowers so fragrant that none such are ever produced by the scented sands of India or Arabia. As for describing their pleasure, better to leave it to them—the more so as they frequently had a second tongue in their mouth.]

And not for Ariosto a "divine love street" ("divina strada amorosa": *Libro del cortegiano*, IV. 62) leading to the real world of Truth and Beauty, of which this world is but a pale and imperfect reflection. Instead his world above (which is reached, as we have seen, by public transport) is a lost luggage office, and merely a confusing reflection of an errant world below. But above all *Orlando furioso* is a condemnation of the *Commedia*. To Dante, who had been lured to Heaven by a woman not his wife with the assurance that the next world was better and more important than this one, Ariosto responds with the assertion that Paradise is well and truly of this world, in the seductive features of one's beloved, and that the highest goal to which any lover must aspire is the "fertile bridal bed" ("genial letto fecondo": XLVI. 77).[2]

Recent studies have shown that Ariosto was well aware of precisely where he stood in the literary tradition of his country and that he was proudly conscious of his originality within that tradition.[3] While paying homage to his predecessors, he also wished to make it clear that he had overtaken them and was

---

1   The edition I quote from is B. Castiglione, *Il libro del cortegiano*, edited by
     E.□Bonora (Milan, Mursia, 1981). The translations are my own.
2   On Ariosto's novel conception of love see A. Scaglione, "*Amori e dolori* in the
     Orlando furioso", *Italica*, 73 (1996), 1–10.
3   See M. Beer, *Romanzi di cavalleria*, p. 35.

leaving them behind. That is why he parodied them. By parodying Dante, he was responding to the threat posed to his own and Ferrara's cultural (and political) pre-eminence by Landino's edition of the *Commedia*. Just as Dante had attempted to highjack the epic for unworldly ends, so Landino had used it to claim the high ground for Florentine ends. And so *Orlando furioso* "di messer Ludovico Ariosto nobile ferrarese", which wants to mark a new beginning in Italian literature, is and cannot but be a resounding "To Hell with Dante... and Landino!"[1]

1   For the preparation of this essay I was unfortunately not able to consult Paolo Procaccioli's recent edition of Landino's commentary: C. Landino, *Comento sopra la Comedia*, edited by P. Procaccioli, 4 vols (Rome, Salerno, 2001). That edition, with its detailed introduction and critical apparatus, should be the point of reference of any further study of Landino's commentary.

DANTE IN THE POETIC THEORY AND PRACTICE OF TOMMASO CAMPANELLA

Enzo Noé Girardi

Campanella refers to Dante in many of his works, both verse and prose, Latin and Italian. The most important references are undoubtedly those in his Latin *Poetica*, in an appendix to the eighth chapter, where he deals with the following three questions: "Utrum comoedia aliis modis fieri possit; et de Dantis poemate et cur *Comoedia* nuncupatur; et de universitatis rerum humanarum comoedia" ["Whether there are other ways of producing comedy; and on Dante's poem, and why it is entitled *Commedia*; and on the comedy of all human matters"].[1]

Regarding the first two questions, Campanella notes that Dante called his poem a comedy because it has the basic structure of comedy: its beginning is sad and its conclusion happy. But, he adds, this comedy is of another kind:

> Est enim exemplar totius universitatis hominum, quorum gratia cum omnes res sint, de omnibus tractat rebus, et principium, medium et finem cunctorum hominum docet, poenas et praemia singulis virtutibus et actionibus convenientes, iniquos damnat, bonos laudat, religionem roborat, secreta naturae pandit: tantaque varietate ac unitate simul constat, ut nihil melius audiri possit neque admirabilius [...] Et quia consideratio comoediae universalis ab ipso Dante fit, ipse est persona loquens videns et referens, vocaturque ab ipso etiam poema sacrum et universale: "Se mai continga ch'il poema sacro, / a cui han posto mano e cielo e terra [...]."

1   See T. Campanella, *Opere letterarie*, edited by L. Bolzoni (Turin, UTET, 1977), p. 612. Translations into English are my own, except for the translations of Dante, which are taken (with the occasional modification) from Dante Alighieri, *The Divine Comedy*, translated by J. D. Sinclair (London, Oxford University Press, 1971).

[It is indeed an exemplar of all mankind, for whose sake all things exist, and since that is so, it deals with all things, and teaches the beginning, middle and end of all men, and the rewards and punishments meet for each virtue or action, condemning the wicked, praising the good, strengthening religion and revealing the secrets of nature: such is its variety and also its unity that one may hear nothing better or more remarkable (...). And since the presentation of the universal comedy is made by Dante himself, it is he who speaks, sees and tells; and it is he who calls the poem sacred and universal: "If it ever come to pass that the sacred poem to which both heaven and earth have set their hand (...)".]

Dante's *Commedia*, therefore, reports on the totality of material and spiritual things, summarizing and bringing together the subjects of many other literary and scientific works, and enacting objectively—and this is the third question—the real comedy of the world:

> Arbitror legislaturae, et philosophiae physicae et moralis, et mathematicae, et politicae poemata ita in hoc uno conflata esse, ut non nisi unum esse videatur. Habes in eo comoedias, satiras, tragoedias, elegias, epitaphia, elocutionis proprietates, utilitates, figurationes, mutationes fluentes, quasi natura, non arte compactas.
>
> Sed plebecula et grammatici insulsi, qui vocabulis afficiuntur delicatis, non vere significantibus quod oportet, fastidiunt Dantem, qui, ut ante oculos ponat scientias et rerum veritates, in personis variis eas exprimit vocibus tam vivis, ut res potius quam voces ipsae voces videantur.
>
> Nos autem in *Canticis* mundum esse comoediam universalem docuimus [...] coelum et terram theatrum, scenas vero civitates et Inferos et Purgatorium, et in fine mundi felicitatem, quae ex tot actionibus passionibusque expectatur, prodituram, iudicante Deo et angelis spectatoribus, quis melius suas partes in scenis prosecutus sit, poenis premiisque distributis.[1]

[I am of the opinion that this one poem brings together poems about laws, natural and moral philosophy, mathematics and politics in such a way that they all seem but one. It combines comedies, satires, tragedies, elegies, epitaphs, the proprieties of speech, useful things, figures, flowing metaphors, as though they had been produced by nature, not by art.

1   T. Campanella, *Opere letterarie*, pp. 614–15.

But the common people and dull grammarians, who are moved by pretty words and not by words that truly mean what they should, have little time for Dante, who puts the sciences and the real truth of things before our eyes, depicting them by means of various characters and in such lively words that they seem to be things rather than words.

In my *Cantica* I explained that the world is a universal comedy (...) with the sky and the earth as its theatre, and cities, Hell and Purgatory as its stage, and with the happiness we expect emerging from all the action and suffering at the end of the world, when God in the presence of angels will judge as to who played his part on the stage best and will distribute rewards and punishments.]

To these passages we may add one from the second part of the Italian *Poetica* (Chapter 12), where Dante is declared superior to Homer and to modern poets, who,

a petto a Dante, tutti sono poetucci e differenti quanto la gondola dal galeone per la grandezza della materia e per lo molto utile e gusto, che da lui ricevono l'orecchie purgate e filosofiche, non le pedantesche.[1]

[by comparison with Dante, are all poetasters, and as different from him as a gondola is from a galleon, bearing in mind the greatness of his subject-matter and the considerable utility and pleasure that purged and philosophic, though not pedantic ears derive from him.]

Before discussing these and other, equally important and more specific opinions on Dante, nearly all of which are favourable, I should like to stress how Dante's exaltation by Campanella is in marked contrast to Dante's denigration at the hands of most of the readers and writers of the seventeenth century, which Firpo has called "the century without Dante", and Maggini, "the most unfortunate century" in the history of the great poet's fortunes.[2] As

---

1   T. Campanella, *Opere letterarie*, p. 369.
2   See F. Maggini, "La critica dantesca dal '300 ai nostri giorni", in *Questioni e correnti di storia letteraria*, edited by U. Bosco (Milan, Marzorati, 1949), p. 133; L. Firpo, "Dante e Campanella", *L'Alighieri*, 10, ii (1969), p. 31. These statements, however, are strongly contested by U. Limentani, "La fortuna di Dante nel Seicento", *Studi secenteschi*, 5 (1964), p. 4: "Dante's strong presence could not be ignored [...], and it is perceptible in many authors, so deeply was the soul of Italy penetrated, consciously or unconsciously, by

a consequence of this contrast, modern critics and scholars have had great difficulty in defining the value and meaning of Campanella's view of Dante from a historical and critical point of view.

Just how great the contrast is between Campanella's attitude towards Dante and that of most *secentisti* is clear from a comparison of the two passages quoted above and what Maggini writes with regard to *secentisti* and Dante:

> I seguaci della poetica classica non potevano rassegnarsi a trovar bello un poema che contravveniva alle regole aristoteliche [...]. D'altra parte [...] la smania di cambiare e di sottrarsi alle regole, l'esaltazione dei moderni di fronte agli antichi non riuscirono motivi favorevoli a Dante, perché l'opera sua parve vieta, rozza e antiquata, priva di eleganza e di gusto, insomma il contrario di ciò che più si ammirava da quegli ingegni.[1]

> [The followers of classical poetics could not reconcile themselves to finding a poem that transgressed the rules of Aristotle beautiful (...). On the other hand (...), the obsession for changing or eluding the rules, the extolling of modern as opposed to ancient writers, did not work in Dante's favour, for his writings seemed old-fashioned, coarse and antiquated, and lacking in elegance and taste: the exact opposite, in short, of what was most admired by such minds.]

Maggini makes the point by quoting the opinions of Paolo Beni (an Aristotelian), who wrote that Dante is "a poet with no sense or talent" ("poeta di niun giudizio e ingegno"), his language "the roar of a croaking and boring crow" ("strepito di crocitante e noioso corbo"), the *Commedia* "a medley or a whim with no measure and no form in its poetic action" ("un miscuglio o capriccio senza regola e senza forma di poetica azione"), and of F. F. Frugoni (a modernist), who wrote: "I prize more a strophe from the odes of Vitali, of Santinelli, of Ciampoli, of Testi, a sonnet by Ciro di Pers, Ceuli, Torcigliani, Rubilli, an octave by Tasso, Ariosto, Tassoni, Chiabrera, than all of Dante's *Commedia*."[2]

Dante's poetry." According to Limentani, "Campanella's admiration for Dante is based above all on religious and moral reasons which have no part in the spirit of Renaissance criticism" (p. 23).

1   F. Maggini, "La critica dantesca", p. 133.
2   F. Maggini, "La critica dantesca", p. 134.

Strangely, when he comes to review the few admirers of Dante that the century produced, Maggini entirely ignores Campanella, mentioning only "level-headed scholars" ("studiosi equilibrati") such as Guarini, Villani and especially "Florentines" such as Dati and Buonmattei, who, although they expressed favourable judgements on Dante, were nonetheless unable "to influence other critics, and alter the prevailing opinion of his detractors", and Magalotti, "who knew by heart nearly the entire *Commedia*", and Ubaldini, "who made important annotations to it".[1] Nor does Maggini's bibliography include the essay by Spampanato, "Il culto di Dante in Campanella", which was the first contribution on the subject and up to now has remained the most complete and useful one from an analytical and historical point of view.[2] Umberto Cosmo also ignores Campanella in his book *Con Dante attraverso il Seicento*;[3] and in both these cases it is difficult to establish—since we are dealing with two very serious scholars—whether their silence is imputable to negligence or whether it is the logical consequence of a low estimation of the significance of Campanella's views on Dante in the history of literary criticism.

On the other hand, the contrast between Campanella's views on Dante and the prevailing views of the time has been strongly stressed in recent studies, though almost as if to argue that such a contrast is what is most significant about Campanella's presence among the critics of his time. "Campanella," writes Firpo, "breaks the wall of incomprehension and indifference by his solitary passion as an assiduous reader and supporter of Dante's"; and Negri states that "the famous philosopher's strong approval of Dante was exceptional in those times."[4] Both Negri and Firpo do try to explain this "strong approval" ("viva adesione"), Negri referring above all to the proud and visionary quality of Campanella's genius and to his idea of the poet as a new prophet, whose model has to be the Holy Scriptures, and Firpo mentioning his keen espousal of civic virtue and creative freedom. But both seem to place the emphasis more on the use Campanella made of Dante in his struggle to renew Christian society than on the value of his

1 F. Maggini, "La critica dantesca", pp. 134–35.
2 V. Spampanato, *Sulla soglia del Seicento* (Milan–Rome–Naples, Albrigi and Segati, 1926), pp. 127–60.
3 U. Cosmo, *Con Dante attraverso il Seicento* (Bari, Laterza, 1946).
4 L. Firpo, "Dante e Campanella", p. 31; R. Negri, "Campanella, Tommaso", in *Enc. dant.*, I, 780.

contribution to a deeper understanding of Dante's poem. Other critics have tended to highlight what unites Campanella with his contemporaries rather than what separates him from them. Mattalia, for instance, quotes only one of the two or three reservations Campanella expresses regarding Dante: that of having neglected elegance ("solus elegantiae neglectus illi obest").[1] Only Aldo Vallone, among recent critics, explains the essential points of Campanella's views on Dante, emphasizing above all their merit in anticipating the sensibility of the Romantics.[2]

We must therefore ask ourselves what is the reason for the prevailing trend among critics to ignore or to underestimate, in the guise of celebrating it, Campanella's singular attitude towards Dante, even though Campanella was one of the most representative and heroic exponents of the cultural, religious, philosophical and literary history of Europe during the period of the Renaissance. Can Campanella's enthusiasm for Dante be explained simply in terms of psychology, of his impetuous personality and his need to go against the taste and judgements of the majority, or is it also grounded in and justified by a logical vision of the meaning and function of poetry in the world?

Since my answer to these questions will be that Campanella's Dante criticism, independently of any polemical intent it may have had, has a solid foundation, from both a historical and a theoretical point of view, it should be pointed out at once that on the matter of Campanella and Dante modern criticism has revealed its limitations more than its insight. On the one hand it has shown a degree of unwillingness to recognize and understand that particular kind of criticism that is "poets' criticism"—and Campanella both as critic and as philosopher *is* a poet—, and on the other hand it has revealed an inadequate grasp of poetry in terms of what it truly is and of its historical evolution.

What I am saying may become clearer if at this point I refer to the figure of T. S. Eliot. He too was both a critic and a poet, he too regarded Dante as one of the greatest poets of all time, making extensive use of themes and expressions from the *Commedia* in his own poetry, and he also shared with Campanella the idea that poetry and beauty are not simply objects of pleasure but have, or

1   See *I classici italiani nella storia della critica*, edited by W. Binni (Florence, La Nuova Italia, 1954), p. 37.
2   A. Vallone, *Storia della critica dantesca dal xiv al xx secolo* (Milan, Vallardi, 1981), pp. 578–83.

may have, the function of morally and socially improving human life, which is an idea that Dante was the first to introduce into European literature—witness the *Letter to Cangrande*: "Finis [huius operis] est removere viventes in hac vita de statu miserie et perducere ad statum felicitatis" ["The aim of (this work) is to remove those living in this life from a state of misery, and to bring them to a state of happiness"].[1] Moreover, like Campanella, Eliot elaborated a project for social and political renewal, *An Idea of a Christian Society*, which, although expounded with much greater caution and awareness of the improbability of its realization, is no less Utopian than *La città del sole*.

More fortunate than the seventeenth-century Calabrian friar, Eliot did not suffer imprisonment and torture because of his religious, social and literary views. Nevertheless, the assessment of those views and of Eliot's literary theories, especially by American scholars, appears possibly more restrictive than that given by Italian scholars on Campanella as a Dante critic. Apart from Northrop Frye, who (wrongly) interprets both Eliot's poetry and his literary criticism in the light of his later Utopianism, calling him a "drum of other times" (whereas in fact that Utopianism ought to be seen as no more than a by-product of Eliot's great work as a poet), American scholars such as Wellek and Austin, and Italian ones such as Rosati, lament the fact that Eliot's criticism is not grounded in a coherent aesthetic system, that his theories on "impersonality" and the "objective correlative" are inaccurate and contradictory, and, in short, that his criticism is the criticism of a poet, which he practised as a means of mastering and promoting his own poetic craft. This is also the opinion one may deduce from the statements of Italian scholars on Campanella's Dante criticism: it is worship, not criticism, aimed more at bolstering his own ideas and actions for social renewal than at achieving a deeper knowledge of Dante. It is as though modern critics, who base their presumption as to the objective and scientific nature of their work on some preexistent aesthetics or methodology, do not feel as bound as other critics to defend their criteria; it is as though, being convinced that in any reasoned and valid critical inquiry there is a mixture of objectivity and subjectivity, they believe that greater objectivity must of necessity be found in the work of critics who are expert in some aesthetic, ideological or methodological doctrine than in the

---

1 *Epist.*, XIII. 39.

work of critics who, being poets, are above all expert in poetry and literature, that is, in the specific object of literary criticism.[1]

It is not an aesthetics but "a very highly developed sense of fact" (as Eliot writes in his essay on *The Function of Criticism*) that is the most important qualification for a good critic, whether or not he or she practises as a poet, that is, whether his or her "sense of fact" in art is active and productive or simply passive and receptive. Like Eliot in our times, Campanella in his was one of Europe's greatest poet-critics. Like Eliot, he was not always free of personal interest, contradictions and changes of mind, but, like Eliot, he was endowed with a great "sense of fact": not only the fact "of his own work" but also the fact of Dante and other poets, and not least the fact of poetry considered in its primary and essential nature as a productive activity, which creates and transforms language and, through language, civilization.

Like Eliot, who plays down Milton's responsibility for the development of a certain rhetorical trend in modern English language and poetry, while looking back to Dante as the model for a language and poetry not "of words" but "of things", so Campanella downgrades Tasso and the main poets of his time, whose distinctive mark he sees as an exquisite elegance which however remains an end in itself, and contrasts them with Dante, "qui ut ante oculos ponat scientias et rerum veritates" ["who sets the sciences and the real truths about things as though before our eyes"] and gives the reader much enjoyment with "finzioni [...] le quali, quanto piú insegnano, tanto piú son belle" ["fictions (...) which, the more they teach, the more they are beautiful"].[2]

Certainly the return, on the part of both Campanella and Eliot, to the origins of the national and European tradition should also be seen as the reaction of two Christian writers to moral decadence in their own times, but at all events it is the sense of fact and a true, albeit intuitive rather than reasoned understanding of poetry and its principal function that drove them to become "drums", not "of other times", but of better times.

But let us now leave Eliot aside and turn to a more particular definition of the critical sense of Campanella's worship of Dante. First of all, I think there is no need to emphasize the exceptional

1   On these and other references to Eliot and his critics see my "Letteratura e critica nel pensiero di T. S. Eliot", *Testo*, 25 (Jan–June 1993), 3–21.
2   T. Campanella, *Opere letterarie*, pp. 615, 409.

nature of Campanella's attitude towards Dante compared to that of his contemporaries, not only because Campanella shares the reservations common to all admirers of Classicism, from Bembo to Leopardi, regarding Dante's lack of elegance, or because his view of Dante's realism may also be found in other readers of the time (for example, Chiabrera, who to Dante "dava gran vanto per la forza del rappresentare e particolareggiar le cose" ["gave great credit for his power to represent and individualize things"]),[1] but because Campanella's criticism appears historically more comprehensible in a diachronic than in a synchronic perspective, that is, when it is linked with preceding and following, rather than with contemporary criticism. What I am here referring to is the question of Christian poetry, which arose around the middle of the fourteenth century, in the context of discussions among the so-called Paduan pre-Humanists and theologians, mostly Dominican or Augustinian, resurfaced towards the end of the fifteenth century with Savonarola and his struggle against the rhetoricism and neo-paganism of the new Humanists, and, quietly submerged throughout the Classical age, came out into the open again during the Romantic era, with Manzoni and his rejection of the classical tradition and methodology. Dante's function in this debate was at first wholly negative. Brother Guido Vernani, in his short book *De Reprobatione Monarchiae Compositae a Dante* (1327–1334?), branded the author of the *Commedia* a "vas diaboli" ["vessel of the devil"].[2] In 1335 the Dominican chapter of Florence forbade friars to hold "poetical books or tracts composed in the vernacular by one named Dante".[3] Some twenty years later, Boccaccio in his *Trattatello in laude di Dante*, the first monographic biography of the poet, reversed the sentence, making Dante into a "theologian-poet" and calling his poem "divine".[4] Since he did this, however, not so much on account of the specifically Christian or theological character of the poem as on the ground that theology and poetry are almost the

1   G. Chiabrera, *Vita scritta da lui medesimo*, in his *Opere*, edited by M. Turchi (Turin, UTET, 1977), p. 521.

2   Edited by T. Kaeppeli in *Quellen und Forschungen aus Italienischen Archiven und Bibliotheken*, 28 (1937–38), 107–46, and reproduced in N. Matteini, *Il più antico oppositore politico di Dante: G. Vernani* (Padua, Cedam, 1958), pp. 94–118 (p. 94).

3   See I. Venchi, "Domenicani", in *Enc. dant.*, II, 542–46.

4   G. Boccaccio, *Trattatello in laude di Dante*, edited by D. Guerri (Bari, Laterza, 1918), p. 87.

same thing (in the sense that theology too is poetry, "the poetry of God"), it is the starting-point not for a religious interpretation of the poem but for a rhetorical and literary one. This is the interpretation shared by those Humanists who, disagreeing with Niccoli that Dante "must be left to shoemakers and bakers",[1] assimilate him, as Landino does in his *Comento,* to the poets of ancient times: Orpheus, Homer, Hesiod and Pindar.[2]

At the end of the fifteenth century, in that atmosphere of spiritual renewal which the preaching of Savonarola had begotten in Florence, another Humanist and Latin poet, Ugolino Vieri, a friend of Savonarola's, proposed to him the idea of a new poetry, in which the "diserte et ornate loqui", the eloquent and ornate style of modern Latin poets, was to be placed at the service not of pagan fables but of truth and people's Christian happiness. Savonarola replied to Vieri with a short work, *In Poeticen Apologeticus* [*Apologia of Poetry*],[3] which to the "diserte et ornate loqui" opposed immediacy and simplicity, that is, the peculiar characteristics of the only kind of poetry which according to Savonarola was permissible within the system of sciences: poetry for the "simplices", the simpleminded people who did not know Latin and philosophy and needed examples and metaphors in order to understand the lofty truths of the Christian faith.

Since Dante puts the very same poetics into the mouth of Beatrice in the fourth canto of *Paradiso* and it was that which inspired all his work as "fabbro del parlar materno" ["craftsman of the mother tongue"; *Purgatorio,* XXVI. 117], we might expect Savonarola to acknowledge Dante as a most Christian poet and put him forward as an example. Yet Dante is not even mentioned in the *Apologeticus.* There may be two reasons for this. Firstly, Savonarola may have been unable to escape the influence of the majority of his contemporaries, who, through Boccaccio and Petrarch, connected Dante with Virgil and Cicero, that is, with a rhetorical view of his

1   See L. Bruni, *Dialogus ad Petrum Paulum Histrum,* in *Prosatori latini del Quattrocento,* edited by E. Garin (Milan–Naples, Ricciardi, 1952), p. 70.

2   See "Proemio al Commento dantesco", in C. Landino, *Scritti critici e teorici,* edited by R. Cardini, 2 vols (Rome, Bulzoni, 1974), I, 137.

3   G. Savonarola, *Opus [...], In Poeticen Apologeticus* (Venice, Giunti, 1542); translated into Italian by V. Mattii (Siena, Tipografia dell'Ancora di G. Bargellini, 1864). See my "L'*Apologeticus* del Savonarola e il problema di una poesia cristiana" [1952], now in my *Letteratura come bellezza* (Rome, Bulzoni, 1991), pp. 45–67.

poem. Secondly, although Savonarola had himself composed a few poems and religious *laude*, he may in fact have had no real interest in poetry, even as a means of edification.

Nevertheless, the concurrence between Dante's poetry and Savonarola's poetics became evident in some of the latter's early disciples, such as Benivieni, and somewhat later in Michelangelo, in whose cultural formation it acted as a determining factor. In due course it was given its best critical expression, from about the middle of the sixteenth century onwards, in the work of Gelli, the hosier-cum-philosopher and lecturer on the *Commedia* in the Accademia Fiorentina, and other famous critics and Dante scholars such as Tomitano, Salviati and Borghini, in whose writings many of the positions held by Campanella are put forward. For instance, applying to Dante Savonarola's idea of poetry as a form of logic ("demonstrative logic" or, as Savonarola called it, "the logic of example"), Gelli identified the greatness and beauty of the *Commedia* as a "harmony not of words but of things" and declared: "If the main duty of the poet is to give pleasure and to be useful, no poet, whether ancient or modern, has ever invented anything more beautiful or delightful than the subject of the *Commedia*."[1] To remarks of the same kind Salviati added that Dante had achieved "the highest degree of poetic perfection according to Plato".[2] For Tomitano, a doctor and master of logic at Padua, Dante was

> un oceano di dottrine, teologia, filosofia, astrologia, cosmografia ed altre sí fatte cose, per lo cui aiuto quelle cose cantò, che alli tre stati dell'anime s'appartengono, con tanta altezza e profondità d'ingegno, con quanta né greco né latino, poetando, ebbe mai forza poter di cantare.[3]

> [a sea of learning, theology, philosophy, astrology, cosmography and other such matters, thanks to which he sang of those things pertaining to the three states of souls with such breadth and depth of mind as no Greek or Latin poet ever had the power to sing with.]

1   G. B. Gelli, *Letture edite e inedite sopra la "Commedia"*, 2 vols (Florence, Bocca, 1881), I, 327–28. See also my "Dante nell'umanesimo di G. B. Gelli: le 'Letture sopra la *Commedia*'" [1953], now in my *Letteratura come bellezza*, pp. 191–232 (pp. 223–25).

2   *Opere del Cav. Lionardo Salviati*, edited by L. Manzoni, 5 vols (Milan, Classici Italiani, 1809–10), V, 73–74.

3   B. Tomitano, *Quattro libri della lingua thoscana* (Padua, Marcantonio Olmo, 1570), p. 75.

Finally, the great Florentine Dantist Borghini, in his *Difesa di Dante come cattolico*, underlined the Christian character of Dante's poem, which, on the whole,

> si può dire un'etica cristiana compita e perfetta, conforme all'E-vangelio e legge cristiana e a quello che hanno scritto i Santi Pa-dri e ancora alle veritadi de' filosofi dove ha potuto la ragione u-mana.[1]

> [may be called a complete and perfect Christian ethics, in accord-ance with the Gospels and Christian law and the writings of the Holy Fathers, as well as the truths of philosophers going as far as human reason could reach.]

Campanella definitely knew Tomitano, whom he quotes in the Latin *Poetica*, and it is likely that he also knew Gelli and the others mentioned above. It is certain that he knew the ideas of his more unfortunate brother from Ferrara: in the Italian *Poetica* he refers to a passage of the *Apologeticus* where "the good Savonarola cautions his readers that poets tell through examples and songs what learned men tell through doctrine."[2] But although he establishes a link, in this respect, with Savonarola's poetics, he in fact goes one step further, viewing Dante in the same perspective as Gelli, To-mitano, Salviati and Borghini, and applying to him, in a truly Christian sense, the "poeta-theologus" qualification of Boccaccio and Landino. Furthermore, assimilating Dante once again to the pagan poets of ancient times, he makes him the very touchstone of the poetry of the ancients.

In Landino's view, Homer, Orpheus and Hesiod were all poets and theologians, their poems all sacred poems. Campanella, on the other hand, makes a distinction. As Dante teaches through many episodes of his poem,

> Dal poeta sempre si deve dir bene del bene e male del male, e quando s'introduce uno che dica male del bene e bene del male, mostrare che a pessimo fine è per venire [...]. Ora, se il libro di Lancellotto ha fatto due cognati, con leggi cristiane avvinti, in-sieme congiungere, ed essere ammazzati, e andare all'Inferno, che farà Omero, che gli adultéri di Venere, di Teti e di Giove e

---

1   V. Borghini, "Difesa di Dante come cattolico", in M. Pozzi, *Lingua e cultura del '500* (Padua, Liviana, 1975), p. 347.
2   T. Campanella, *Opere letterarie*, p. 406.

quel nefando vizio del medesimo con Ganimede e altri simili racconta? Perché invero, se li dei ciò fanno, non è dubbio che piú lo dobbiamo far noi, essendo noi obligati ad imitare li dèi.[1]

[The poet must always speak well of good and ill of evil; and when he introduces a character who speaks ill of good and well of evil, he must show that he will come to a bad end (…). Now, if the book of Lancelot caused a brother- and sister-in-law, bound by Christian laws, to couple, be murdered and go to Hell, what will Homer do, who tells of the adulteries of Venus, Thetis and Jupiter, and of that wicked vice of Jupiter's with Ganymede, and of other such things? For in truth, if the gods do it, there is no doubt that we must do it ourselves, being obliged, as we are, to imitate the gods.]

Therefore Campanella warns:

Non vi curate […] di far poemi a modo delle regole d'Aristotile e d'Omero, ma piú tosto imitare Esiodo e Orfeo e Lino e, tra ' nostri, Dante, lo cui poema invero è sagro.[2]

[Do not bother to write poems following the rules of Aristotle and Homer, but rather imitate Hesiod, Orpheus and Linus and, among our own, Dante, whose poem is indeed sacred.]

In the same way and for the same reasons Campanella proclaims and justifies his preference for Latin over Greek poets:

Leggendo alcuno il libro di Lucrezio, sempre riceverà piú gusto che da Omero, perché da quello resta l'uomo ammaestrato a vivere e onorato da chi per tale lo conosce, e da questo ammaestrato all'avarizia e fierezza d'Achille, alla stoltezza di Agamennone, all'impietà e poca stima de' giuramenti di Sinone.[3]

[If someone reads the book of Lucretius he will derive more pleasure from that than from Homer, because the former will have taught him to live and be honoured by those who recognize that he has been so taught, whereas the latter will have schooled him in the avarice and pride of Achilles, the foolishness of Agamemnon and the impiety of Sinon and his scant regard for oaths.]

---

1   T. Campanella, *Opere letterarie*, pp. 357, 371.
2   T. Campanella, *Opere letterarie*, p. 368.
3   T. Campanella, *Opere letterarie*, p. 370.

Among the Latins he recommends the most ancient:

> Plauto, Terenzio, Valerio Sorano e altri di quelli poeti che sono
> stati al tempo di Roma santa, secondo le lor leggi e libertà han-
> no poetato piú secondo il vero ammaestramento del popolo,

> [Plautus, Terence, Valerius Soranus and other such poets who
> lived at the time when Rome was hallowed, did write, according
> to their laws and freedom, with greater regard for the true
> instruction of the people,]

rather than

> li scelerati Catulli e Marziali, e li bugiardi Virgilii e Ovidii, i la-
> scivi Galli e Tibulli e Orazii, i quali invero furono uomini d'inge-
> gno, ma l'adoprorno a corrompere la repubblica.[1]

> [the wicked Catulluses and Martials, the lying Virgils and Ovids,
> the lascivious Galluses and Tibulluses and Horaces, who were
> men of talent indeed, but used it to corrupt the republic.]

Considering the above and many other statements of the same
kind, it is easy to understand why almost all Campanella scholars
discuss his criticism in terms of "moralism". But moralism is most
definitely not the correct term to use in this connection, at least in
the usual, modern, heteronymous sense of the word. The truth is
that modern critics tend to see moral *engagement* in poetry as an
external, ideological factor—positive or negative as the case may
be—in literary inspiration, and not as one of its modes of being. Yet
at certain times in the history of literature, and with certain writers,
moral teaching, as well as science, philosophy and theology, is
born and lives together with the unsophistication, inventiveness
and imagination that are peculiar to poetry. In the earlier periods
of any language or civilization, before the natural evolution of
culture into different branches of knowledge and styles of writing
has taken place, science and religion, doctrine and morality become
the very stuff of poetry and literature (as for instance with Dante).
This also happens in ages that are maturer and more advanced, or
even in some sense decadent, with certain writers who feel a need
for renewal, simultaneously proclaiming and achieving it in their
work, by returning to the origins of their tradition and reconstituting

1   T. Campanella, *Opere letterarie*, p. 356.

its original unity in their works of prose or poetry—as is the case with Campanella and, we might add, with Eliot.

So Campanella's criticism, on Dante and in general, is not really the criticism of a moralist, whether in a narrowly Christian sense or in a broader sense, which would include natural ethics. It is, as we have seen, the criticism of a poet, in which religion, morality, philosophy and science live and develop together, as expressions of his poetic personality. It is the criticism of one of the great poets of his time, a time which, in terms of literary history, cannot be reduced to mere *secentismo* and *antisecentismo* and their noisier manifestations, and a time moreover that must be seen as the continuation and development of the Renaissance, that is, of a culture in which art and poetry, craft and creativity assume the task of knowing (or at least searching for) the whole, the microcosm and the macrocosm, a task which in the Middle Ages was performed by theology and scholasticism and in modern times has become the unattainable object of dialectical discourse and the contraposition of empirical science and moral sense.

Just as Michelangelo, a hundred years earlier, had exalted Dante above all men ("Ne'er walked on earth a greater man than he"),[1] for having investigated and informed us of the whole range of visible and spiritual things, and just as he himself used sculpture and poetry to delve into the night and, beyond the night, into the human and cosmic mystery of God and evil, so did Campanella make and use the beauty of poetry to search for, and at the same time make accessible to all, a Christian vision of the universe, in terms which were consistent with the mentality and the sensibility of his time, as Dante had done with his own poem in his own time.

The idea of poetry as the language of the totality of things did not last beyond the seventeenth century: Vico's conception of poetry as the philosophy of primitive peoples and civilizations is something quite different, and already according to that conception when Dante philosophizes or theologizes he ceases to be a poet. But the idea of Dante as the poet of the totality of things endures for longer, as may be seen in the discourse *Sull'"Endimione" del Guidi* by Gravina, one of the most important critics of Arcadia:

---

1   See the sonnet "Dal ciel discese" (no. 248) in Michelangelo Buonarroti, *Rime*, edited by E. N. Girardi (Bari, Laterza, 1960); and my "Michelangelo e Dante" [1976], now in my *Letteratura come bellezza*, pp. 89–102.

Largamente spiegò le piume del suo ingegno Dante, il quale felicemente ardí di sollevar le forze del suo spirito all'alto disegno
di "descriver fondo a tutto l'universo"; sicché in un'opera non
solamente le umane e le civili cose, ma le divine e le spirituali mirabilmente comprese. E fu egli cosí avventuroso in quest' impresa, che gli riuscí di esprimere al vivo con incredibile verità ed
evidenza tutti i costumi, le condizioni e gli affetti con parole pregne d'immagini, e con colori poetici sí gagliardi e vari, che scolpiscono i geni, gli atti, i pensieri e i gesti di tutte le persone. Onde si vede in un poema tentato ogni genere di poesia, ogni maniera di dire, ogni stile, ogni carattere, con parole tali che spesso si cangiano nel proprio essere delle cose. Si sforza egli di aggiungere a questi pregi il maggiore, ch'è quello delle scienze.[1]

[Broadly did Dante spread the wings of his mind, successfully
daring to make the strength of his spirit equal to the grand design
of "describing the bottom of all the universe", so that in a single
work he miraculously managed to include not only human and
civic matters but divine and spiritual ones as well. And he was
so successful in this undertaking that he managed to give life,
with amazing truth and clarity, to every kind of behaviour,
condition and feeling, by means of words pregnant with images
and of such bold and varied poetic colours that they depict the
personality, the actions, the thoughts and the gestures of every
person. Wherefore in a single poem every type of poetry can be
seen to have been attempted, every manner of speech, every
style, every figure, and with words so chosen that often they turn
into the things themselves. To all these qualities he attempts to
add the greatest, which is the quality of science.]

These words reproduce and summarize the basic thought on
Dante of Campanella and his sixteenth-century predecessors whom
we quoted above. At a later stage, in his major work, *Della ragion
poetica*, Gravina will once again put forward Landino's and Campanella's likening of Dante to the primitive theologian-poets,
Orpheus, Linus, Museus and Homer. But—Gravina stresses—
Dante surpassed them in knowledge and art, because "volle la sua
poesia consecrare colla religione e con la teologia rivelata e celeste,
molto piú degna della naturale de' filosofi e de' primi poeti" ["he
wanted to consecrate his poetry with religion and with revealed

1   G. V. Gravina, *Opere scelte* (Milan, Giusti and Ferrario, 1819), p. 349.

and divine theology, which is far worthier than the natural religion and theology of the philosophers and early poets"].[1]

With Gravina, however, this Humanist and Christian way of interpreting Dante, which reached its apex in Campanella, came to an end. It is true that Manzoni, in the appendix to his *Relazione sull'unità della lingua*, says that Dante "gathered together in one stupendous work memories, taken from many ages and many places, of the most varied deeds and thoughts, of vices and virtues, of joys and sufferings, of fortunes and misfortunes, of ideas and errors",[2] but he also says more or less the same thing about Petrarch and Boccaccio, in what is a generic appraisal of these writers as creators and promoters "of the mother tongue", rather than a specific consideration of their respective poetry. What is more, after his religious and literary conversion—from agnosticism to Catholicism and from Neoclassicism to Romanticism—Manzoni took only a limited interest in the Italian literary tradition and its poets: his favourite poets were Virgil and Shakespeare. He did not share in Dante's—or Campanella's—exaltation of Rome and Rome's imperial mission. In 1865, according to Cantú, he even refused to sign a petition calling for Dante's birthday to be declared a public holiday. And regarding the question of Christian poetry, and more generally of the relationship between poetry and doctrine, Manzoni represented and held to a vision which was quite the opposite of Campanella's and to all intents and purposes similar to Savonarola's. Knowledge and moral action no longer drew their impulse and character from poetry; on the contrary, poetry must now conform to principles of truth and goodness. As a consequence, in Romantic and modern criticism, the sense of the unity of Dante's poetic world appears to be lost for good, both from an ideological and from an aesthetic point of view. Rossetti turned Dante into a sectarian, the forefather of the Italian Risorgimento, opposed to the temporal power of the papacy. For De Sanctis, Carducci and Croce, Dante's poetry lived on for ever, but *in spite of* its medieval, theological and philosophical form.

On the other hand, Romantic and modern critics have promoted analytical readings and interpretations of the poem, as well as aesthetic evaluations—but according to perspectives and prefer-

1   G. V. Gravina, *Della ragion poetica*, edited by G. Natali (Lanciano, Carabba, 1920), pp. 143–44.

2   A. Manzoni, *Tutte le opere* (Rome, Avanzini and Torraca, 1965), p. 1231.

ences of taste that in some cases were those of Campanella. An example of this may be found in the modern critical motif of Dante the character and his unifying function in the poem's structure. Dante, Campanella writes in the Italian *Poetica*,

> parla di cose infinite diversissimamente in sostanza, luogo, natura e tempo: nondimeno tutte le riferisce al suo passaggio, che ha fatto per considerazione delle cose dell'Inferno, Purgatorio e Paradiso, le quali sono come tre parti integrali di tutta la *Commedia*, unite in corpo di considerazione rappresentativa di tutta l'università mondana e umana.[1]

> [speaks of countless things in very many different ways regarding substance, place, nature and time; nevertheless he refers them all to the journey he made to consider matters in Hell, Purgatory and Paradise, which, as the three integral parts of the *Comedy*, are united into one body with a view to representing the whole world and humanity.]

Similarly Campanella, like Romantic readers and—we may add—like Eliot, prefers *Inferno* to the other two *cantiche*, because beauty in art "non consiste nello soggetto materiale, ma nell'imitazione [...]; è Tersite buffone in scena bene imitato, piú bello d'Agamennone re, mal imitato" ["does not reside in the subject-matter but in imitation (...); the buffoon Tersites well imitated on stage is more beautiful that King Agamemnon badly imitated"].[2] Equally, the episodes of the *Commedia* which he quotes most frequently in his *Poetica* are those which will also be the favourites of Romantic readers, such as the entry into Hell (*Inferno* III), Paolo and Francesca (*Inferno* V), Ulysses (*Inferno* XXVI), Count Ugolino (*Inferno* XXXIII), as well as those passages in *Purgatorio* and *Paradiso* which demonstrate Dante's ability to translate concepts into images, characters and scenes (what Croce calls "poetry"), such as the sculptures in *Purgatorio* X, the procession in *Purgatorio* XXIX and the story of the Roman eagle in *Paradiso* VI, rather than the merely doctrinal passages (what Croce calls "structure"). Campanella, though, has too developed a "sense of fact" to separate poetry from structure, that is, to separate poetry from its very body.

---

1   T. Campanella, *Opere letterarie*, p. 400.
2   "Poesie filosofiche", Canzone 29, Madrigale 5, in T. Campanella, *Opere letterarie*, p. 165.

Among other references to Dante that could be mentioned, one in particular deserves attention, since it appears to contradict Campanella's praise, in the Italian *Poetica* (p. 451), of Dante as the greatest "craftsman of the mother tongue" and also to contradict his own poetry. In the preface to his *Commentaria* on the Latin poems composed by Maffeo Barberini before he became Pope Urban VIII, Campanella writes that the Pope's poetry is even better than Dante's, being written in Latin: "Dantes, poetarum optimus, christiano ritu cecinit, sed vulgari nec satis culto sermone" ["Dante, the best of poets, sang according to Christian custom, but in the vernacular and in a language which was insufficiently refined"].[1] Anyone who knows that Campanella escaped ending his days at the stake by virtue of his diplomacy and his capacity for befriending the mighty will understand that little notice should be taken of this statement!

Finally, a few words should be said about Dante's presence in and influence on Campanella's poetry. Firpo points out that the presence is evident above all in "transparent and explicit quotations, which are however more than casual or convenient appropriations".[2] Sometimes Campanella himself underlines his debt in his footnotes, as in the closing line of Sonnet 5 ("sol certo e lieto chi s'illuia e incinge" ["only he is safe and happy who makes himself him (i.e. God) and becomes impregnated with him"]), derived from *Paradiso*, IX. 73 ("Dio vede tutto, e tuo voler s'inluia" ["God sees all, and thy seeing gets inside Him"]) and *Inferno*, VIII. 45 ("Benedetta colei che 'n te s'incinse" ["Blessed is she who bore thee"]). *Illuiare* and *incingersi*, Campanella notes, "are Dante's own coinages and marvellously apt" ("son vocaboli di Dante, mirabili a questo proposito"), apt, that is, for the subject of the human soul's divine destiny. More often the borrowing is not declared, yet it is equally indicative of the great debt owed by Campanella to Dante, especially to that part of Dante's lexicon which serves to represent spiritual processes, for example in *Canzon d'amor*, 28 ("all'alto volo gli vestí le penne" ["he clothed him with feathers for the lofty flight"]), derived from *Paradiso*, XV. 54 ("ch'a l'alto volo ti vestí le piume" ["who clothed thee with feathers for the lofty flight"]), or in Sonnet 95 ("purgate le caligini del mondo" ["cleansed of the mists

---

1   T. Campanella, *Opere letterarie*, p. 672.
2   L. Firpo, "Dante e Campanella", p. 36.

of the world"]), derived from *Purgatorio*, XI. 30 ("purgando la caligine del mondo" ["cleansing the mist of the world"]).

There is a great difference, however, between Dante's poetry and Campanella's, not only from a structural point of view, in that the *Commedia* belongs to the epic genre while the *Cantica* belongs to the lyric one, but also and above all by virtue of the different relationship in each poet between the message conveyed and the beauty offered for the reader's enjoyment. In Dante the message is conveyed and governed by a poetic structure which is intended above all to provide enjoyment while representing the totality as a whole and in its many parts. Dante's own religious and political polemizing is subject to this poetic concern, which is peculiar to a poem designed, in the wake of the *Convivio*, as a response to the demand for a new language on the part of a new people in need of material and spiritual improvement. In short, it is more important for Dante to give the greatest number of vernacular names to existing and known things, many of them never written about before except in Latin, than to use these names for inquiring into, heralding or bringing about new things. His task is cultural popularization, and as a consequence of this the beauty of his poem resides in its being wholly soothing, tranquil, objective—capable of imposing its rule of detachment and harmony even on the personal displays of indignation or excitement in which the poet-pilgrim sometimes indulges.

On the other hand, at a time when the entire structure of the universe, both natural and human, is once again in discussion, the philosophical and literary condition in which Campanella finds himself is quite different, and as a result the beauty of his poetry is also different. For Campanella it is no longer a question of giving new names to old things but of giving new things to old names, that is, of once again giving to words, which "modern poets" now use only for play or for lying, a sense of reality and truth and the function of bringing about religious, moral and social renewal, as it was for the poets of earlier times. In the *Cantica*, therefore, the relation between message and beauty, truth and pleasure, is reversed. The message prevails over beauty, truth over pleasure. Campanella's philosophical, moral and religious message, charged as it is with mental strain, painful experience and the messenger's moods and disdain, determines the structure of his work, both as a whole and in the succession of its parts, and therefore the nature of its beauty.[1] Gone is the tranquil, detached, objective beauty which corresponds to a clear and solid totality which has been revealed in full and is thoroughly accessible to both sense and intellect. Beauty in Campanella corresponds to a totality which is partly known and partly unknown, was not created once and for all but is *in fieri*, and is no longer accessible solely to man's contemplative intelligence but also—and even more so—to his volitive and creative intelligence. It is therefore a restless and tense beauty, always torn between earth and Heaven, sorrow and hope. The poetry, too, is divided, between philosophy and poetry, and this is expressed partly through the discursive terms and common speech of prose and partly through the rhythmic and metaphorical devices which are peculiar to poetry.

Rather than the quotations we looked at earlier, it is this idea, freely and aptly flowing through the sonnets and *madrigali* of the *Cantica*, that is in my view the most obvious indication of Dante's presence in Campanella's poetic writing.

---

1   Lina Bolzoni, in her introduction to Campanella's *Opere letterarie* (p. 27), perceptively notes that in Campanella's poetry the basic outline of the *Commedia* is repeated ("The poet's experience becomes the exemplary expression of a universal event and law"), thus underlining the difference between Dante and his follower in terms not too dissimilar from my own.

"AN ITALIAN WRITER AGAINST THE POPE"? DANTE IN REFORMATION ENGLAND, *c.1560–c.1640*

Nicholas R. Havely

The English reception of Dante during the sixteenth and early seventeenth centuries has not been thought worthy of much close critical attention. In the most authoritative recent survey of Dante's *fortuna*, Michael Caesar argues that "there is [...] no sign of any real knowledge of Dante in English Renaissance literary circles."[1] Yet there is a danger that the concept of "literary circles" can engender a rather narrow sense of what literature may be. On the same page Caesar seems implicitly to recognize that danger by going on to acknowledge the importance of religious polemic in shaping perceptions of Dante during the Reformation period. He quotes an early and influential description of the poet by the Protestant polemicist Mathias Flacius (1520–75) in the first edition (1556) of the latter's *Catalogus Testium Veritatis Qui ante Nostram Aetatem Reclamarunt Papae* [*Catalogue of Witnesses to the Truth Who before Our Age Spoke Out against the Pope*]:

> Dante of Florence flourished 250 years ago; he was a pious and learned man, as many writers and above all his own writings testify. He wrote a book, which he called the *Monarchy*. In it he showed that the Pope was not superior to the Emperor, nor had he any rights in the Empire, wherefore he is condemned by some as a heretic. He also wrote not a little in the Italian tongue, in which he censured many things in the Pope and his religion. In one place [i.e. *Paradiso*, XXIX. 103–08] he lamented at length that the preaching of the word of God had been allowed to lapse and instead vain fables were being preached by the friars, and

---

1   *Dante: The Critical Heritage*, edited by M. Caesar (London, Routledge, 1989), p. 30.

nonsense in the place of faith [or more accurately: "and that trust is being placed in their frivolities"]: and thus the sheep of God were being fed not with the true fodder of the Gospel, but with wind. Elsewhere [i.e. *Paradiso*, IX. 127–38] he states that the Pope had been turned from a shepherd into a wolf, that he was laying waste to the Church, that along with his cardinals he was not concerned with the word of God, but only with the Decretals. Elsewhere, in the Banquet of Love [i.e. *Convivio*, perhaps IV. 28. 9–10], he equates the married with the celibate state.[1]

Flacius's views on and uses of Dante will be given closer attention here, since (as Caesar argues) they contained the seeds of later Protestant appropriation of the *Commedia* and *Monarchia*.

More evidence of that appropriation—and of Roman Catholic responses to it—has recently been collected by Jackson C. Boswell.[2] Boswell is not a Dante scholar, an Italianist or a Latinist and hence makes no attempt to contextualize his material in the way that Paget Toynbee and Michael Caesar were able to do; and the value of his work is further limited by some methodological oddities and a few mistranslations and mistranscriptions.[3] Nonetheless, his collection is an important new resource for research; and the following discussion is an attempt to construct a narrative out of this evidence and that which my own further investigations have brought to light.

This essay, therefore, seeks to interpret the new material as evidence of reception in a period when, it is often assumed, Dante's work was not much read. It touches on the critical standards and textual culture of the period, taking account of the temper of

---

1   M. Flacius, *Catalogus Veritatum* (Basel, Oporinus, 1556), p. 868 (translated by
     Caesar in *Dante: The Critical Heritage*, pp. 30–31). Flacius's later edition (Argentina [Strasbourg], Paulus Machaeropoeus, 1562) includes substantially
     more discussion of Dante, especially *Monarchia* (pp. 409, 505), the text and
     Latin translation of *Par.*, IX. 126–42, XVIII. 127–36 and XXIX. 88–126 (pp. 505–
     07) and an interpretation of the "puttana sciolta" of *Purg.*, XXXII. 149 as the
     Papacy (p. 507).
2   *Dante's Fame in England: References in Printed British Books 1477–1640*, edited
     by J. C. Boswell (Newark, NJ, University of Delaware Press; London,
     Associated University Presses, 1999).
3   See N. Havely, review of J. C. Boswell, *Dante's Fame in England*, in *Analytical
     and Enumerative Bibliography*, new series 11, iv (2000), 318–22. There are
     serious mistranslations of Latin quotations on pp. 69 and 90 of Boswell's
     volume. P. Toynbee, *Dante in English Literature from Chaucer to Cary (c.1380–
     1844)*, 2 vols (London, Methuen, 1909) remains useful for this period.

religious debate (especially around the time of Elizabeth I's ex-communication and the accession of James I), and it tries to map a little more precisely the ideological hinterland of a major poem of the 1630s, Milton's "Lycidas". In so doing, it addresses a number of related questions. In what form and with what critical baggage did texts of Dante's work reach English Renaissance readers? How did Dante come to be incorporated into the scheme of Protestant history? What particular anti-Catholic topics are his representa-tions of the Church made to serve? How did English Catholics respond to the construction of Dante as an "Italian writer against the Pope"? Does the polemical controversy about the poet's work affect its wider dissemination and the responses to it on the part of an imaginative writer such as Milton?

In the first place, then, we need to take some note of the critical temper of the time. In general Dante's fame over this period was not what it had been or later was to be. During the sixteenth century the *Commedia* certainly continued to be read by those of status and influence, and its writer has been called "the poet of the powerful" of that period.[1] From the sixteenth to the later eighteenth century, however, Dante's standing as an author was largely over-shadowed by other Italian writers, especially Petrarch.[2] One reason for this decline in his status as poetic model was concern (expressed by a number of Italian Humanists) about his style and language. For example, Giovanni Della Casa's influential guide to manners, *Galateo* (1552), objects to linguistic coarseness throughout the *Com-media*; and its concern was literally echoed in England, where the Elizabethan translation of Della Casa spoke of "unhonest and filthie talke" in *Inferno* and "base" and "uncomely" words in *Pur-gatorio* and *Paradiso*.[3] In the earlier sixteenth century an important contribution to the wider circulation of the *Commedia* had been

---

1   See B. Richardson, "Editing Dante's *Commedia*, 1472–1629", in *Dante Now: Current Trends in Dante Studies*, edited by T. J. Cachey Jr (Notre Dame–London, University of Notre Dame Press, 1995), pp. 237–62 (p. 247, quoting C. Dionisotti).

2   For evidence of Petrarch's "ascendancy" over Dante in terms of editions and readership see D. Parker, *Commentary and Ideology: Dante in the Renaissance* (Durham, NC, Duke University Press, 1993), pp. 132, 216 n. 67.

3   The translation is by Robert Peterson, *Galateo of Maister John Della Casa: Or rather, a Treatise of Manners* (London, Newbery 1576: STC 4738). The phrases quoted may also be found in P. Toynbee, *Dante in English Literature* (I, 61–62), *Dante: The Critical Heritage* (p. 269) and *Dante's Fame in England* (pp. 51–52).

made by the octavo, plain-text edition of the poem published by Aldo Manuzio in Venice in 1502 and edited by the Humanist Pietro Bembo.[1] Yet even Bembo had a marked preference for Boccaccio and Petrarch as stylistic models. In his later critical pronouncements he regretted Dante's reluctance to adopt "more pleasing and honourable words" at nasty moments in Hell and deplored his tendency to "let himself fall […] into writing the lowest and basest things". He went on to compare the *Commedia* "to a beautiful, spacious field of wheat which is interspersed all over with oats, tares and sterile harmful grasses".[2] Bembo was both fairly typical of and highly influential on sixteenth-century criticism (it was he, in fact, who shaped Della Casa's views); and with this kind of response from an authority regarded as a defender of vernacular writing, Dante's plurilingualism and mixture of styles were unlikely to find a sympathetic audience.

As a vernacular author Dante nonetheless continued to share some of the common glory, together with Petrarch and Boccaccio, of the "three crowns of Florence"; and this is also reflected in sixteenth-century England. Signs of the "triumph of English" during this period are evident in the aligning of the three Florentine crowns with the home-grown medieval masters: Chaucer, Gower and, on occasion, Lydgate.[3] Cultivation of an English national poetic tradition since at least the time of Henry VIII resulted in this kind of comparison—most famously in Sidney's *Apologie for Poetrie* of 1595—, and here Dante provided a convenient yardstick for poetic status, as he had done for Chaucer himself.[4] Comparison

1   On the importance of the 1502 Aldine edition (based on a manuscript owned by Bembo) see D. Parker, *Commentary and Ideology*, pp. 137–41 fig. 2, p. 202 n. 51; also B. Richardson, "Editing Dante's *Commedia*", pp. 238, 241–44, 246.

2   The phrases are from Bembo's *Prose della volgar lingua* (published in 1525, but begun between 1506 and 1511); the translation is in *Dante: The Critical Heritage*, pp. 234, 236–37. See also B. Richardson, "Editing Dante's *Commedia*", pp. 248, 260 n. 17.

3   An early example of this kind of alignment (Dante, Petrarch, Boccaccio; Chaucer, Gower, Lydgate) may be found in William Horman's Latin–English phrasebook of 1519: see *Dante's Fame in England*, p. 9.

4   Sidney appears to have read at least the proem to Landino's 1481 edition of Dante, since, at the end of the *Apologie*, he alludes to its view of poets as "beloved of the Gods": see Sir Philip Sidney, *An Apology for Poetry: Or the Defence of Poesy*, edited by G. Shepherd (London, Nelson, 1965), pp. 142, 236. On Chaucer's (explicit and implicit) awareness of Dante's work as poetic precedent see for instance *The House of Fame*, lines 447–50, 1091–1109.

between Chaucer and Dante, especially as revivers of the vernacular, is recurrent throughout the century, and reference is also made to the belief that Chaucer had actually translated the Italian poet.[1] A similar confidence-building purpose is served by the comparison of Dante and other Italians with masters of the sixteenth-century English vernacular and (to use George Puttenham's phrase) "reformers of our English meetre and stile", such as Wyatt, Surrey, Skelton, Drayton and, a little less resoundingly, "Mathew Roydon, Thomas Atchelow [and] Thomas Watson".[2] Appropriation of Dante is also evident in a few examples of English translation, such as James Sanford's partial *terza rima* versions of passages from *Inferno* and *Purgatorio* in his 1573 translation of Lodovico Guicciardini's *Houres of Recreation* (*L'hore di ricreatione*) and George Pettie's briefer snatches from *Inferno* and *Paradiso* in his own translation, dating from 1581, of Guazzo's *Civile Conversation* (*La civil conversatione*).[3] But, compared with the huge amount of translation from other Italian authors in the Tudor period, such pickings are relatively meagre, and they do not indicate that the translators had necessarily read any of the *Commedia* in the original. More significant sixteenth- and seventeenth-century translations can, I shall argue, be found elsewhere.

There is thus some respectful and some hostile reference to Dante as vernacular author during this period—along with evidence of some second-hand translation. But who, if anyone, was actually reading the text, and in what form might they have been doing so? Certainly, a fair number of printed editions of the *Commedia* were produced during the fifteenth and sixteenth centuries; and in his own city, Florence, during the sixteenth century, Dante's poem was, according to a recent estimate, "the most frequently possessed single text apart from the Bible".[4] More

---

1   Such comparisons may be found, for instance, in Bale, Leland and Speght (P.□Toynbee*Dante in English Literature*, I, 37–38, 31, 100). See the same work (I, 71) on Chaucer as "translator" of Dante.

2   P. Toynbee, *Dante in English Literature*, I, 30–31, 82 (Leland, comparing Wyatt to Dante and Petrarch), 79 (Puttenham, on Wyatt and Surrey as "reformers" of English), 99–100 (Meres, on Roydon and others as English equivalents to the Italian pantheon), 116 (William Burton, comparing Drayton to Dante, Petrarch and others).

3   *Dante's Fame in England*, pp. 45–48; P. Toynbee, *Dante in English Literature*, I, 66–68.

4   See the statistics in B. Richardson, "Editing Dante's *Commedia*", pp. 255–57, and D. Parker, *Commentary and Ideology*, pp. 132–34. On the ownership of

research on the ownership of such editions in England needs to be done, but we know a number of English inventories, especially from the late sixteenth century onwards, that include works of Dante along with other Italian books. The cathedral library at Wells during the 1530s had a copy of Serravalle's Latin translation of the *Commedia*, which had been commissioned by the Bishops of Salisbury and Bath and Wells at the Council of Constance around 1415; and Henry VIII's library in 1542–43 contained "Danti's works in the Castilian tongue" (which must be Villena's prose translation of 1428).[1] The library of John, Baron Lumley catalogued in 1596 included an early sixteenth-century edition of the *Commedia*; John Donne owned a copy of the 1531 Venice edition of the *Convivio*; Milton (around 1635–38) was using an edition of the *Commedia* with commentary by Daniello (1568); and among the quite large number of Italian books owned by the prominent lawyer and judge Sir Edward Coke at his death in 1634 was an unnamed edition of the "Poet Dante's Workes" of 1568 or 1578.[2] Dante's name (at least) also appears in lists of authors consulted by some writers in this period, from Foxe's 1570 edition of *Actes and Monuments*, through Florio's sources for his new Italian and English dictionary in 1611, to Milton's *Commonplace Book* in the 1630s.[3] Providers of such texts included the bookseller Robert Martin, who listed sixteenth- and seventeenth-century editions of the

    texts of the poem in sixteenth-century Florence see *Dante: The Critical Heritage*, pp. 27, 77 n. 47.

1   P. Toynbee, *Dante in English Literature*, I, 29–30, 32.

2   See J. L. Lievsay, *The Englishman's Italian Books 1550–1700* (Philadelphia, University of Pennsylvania Press, 1969), pp. 52–56, 48–50. On Donne's copy of the *Convivio* (now in the Bodleian Library, Oxford, at 8° D 19 Art. Seld.) see F. P. Wilson, "A Supplement to Toynbee's *Dante in English Literature*", *Italian Studies*, 3 (1946), 50–64 (p. 51). This octavo volume is signed by Donne at the foot of the title page, and at the head of the verso blank opposite is inscribed the motto: "per Rachel ho seruito e non per Lea." Milton's use of the quarto edition of the *Commedia* with commentary by Bernardino Daniello (Venice, for Pietro da Fino, 1568) is indicated by a reference on p. 160 of his *Commonplace Book* (see n. 3 on this page).

3   For Foxe and Florio see P. Toynbee, *Dante in English Literature*, I, 57–59, 84–88. For Milton's *Commonplace Book* see: the facsimile edition (London, Royal Society of Literature, 1876); *The Works of John Milton*, edited by F. A. Patterson, 18 vols in 21 (New York, Columbia University Press, 1931–33), XVIII, 128–227; *Complete Prose Works of John Milton*, edited by D. M. Wolfe, 6 vols (New Haven, Yale University Press, 1953–73), I, 344–513. For the Dante items only see P. □Toynbee*Dante in English Literature*, I, 121–22.

Commedia in his catalogues up to 1640; and the items mentioned here include relatively small, portable editions (such as Daniello's quarto of 1568), as well as the fine folio volumes (such as those of Landino and Vellutello) which may possibly have lain undisturbed on the shelves of aristocratic libraries.[1]

We also have evidence of Dante's presence on the shelves of a working library, the Bodleian at Oxford, in catalogues from 1602 onwards.[2] The author of these Oxford catalogues, Thomas James, is of interest here for several reasons. He was Bodley's first librarian (from 1602 to 1620) and he also published one of Wyclif's anticlerical treatises, as well as anti-Catholic works. Like a number of Protestant writers during this period, James found his interest in Dante and other authors sharpened by their exposure to censorship or prohibition in the various Catholic Indices. Thus, in a polemical work of 1625, James lists "Dantes" along with Ariosto, Petrarch, Valla and others as "Authors [who] with their seuerall bookes, are rescued out of the Papists hands, and restored by me".[3] Precisely what this process of "restoration" entailed is not entirely clear, but by the time James was writing, Dante's major political work, *Monarchia*, had been on the Index of prohibited books for three-quarters of a century, following the Roman Church's official Index of 1554. The *Commedia* itself had been subject to some expurgation, for instance in the Lisbon supplement to the Index of 1581 and the Madrid *Index Expurgatorius* of 1614.[4] Part of what James may be congratulating himself upon here is probably the acquisition of several important editions of *Monarchia*, which were published in Switzerland and Germany and appear, along with various editions of the *Commedia*, in the Bodleian catalogues for 1602–03 and 1620.[5]

1   See J. L. Lievsay, *The Englishman's Italian Books*, pp. 43–48; *Dante's Fame in England*, pp. 197, 208, 214.

2   See P. Toynbee, *Dante in English Literature*, I, 103–05; J. L. Lievsay, *The Englishman's Italian Books*, pp. 35–40; *Dante's Fame in England*, pp. 127, 169–70.

3   The work is *An Explanation or Enlarging of the Ten Articles in the Supplication of Doctor James, lately Exhibited to the Clergy of England* (Oxford, Lichfield and Turner, 1625), pp. 7–9 (quoted in *Dante's Fame in England*, p. 185).

4   On *Monarchia* in the fifteenth and sixteenth centuries see *Dante: The Critical Heritage*, pp. 30–31, 216–18, 273–76. On the expurgation of the *Commedia* see P. Toynbee, *Dante Studies* (Oxford, Clarendon Press, 1921), pp. 111–12, and L. Martinelli, *Dante* (Palermo, Palumbo, 1966), p. 75.

5   See P. Toynbee, *Dante in English Literature*, I, 103–04, and *Dante's Fame in England*, p. 170. The rare 1610 Offenbach edition of *Monarchia*, to which both

Monarchia is a crucial text in the Protestant construction of Dante's identity as (to use Foxe's term) "an Italian writer against the Pope".[1] Its treatment—particularly in its third and final Book—of the bases of papal authority and the relationship and potential conflicts between ecclesiastical and secular power had early on drawn official opposition and condemnation. Shortly after Dante's death in 1321 and in the midst of the conflict between John XXII and the Holy Roman Emperor Ludwig of Bavaria, *Monarchia*'s relevance to the dispute was acknowledged by two attacks upon it from within the Church. One was from a papal legate who, in 1328 or 1329, ordered it and its author's remains to be burnt.[2] The other was from a Dominican apologist for the Papacy, Guido Vernani, who (some time between 1327 and 1334) argued that it would indeed be a good thing for the world to have a single ruler, as Dante had argued in Book I, but unfortunately "the spirit of faction [had] darkened his foolish mind and he was unable to discover the true monarch", namely (as Vernani not unexpectedly concludes) "the supreme pontiff of the Christians, the vicar-general of Jesus Christ".[3] Such adverse judgements did not prevent Dante's treatise from continuing to be read and even translated in Catholic Italy during the fifteenth century.[4] They also sharpened an interest in Dante among the early Protestant anti-papal writers.

One such writer—and possibly the earliest Protestant con-scriptor of Dante—was one to whom this essay has already referred: Matthias Vlachich (1520–75), widely known to his allies and adversaries by his Latinized name of Flacius or Flacius Illyricus

---

Toynbee and Boswell refer, is not listed under "Dante" in the current Bodleian catalogue. There are, however, two copies now under the heading "Engelbertus" (Engelbert of Admont); one of these is the copy to which James refers and which (after some 400 years) still carries the same shelfmark.

1   Foxe's phrase appears in a shouldernote on p. 485 of the second edition of his *Ecclesiastical History* (London, Day, 1570).

2   See Boccaccio's *Trattatello in laude di Dante*, edited by P. G. Ricci, in G. Boc-caccio, *Tutte le opere*, edited by V. Branca, 10 vols (Milan, Mondadori, 1964–98), III, 487–88, §§ 195–97.

3   Translated by Caesar in *Dante: The Critical Heritage*, pp. 110–14. For the original see N. Matteini, *Il più antico oppositore politico di Dante: Guido Vernani da Rimini: testo critico del "De Reprobatione Monarchiae"* (Padua, CEDAM, 1958).

4   Marsilio Ficino translated *Monarchia* into Tuscan in 1467–68. For an edition see P. Shaw, "La versione ficiniana della *Monarchia*", *Studi danteschi*, 51 (1978), 289–408. For a translation of the Preface see *Dante: The Critical Heritage*, pp. 217–18.

(Illyria being his birthplace). Flacius studied in Venice, Basel and Tübingen, and was active as leader of the conservative Lutheran faction around the middle of the century at Wittenberg, Magdeburg and Jena.[1] His *Catalogus Testium Veritatis* appeared first at Basel in 1556, and an enlarged edition was published at Strasbourg in 1562.[2] It presents an account of witnesses who, according to the title page, "before our age spoke out against the Papacy". "Dantes Florentinus" appears in the book's initial list of these, and in the 1556 edition he is subsequently referred to in three passages, not all of which have been noted in the reference books. The first of Dante's works to be mentioned is *Monarchia*: "In this," says Flacius, "he proved the Pope not to be superior to the Emperor, nor to have any jurisdiction over the Empire, because of which he was by certain persons convicted of heresy" (p. 868). This is part of the best-known passage about Dante in the 1556 edition of the *Catalogus*, but the work had also, earlier on, mentioned papal conflicts with emperors, such as Fredrick II, Henry of Luxemburg and Ludwig of Bavaria. It is when discussing Ludwig's dispute with John XXII that Flacius twice (on pages 815 and 819) enlists Dante among the "learned men" and "friends" of the Emperor—clearly once again with *Monarchia* chiefly in mind, since he immediately goes on to reproduce at length Ludwig's defence against the Pope's "calumnies" (pages 820–31). Dante had of course been dead for several years before this particular quarrel erupted, and Flacius's enlistment of him as a participant is probably based upon a misreading (or at least a judicious stretching) of Boccaccio's account of *Monarchia*'s afterlife as a contentious text in the mid-fourteenth century.[3]

What made *Monarchia* a yet hotter property for such Protestant writers was that at roughly the same time (the mid-sixteenth

---

1   On Flacius and his career see H. J. Grimm, *The Reformation Era 1500–1650* (New York, Macmillan, 1973), pp. 398–401, 490–91; E. Cameron, *The European Reformation* (Oxford, Clarendon Press, 1991); C. Lindberg, *The European Reformations* (Oxford, Blackwell, 1996), pp. 6–7, 242–45, 374.

2   I have also seen subsequent editions of the *Catalogus* dating from 1597 and 1608, and there may well be more.

3   For Boccaccio's reference to Ludwig of Bavaria and *Monarchia* see his *Trattatello* (as in n. 2 on p. 134). Flacius's contemporary, Johann Herold, in the biography of the poet appended to his German translation of *Monarchia* (1559), extended Dante's life till 1341 for the purpose (it seems) of linking him with Ludwig of Bavaria: see W. P. Friederich, *Dante's Fame Abroad, 1350–1850* (Chapel Hill, NC, University of North Carolina Press, 1950), pp. 348–49.

century) it was appearing in the official Indices of prohibited
books. This fact was highlighted by the appearance in 1560 of an
edition of the most recent (1559) Index, together with annotations
by the Italian Protestant convert, Pier Paolo Vergerio.[1] Vergerio
was himself a good catch for the Protestants: he had been papal
nuncio in Germany and Bishop of Capodistria, before being
subjected to a protracted heresy trial and fleeing from Italy to
Switzerland and Germany in 1549.[2] His annotations on Dante in
the 1560 volume cover about four pages and focus almost entirely
upon *Monarchia* (mentioning only briefly that the poet "wrote
much in Italian"). Once again (perhaps following Flacius) Dante is
linked with Ludwig of Bavaria. Vergerio also finds a parallel
between Ludwig's dispute with John xxii and the contemporary
quarrel between Ferdinand i and Paul iv over the Pope's right to
authorize the election of an Emperor.[3] For the Protestant pro-
ponents of what is called "magisterial reformation", with their
emphasis on the role of secular powers, *Monarchia*'s assertions
about the limitations of papal power were obviously attractive,
since such claims could be—and were—also advanced on behalf of
other rulers besides the Emperor. Thus in England, a very few
years before Pius v formally revoked Elizabeth i's authority through
the Bull *Regnans in Excelsis* of 1570, we find several Protestant
apologists citing Dante to their Catholic adversaries in defence of
"the Q[ueene's] maiestie's Lawfull and due authoritie" and against
"the Tyrannie of the *Bisshoppes* of Rome and their Barbarous
Persianlike Pride". The apologists quoted here are Robert Horne,
Bishop of Winchester, writing in 1566, and John Jewel, Bishop of
Salisbury, writing in 1567.[4] Both had been among the Protestant
exiles who had taken refuge in Germany and Switzerland during

---

1   See P. Vergerius, *Postremus Catalogus Haereticorum Romae Conflatus, 1559*
     [...] *cum Annotationibus Vergerii* MDLX (Pforzheim, Corvinus, 1560), ff. 18r–
     19v. Excerpts are translated by Caesar in *Dante: The Critical Heritage*,
     pp. 274–75.
2   On Vergerio and the context of Italian religious dissent see H. J. Grimm, *The
     Reformation Era*, pp. 228–29, and E. Cochrane, *Italy 1530–1630*, edited by
     J. Kirshner(Harlow, Longman, 1988), pp. 141–43.
3   P. Vergerius, *Postremus Catalogus*, f. 18v (translated by Caesar in *Dante: The
     Critical Heritage*, p. 274).
4   R. Horne, *An Answeare Made by Rob. Bishoppe of Wynchester to a Booke
     Entituled The Declaration of Suche Scruples, Touchinge the Othe of Supremacy, as
     Iohn Fekenham by Writing Did Deliuer unto the L. Bishop of Winchester, with his
     Resolutions Made thereunto* (London, Wykes, 1566), f. 130r; J. Jewel, *A Defence*

Mary Tudor's reign.[1] They would have been familiar with the work of both Flacius and Vergerio; indeed Jewel cites both in his *Defence of the Apologie of the Churche of England* (pages 43–44). Of the two, Horne (as Boswell has established) is slightly earlier in his citation of Dante, but Jewel, whose *Defence* was reprinted four times in the sixteenth and seventeenth centuries, appears to have been the more influential.

Even more influential in the Protestant conscription of Dante during this politically and polemically turbulent period is the martyrologist John Foxe. Like Horne and Jewel, Foxe had been an exile on the Continent during the Marian persecutions; and while at Basel (from November 1555 to October 1559) he was employed as a proofreader by the printer, Oporinus (Johann Herbst), who during those years published both Flacius's *Catalogus* and the first ever printed edition of Dante's *Monarchia*.[2] It is quite possible, therefore, that he was involved on the production side with both these items. He certainly shows the influence of Flacius's views on Dante in the enlarged 1570 edition of his *Ecclesiasticall History*, where he follows Flacius closely in linking Dante to Ludwig of Bavaria and quite literally in asserting that Dante (presumably in *Monarchia*, though Foxe does not say so) "proueth the pope not to be aboue the Emperour, nor to haue any right or iurisdiction in the empyre".[3] Foxe also refers in the same passage to a text (the *Chronica Iordanis*) that was published in the same volume as the 1559 Basel *Monarchia*; and in his initial list of "the Authors alleged in this Booke" he includes both "Dantes Italicus" and "Illyricus", the name by which Flacius is generally known.[4]

Hence, by 1570 Dante—Foxe's "Italian writer against the Pope"—has come to be written into the English Protestant scheme of history as he had been in Flacius's *Catalogus* and would continue

---

of the Apologie of the Churche of Englande: An Answeare to a Certaine Booke by M. □Harding⟨London, Wykes, 1567), p. 457.

1   On Horne and the Marian exile see M. R. O'Connell, *Thomas Stapleton and the Counter-Reformation* (New Haven–London, Yale University Press, 1964), pp.□158–63 and n. 7; C. Cross⟨Church and People: England 1450–1660*, second edition (Oxford, Blackwell, 1999), pp. 104–10.

2   See *DNB*, under "Foxe, John (1516–87)", pp. 583–84; P. Toynbee, *Dante Studies*, pp. 109–10.

3   J. Foxe, *The Ecclesiasticall History Contaynyng the Actes and Monumentes of Thynges Passed in Euery Kynges Tyme in This Realme especially in the Church of England. Newly Recognised and Inlarged* (London, Day, 1570), p. 485.

4   J. Foxe, *The Ecclesiasticall History*, sig. ¶ 1v.

to be in later Protestant polemic. Within this scheme, he was, as Michael Caesar has pointed out, "one of a number of medieval writers [...] invoked by Protestant reformers to support the thesis of a long-established anti-papal tradition".[1] Within the broad historical framework adopted by Flacius, Foxe and their followers, Dante forms part of a procession of proto-Protestants that includes a number of radical apocalyptic and polemical writers familiar to medievalists, such as Joachim of Fiore, William of Saint-Amour, Marsilius of Padua, William of Ockham, John of Rupescissa and Wyclif—as well as writers such as Petrarch, Boccaccio, Chaucer and Langland.[2]

What must have been particularly attractive about Dante for Northern European Protestant writers is that he is not just a "writer against the Pope" but that he is an Italian and a writer whose work addresses the whole structure of Catholic doctrine. He thus becomes particularly useful in the process of breeding the virus that Protestant polemicists sought to implant within Rome's ideological system. This process is quite explicit in the discourse of a number of English Protestant texts. For instance, Bishop Jewel, directly confronting his Catholic adversary (Thomas Harding) in 1567, fires off at him "*Petrarcha, Dantes*, and a greate number of other *youre owne Doctours*".[3] In 1610, John White names Dante resoundingly among those by whom "the present religion of the Romane Church was observed and resisted in all ages", and having linked him with the usual fourteenth-century suspects (such as Marsilius, Ockham, Wyclif), he immediately comes in with (as he sees it) the clincher: "For *in the Popes owne Librarie* are bookes both Latin and Greeke written against his Primacie."[4] Dante thus comes to be subsumed within a common ideological trope—which might go by the name of "Even Their Own People".

There are at least two further topics of Protestant polemic which Dante in Reformation England is made to illustrate. These may be identified as, first, the representation of "the Pope as Antichrist and Rome as Babylon or Scarlet Woman", and secondly the

1   *Dante: The Critical Heritage*, p. 273.
2   For some examples see *Dante's Fame in England*, pp. 40–41, 63, 64, 132–33, 187.
3   J. Jewel, *Defence of the Apologie*, p. 721 (*Dante's Fame in England*, p. 28). Earlier, Jewel refers to Nicholas of Lyra as "one of your owne late Doctours" (p. 243).
4   J. White, *The Way to the True Church* (London, Bill and Barret, 1610), p. 386; my italics.

concern with magical practices and delusion. In the first case, there were, as the Reformation writers knew, precedents in some medieval apocalyptic exegesis for the identification of Babylon, the Antichrist and the "meretrix magna" with Rome and the Papacy.[1] The titles alone of some of their works give one a clear idea of the kind of resources and discourse they drew upon, for instance: *De Turcopapismo, Mysterium Iniquitatis seu Historia Papatus* and *Antichrist the Pope of Rome: Or the Pope of Rome is Antichrist, Proved in Two Treatises*.[2] Within this apocalyptic context, references to Dante are very often accompanied by ones to Petrarch, especially to the latter's anti-Avignon sonnets and the invective of his *Sine Nomine* letters. Jewel and Foxe, for example, once again follow Flacius's lead in citing Petrarch's sonnet about the papal curia as "impious Babylon".[3] Towards the end of the century, one of the most prolific and energetic of the English "writers against Rome", Matthew Sutcliffe, quotes at some length and with some precision Petrarch's views of Rome as "school of error" and "temple of heresy".[4]

Dante, as "writer against the Pope", is linked or (as Foxe puts it) "adioyned" quite closely with Petrarch throughout the period.

1   For instance, Flacius in the 1556 edition of the *Catalogus* cites Petrus Iohannis Olivi as one of his "witnesses" (pp. 872–73). By associating the "meretrix magna" of Revelation 17 not only with the reprobate in the Church but with Rome "as it subsequently was through the Christian religion", Olivi in his Apocalypse commentary came close to identifying her with the institutional Church and the Papacy; and his followers had no qualms about going the full distance. See *Lectura super Apocalypsim*, in Rome, Biblioteca Angelica MS 382, ff. 103vb–104ra; D. Burr, *Olivi's Peaceful Kingdom* (Philadelphia, University of Pennsylvania Press, 1993), pp. 91–98; *Manuel de l'Inquisiteur*, edited by G. Mollat, 2 vols (Paris, Champion, 1926), I, 142.

2   These are the titles of works by, respectively, Matthew Sutcliffe (1599), Philippe de Mornay (published in Latin and French in 1611, and translated by Sampson Lennard as *The Mysterie of Iniquitie* in 1612) and Thomas Beard (1625). On the widespread trope of Catholic Rome as Whore/Babylon and the Pope as Antichrist see A. Shell, *Catholicism, Controversy and the English Literary Imagination, 1558–1660* (Cambridge, Cambridge University Press, 1999), pp. 24–33.

3   For the references to Petrarch see M. Flacius, *Catalogus* (1556 edition), pp. 871–72; J. Jewel *Defence of the Apologie*, p. 460 (*Dante's Fame in England*, p. 28); J. Foxe, *Ecclesiasticall History* (1570 edition), p. 486 (*Dante's Fame in England*, p. 42).

4   M. Sutcliffe, *Mattaei Sutliuii de Catholica, Orthodoxa et Vera Christi Ecclesia, Libri Duo* (London, Reg. Typog., 1592), p. 53. See also T. Beard, *Antichrist the Pope* (London, John Bellamie, 1625), p. 104.

Thus Jewel asserts that "*Dantes* an *Italian Poete* by expresse woordes calleth Rome the Whore of Babylon", and he specifically cites Canto xxxII of *Purgatorio*, where the vision of the giant and the prostitute on the chariot of the Church may be thus construed; while Foxe less precisely refers to the same idea in "the canticle of purgatory".[1] Both are plainly influenced by the account of the episode in *Purgatorio* xxxII that had appeared in the second (1562) edition of Flacius's *Catalogus*.[2] Other, more explicitly anti-papal passages from the *Commedia* come to be quoted and even translated in subsequent English Protestant polemic. These include the attack on Nicholas III and other avaricious popes in *Inferno* xix, and, with increasing frequency, the passage at the end of *Paradiso* ix, where the corruption of the Papacy is envisaged as the transformation of the shepherd into a wolf.[3] The second of these (*Paradiso*, ix. 126–42) had actually been quoted and translated by Flacius in the second edition of the *Catalogus*.[4] From the mid-sixteenth century onwards, then, the *Commedia*'s anticlerical and anti-papal imagery reinforces that of Protestant polemic. Citing and translating of passages in relation to this theme (the Papacy as Whore, Babylon, Antichrist or ravening wolf) show that some of the polemicists are reading (or quite closely *mis*reading) parts of the poem's text, and that, in this

1　J. Jewel, *Defence of the Apologie*, p. 460 (*Dante's Fame in England*, p. 28); J. Foxe, *Ecclesiasticall History* (1570 edition), p. 485 (*Dante's Fame in England*, p. 41).

2　See M. Flacius, *Catalogus* (1562 edition), p. 507: "In cantione 32. purgatorii non obscurè ostendit Papam esse meretrice Babylonam."

3　For references to Nicholas III and *Inferno* xix see *Dante's Fame in England*, pp. 135 (Alexander Cooke in 1610), 163 (Arthur Duck in 1617), 183 (Thomas Beard in 1625), 202 (Simon Birckbek in 1634). For allusions to the Pope as wolf in *Par.*, ix. 132 see, for instance: M. Flacius, *Catalogus* (1556 edition), p. 868; J. Foxe *Ecclesiasticall History* (1570 edition), p. 485 (*Dante's Fame in England*, p. 41); L. Humphrey, *Jesuitismi Pars Secunda* (London, Middleton, 1584), p. 347 (*Dante's Fame in England*, p. 69, but mistranslated and not attributed to *Par.* ix); P. de Mornay (translated by S. Lennard), *The Mysterie of Iniquitie*, pp. 444–45; S. Birckbek, *The Protestants Evidence, Taken out of Good Records* (London, for R. Milbourne, 1634), pp. 58–60 (*Dante's Fame in England*, pp. 199–202).

4　M. Flacius, *Catalogus* (1562 edition), pp. 505–06. In this edition (pp. 505–07) Flacius substantially enlarges his account of Dante and includes 66 lines of text from *Paradiso* in the original (see above, p. 128 n. 1), together with a brief discussion of how in *Purgatorio* xxxII Dante equates the Pope with the Whore of Babylon (Revelation 17). This Dantean material was subsequently recycled by a number of English Protestant polemicists, including Jewel (1567), Foxe (1570) and Humphrey (1584).

respect, Dante in Reformation England was not merely a useful name to conjure with.

The second topic which leads Protestant polemic to appropriate parts of the *Commedia* is concern with alleged magical and illusory practices on the part of the Roman Church and its priesthood. The association of the "old profession" with the power of superstition and enchantment is well known today, at least since Keith Thomas's *Religion and the Decline of Magic* (1971). It surfaces in a variety of forms within and beyond the period with which we are dealing.[1] The examples of Catholic magic that tend to be focused upon by the polemicists who appropriate Dante are: beliefs about Purgatory, saints' relics and miracles, and the deceptions and fables of the pulpit. Boccaccio also provides good ammunition here, for instance in his tale of Ciappelletto, the "worst of men" who on his death becomes venerated as a saint (*Decameron*, I. 1), and in his story of Frate Cipolla, the itinerant preacher and relic-salesman (VI. 10).[2] In this context the key text from Dante—and the passage from the *Commedia* that is most frequently cited by Protestant writers—is from Beatrice's condemnation of the vanity and "fables" of preachers in Canto XXIX of *Paradiso* (103–08):

> Non ha Fiorenza tanti Lapi e Bindi
> quante sí fatte favole per anno
> in pergamo si gridan quinci e quindi:
>   sí che le pecorelle, che non sanno,
> tornan del pasco pasciute di vento,
> e non le scusa non veder lo danno.

1   "The old profession" is the phrase used to describe pre-Reformation (and particularly monastic) Catholicism in Richard Corbet's ballad "Farewell Rewards and Fairies" (*c.*1625, published in 1647). On English Protestant perceptions of the dangers of traditional Catholicism in the 1560s and 1570s see D. Cressy, *Agnes Bowker's Cat: Travesties and Transgressions in Tudor and Stuart England* (Oxford, Oxford University Press, 2000), pp. 22–24.

2   The *Decameron* had the added advantage of having appeared on Catholic Indices too—for instance in the 1550 Index (see P. Vergerio, *Postremus Catalogus*, p. 6v) and in a later *Index Librorum Authorumque S. Sedis Apostolicae Sacrique Concilij Tridentini Authoritate Prohibitorum* (Munich, s.n., 1582), sig. ☐E 1r (under "Certorum auctorum libri prohibiti")Specific reference to Ciappelletto is made by Matthew Sutcliffe in *De Turcopapismo* (London, G.☐Bishop, R. Newberie and R. Barker, 1599), p. 213; and there is a lively summary of the Frate Cipolla story in Thomas Beard's *Retractive from the Romish Religion* (London, Stansby, 1616), p. 200.

[Even the names Lapo and Bindo aren't so common in Florence
as are these tales that are bawled out year by year from pulpits
everywhere. Thus the poor, unwary flock come back from those
fields fed with wind, but can't be excused for not seeing what is
wrong.][1]

This passage was itself summarized by Flacius in the first edition
of the *Catalogus*; and in the second edition, of 1562, it forms part of
his longest passage of Latin translation from Dante (39 lines). It is
also referred to, quoted and translated by English Protestant
writers a number of times over the period between 1570 and the
1630s. For instance, Foxe in 1570 paraphrases Flacius's 1556
summary of the passage; Humphrey in 1584 quotes from the 1562
translation of it; Sutcliffe in 1599 and 1600 quotes from, translates
or alludes to the original; Beard paraphrases it again in 1616; and
Birckbek in 1634 includes lines 109–26 among the four passages
which he translates from *Paradiso* and *Purgatorio*.[2] The polemicists'
conscription of Beatrice's anticlericalism thus serves to reinforce
their image of the sorcerous Catholic priesthood dispensing what
Sutcliffe called "a dark and mistie cloud of ignorance" and that of
Catholicism in general as—to quote the words of the Puritan
Thomas Beard—the "Religion which nourisheth the most barbarous
and grosse ignorance among the people".[3] We shall return in
conclusion to the influence of this particular passage.

    Meanwhile, from the late sixteenth century into the early
seventeenth, Dante in England has been firmly and repeatedly
written into Protestant history: as a political opponent of papal
supremacy, as a prophetic witness against the Papal Antichrist
and Scarlet Woman and as an unmasker of the obscurantism of the
Roman Catholic priesthood. How then did the Catholic priest-

1   The translation is my own.
2   For Foxe see P. Toynbee, *Dante in English Literature*, I, 58; *Dante: The Critical
    Heritage*, pp. 278, 279 n. 4; *Dante's Fame in England*, p. 41. For Humphrey see
    Dante's Fame in England, p. 69 (Humphrey's Latin is again mistranslated
    here). For Sutcliffe see *Dante's Fame in England*, pp. 110, 111, 114. For Beard
    see *Dante's Fame in England*, p. 153. For Birckbek see *Dante's Fame in England*,
    pp. 200–02.
3   M. Sutcliffe, *A Briefe Replie to a Certaine Odious Libel lately Published by a
    Jesuite, Calling himselfe N. D.* (London, Hatfield, 1600), p. 43; T. Beard, *A
    Retractive from the Romish Religion, Contayning Thirteene Forcible Motives
    Disswading from Communion with the Church of Rome* (London, Stansby,
    1616), p. 345.

hood itself—and especially its dispossessed and exiled English members—react to the conscription of Dante into the ranks of their opponents? Contrary to the impression of a firm "party line" which the successive Indices may generate—and contrary, too, to the English Protestants' tendency to imagine firm diabolical concord holding among their adversaries—, the responses of English Catholic writers are quite interestingly diverse.[1] Several of the Protestant polemicists I have quoted were directly engaged in dispute with specific Catholic opponents. Bishop Horne, for example, was in 1566 answering the objections to the Elizabethan Oath of Supremacy that had been raised by the former Abbot of Westminster, John Fekenham; and the following year he received a response from another Catholic exile, who was to become prominent in English Catholic culture at Douai and Louvain, Thomas Stapleton.[2] Around the turn of the century, one of the most aggressive of the Protestant polemicists, Matthew Sutcliffe, was more than once (in 1600 and 1606) to measure tomes with the Jesuit missionary Robert Parsons, an adversary to whom he refers (perhaps not without a certain rough affection) as "Noddy".[3] There was also an acrimonious dispute *within* the ranks of English Catholics involving the status of Dante's views on papal authority, but that lies beyond the scope of the present discussion.[4]

---

1   An important account of the context here—and of the conflict between the English Catholic "clerks" and "gentry"—is J. Bossy, "The Character of Elizabethan Catholicism", in *Crisis in Europe 1560–1660: Essays from "Past and Present"*, edited by T. Aston (London, Routledge and Kegan Paul, 1965), pp. 223–46 (pp. 230, 238, 243). See also Bossy's account of this dispute in his *The English Catholic Community, 1570–1850* (New York, Oxford University Press, 1976), pp. 37–59; J. C. H. Aveling, *The Handle and the Axe: The Catholic Recusants in England from Reformation to Emancipation* (London, Blond and Briggs, 1976), pp. 68–71. On English Protestant perceptions of the monolithic menace of Rome see especially C. Z. Wiener, "The Beleaguered Isle: A Study of Elizabethan and Early Jacobean Anti-Catholicism", *Past and Present*, 51 (1971), 27–62 (pp. 37–41).

2   On Stapleton see n. 4 on this page.

3   The reference is to Parsons's pen-name, "N[icholas] D[oleman]". See M. Sutcliffe *A Briefe Replie*, for instance pp. 53 ("This personate Noddy [be hee what he will]"), 90, 116 ("the Noddy").

4   This dispute involved particularly the Benedictine "Roger Widdrington" (Thomas Preston) and the Douai and Rheims master, Matthew Kellison: see *Dante's Fame in England*, pp. 142–43, 155–62, 163–64, 173–75. It may well be symptomatic of the conflict between the "gentry" and "clerk" factions among the English Catholics (see n. 1 on this page).

The initial English Catholic response to Bishop Horne's conscription of Dante, then, is that of Thomas Stapleton, who from Louvain in 1567 issued his punningly titled *Counterblast to M[aster] Hornes Vayne Blaste against M[aster] Fekenham.*[1] Here, in the course of answering Horne's points about the rights of the Emperor as secular ruler and arguing that Ludwig of Bavaria was "no lawfull Emperour, but an usurper", Stapleton takes a fairly straightforward line on the authorities (including Dante) that Horne has enlisted in support of his case. For Stapleton, Dante is just one among a motley crew of poets and heretics, and his contemptuous shouldernote here reinforces the point: "M[aster] Horne proueth his new primacie [i.e. that of the Emperor] by poets."[2] This is a tactic that some later Catholic polemicists were also to deploy in response to the citing of Dante as authority on theology and politics.[3] In a work published posthumously (in 1600) Stapleton himself continued to belittle Dante as one of a number of childish rebels, vainly hurling themselves against the solid rock of the Roman Church, "all of whose insults, wrath and rage this Rock of Rome has easily shrugged off, destroyed and dashed to pieces" ("quorum omnium insolentiam, furorem, rabiem, inuicta haec Romana Petra, veluti rupes solidissima facilè decussie, labefactauit, fregit").[4]

A somewhat more sophisticated response on the part of Catholics was to protest against the Protestants' conscription of Dante and to attempt to reclaim him as a Catholic writer. During the later sixteenth century a major polemical voice in this respect, as in others, is that of the Jesuit controversialist Robert Bellarmine; and his approach to Dante is largely shared by his fellow Jesuit, the missionary to England and rector of the English College in Rome,

---

1   On Stapleton's life and his polemic against Horne and Jewel see M.□R.□O'Con-
     nell, *Thomas Stapleton*, pp. 26–52, 56–61, 154–210.
2   T. Stapleton, *Counterblast* (Louvain, Johannes Foulerus, 1567), p. 334r. The
     contemptuous shouldernote about "poets" is omitted in the transcription of
     the passage in *Dante's Fame in England*, pp. 29–30.
3   In the early seventeenth century Dante was described by one Roman
     Catholic apologist as a talented poet but ignorant theologian who should
     have stuck to his trade and not strayed into contentious areas of doctrine:
     see A. Schulckenius, *Apologia Adolphi Schulckenii Geldiensis* [...] *pro Illustrio
     Domino D. Roberto Bellarmino* [...] *adversus Librum falsò Inscriptum, Apologia
     Card. Bellarmini pro Iure Principum, &c. Auctore Rogero Widdringtono Catholico
     Anglo* (Cologne, Hemmerden, 1613), p. 64.
4   T. Stapleton, *Vere Admiranda, seu De Magnitudine Romanae Ecclesiae Libri
     Duo: Editio Secunda Correctior* (Rome, Mutius, 1600), Book i, pp. 27–28.

Robert Parsons.[1] In his *Treatise of Three Conversions of England from Paganisme to Christian Religion* (1603) Parsons undertakes a comprehensive critique of Foxe's scheme of ecclesiastical history—of "the visible succession (forsooth) which Iohn Fox hath deuised to sett downe for the proofe of his new Church".[2] Like Stapleton (to some extent), Parsons dismisses a large number of Foxe's fourteenth- and fifteenth-century witnesses to Protestantism as "paltry heretiks" or "a rabblement of Sectaryes".[3] Unlike Stapleton, however, Parsons objects strongly to the conscription or, as he describes it, "conioyninge" of writers such as Dante and Petrarch among this "company", since, he says, "[they] neuer held any iote of protestant religion in the world. And yet are brought in here by Iohn Fox, as men of his Church and beleefe."[4] Although he does not refer to or quote any of the *Commedia*'s critical passages about the Papacy or the Church, Parsons seems to be taking them into account (along with Petrarch's anti-Avignon invective) when he goes on to claim that for Foxe to build a "visible succession" out of this kind of criticism "is as good an argument, as if a man would proue, that *Saint Paule* was not of the faith, or religion of the *Corinthians*, for that he reprehended them sharpely, for fornication among them".[5] Parsons shows some further signs of having actually read Dante a few years later when, during an argument about Papacy and Empire in 1612, he corrects a Protestant opponent about the identity of Pier delle Vigne (Chancellor to Emperor Frederick II and a prominent figure in *Inferno* XIII). He here twice cites not only Dante himself but also the commentaries on the *Commedia* by Landino and Vellutello, which had first been printed together in 1564.[6]

---

1   On Bellarmine's approach to Dante and its post-Tridentine context see W. P. Friederich, *Dante's Fame in England*, pp. 82–83, and *Dante: The Critical Heritage*, pp. 34–37. On Parsons/Persons, his career and his vision of a restored English Catholic church see J. Bossy, *The English Catholic Community*, pp. 21–24, and J. C. H. Aveling, *The Handle and the Axe*, pp. 57–59, 67–68.

2   R. Parsons [writing as "N. D."], *A Treatise of Three Conversions* (Saint-Omer, s.n., 1603), p. 516 (not in *Dante's Fame in England*).

3   R. Parsons, *A Treatise of Three Conversions*, pp. 353 (not in *Dante's Fame in England*), 514 (in *Dante's Fame in England*, p. 123).

4   R. Parsons, *A Treatise of Three Conversions*, pp. 538–39 (in *Dante's Fame in England*, p. 123).

5   R. Parsons, *A Treatise of Three Conversions*, p. 539 (not in *Dante's Fame in England*).

6   R. Parsons, *A Discussion of the Answere of M. William Barlow D. of Diunity to the Booke Intituled: The Judgment of a New Catholike Englishman* (Saint-Omer,

Evidence of actual close reading of Dante by English Catholics in response to Protestant claims about him continues to be found in the early decades of the seventeenth century. One of Parsons's fellow Jesuits, John Clare, is named as the author of a series of dialogues about Catholicism and Protestantism, called *The Converted Jew: Or Certaine Dialogues betweene Micheas a Learned Jew and Others, Touching Divers Points of Religion Controuerted betweene the Catholicks and Protestants* (1630).[1] In the second of these dialogues, the "learned Jew" Micheas (who by this point shows signs of turning into a Bellarminian Jesuit) continues Parsons's attack on Foxe's "visible" Protestant succession by arguing that even Wyclif "cannot be truly claymed for a Protestant [...] in that (besides he was a Catholicke Priest, and no Church of the Protestants, then known to him) he still retayned many Catholicke Opinions".[2] The "Appendix" to these dialogues is designed as a reply to George Abbot's treatise on "papistry" (1604), which among other things had described *Monarchia* as "a book against the Pope".[3] John Clare (or his ghost-writer) here reviews a number of Abbot's alleged proto-Protestant witnesses (including at some length Chaucer),[4] and in his discussion of Dante and Petrarch he perhaps inherits something of Stapleton's prejudice when he rebukes Abbot for relying on "the testimonies euen of Poets (*as Chaucer, Dantes, Petrarch*)", but he does do something to substantiate his general claim that "what the foresaide Poets did Satyrically wryte, was written only against some disorders in the Church of Rome, and against the presumed faults of some particular Popes; but neuer against their supreme dignity in the Church of Christ."[5] In order to do this, Clare scores off Abbot by going directly to the text of the *Commedia*, quoting several passages from *Inferno* and *Paradiso* and

s.n., 1612), pp. 500 (not in *Dante's Fame in England*), 503 (in *Dante's Fame in England*, p. 146). Landino and Vellutello are referred to twice here: in shouldernotes *m* and *n* on p. 500, and in the text on p. 503. Their commentaries first appeared together in the Venice folio edition of 1564, edited by Francesco Sansovino (see B. Richardson, "Editing Dante's *Commedia*", p. ☐256).

1   The dialogues appeared two years after Clare's death and may not actually be by him.
2   J. Clare, *The Converted Jew* ([printed secretly in England], 1630), p. 49.
3   The appendix is on pp. 121–53 of *The Converted Jew*. For Abbot's view of *Monarchia* see *Dante's Fame in England*, pp. 123–24.
4   J. Clare, *The Converted Jew*, p. 140.
5   J. Clare, *The Converted Jew*, p. 144 (in *Dante's Fame in England*, p. 191).

even translating one of them (the praise of St Peter as "gran viro" in *Paradiso*, xxiv. 34–36).[1]

Such readings (especially Clare's approach to the popes in *Inferno* xix and xxvii) may be somewhat slanted and decontextualized. Clare (page 143) conveniently disregards the specific circumstances in which Dante expresses "reverenza" for Nicholas iii (*Inferno*, xix. 101) and those in which he refers to Boniface viii's "sommo officio" (*Inferno*, xxvii. 91—mistakenly attributed to "Cant.□22. del'Inferno"). But what we have here is, nonetheless, an actual reading (rather than a mere naming) and one which thus shifts the grounds of the debate from the generalities of the "true Church" and the "visible succession" to the actual interpretation of a particular text. It is significant from this point of view that, four years after Clare's discussion of Dante in *The Converted Jew*, there appeared an opposing series of dialogues, Simon Birckbek's *The Protestants Evidence, Taken out of Good Records*.[2] This Protestant work not only goes century by century through the usual succession of "worthy *Guides* of *God's* Church" but also pays close attention to some of its "good records", by translating both from two of Petrarch's sonnets and at some length from Cantos ix, xviii and xxix of *Paradiso* and Canto xix of *Inferno*, thus outdoing its Catholic predecessor (Clare), in quantity at least.[3] Birckbek's text of the *Commedia* (which he also quotes in the original) is somewhat corrupt, but his summary of *Paradiso*'s critique of the Church is reasonably accurate and the couplets of his translation have a certain rude and rollicking energy which is evident in the following sample, taken from the passage about vain preachers in *Paradiso*, xxix. 115–20:

> Now the way of preaching, is with toyes
> To stuffe a sermon; and herein joy's

1   J. Clare, *The Converted Jew*, pp. 142-43 (in *Dante's Fame in England*, pp. 190–91).

2   On Birckbek see above, p. 140 n. 3 and p. 142 n. 2.

3   For the four passages of Birckbek's translation see *Dante's Fame in England*, pp. 200–02. The four passages (which appear in the original and in English translation) are: *Par.*, ix. 130–36, xviii. 127–19, xxix, 94–126, *Inf.*, xix. 106–11. The first three of these had also been translated in the 1562 edition of Flacius's *Catalogus* (see above, p. 128 n. 1 and p. 140 n. 4), and Birckbek may well have used Flacius's line-by-line Latin rendering when producing his own English versions.

> Their teachers; if the people doe but smile
> At their conceits, the Frier i' th' meane while
> Huff'es up his Cowle, and is much admir'd
> For that's his aime; there's nothing else requir'd:
> But in this hood there is a nest
> Of birds, which could the vulgar see,
> They might spie pardons and the rest,
> How worthy of their trust they bee.

Thus, while some of the polemicists of this period—Foxe, Humphrey, Beard and a number of others—may be quoting from or referring to the *Commedia* at second hand (probably by way of "Illyricus"), there are clear signs that a number of others—such as Sutcliffe, Parsons, Clare and Birckbek—were in their various ways engaging directly with Dante's text.

Birckbek's translation of *Paradiso* XXIX's attack on vain preachers in 1634 is only three years away from Milton's reinvention of Beatrice's invective during St Peter's outburst in "Lycidas" (1637):

> Blind mouthes! that scarce themselves know how to hold
> A Sheep-hook, or have learn'd ought els the least
> That to the faithfull Herdman's art belongs!
> What recks it them? What need they? They are sped;
> And when they list, their lean and flashy songs
> Grate on their scrannel Pipes of wretched straw,
> The hungry Sheep look up and are not fed,
> But swoln with wind, and the rank mist they draw,
> Rot inwardly, and foul contagion spread.[1]

This shows that there is a certain continuity in the Protestant appropriation of *Paradiso* XXIX, which may be traced from the polemic of Flacius and Foxe, through Sutcliffe and Beard, to Birckbek and the Milton of the late 1630s.[2] In "Lycidas"—a text that tests the pastoral mode almost to destruction—Milton, characteristically,

1 Milton, "Lycidas", lines 119–27, in *The Poetical Works of John Milton*, edited by H. Darbishire (London, Oxford University Press, 1958), p. 450.
2 Birckbek does not actually translate *Paradiso*'s lines about feeding the flock on wind (which by his time appear to have become something of a commonplace of Protestant polemic), but he paraphrases them earlier, in terms which are clearly based on Sampson Lennard's version in his 1612 translation of de Mornay: "The pore sheep were fed with the puffes of winde, and were pined and consumed away" (p. 57 of *The Protestant's Evidence*: see *Dante's Fame in England*, p. 200, and compare p. 145, §2).

shifts the ideological ground somewhat by making the shepherds who feed their flocks on wind not Catholic friars but Laudian clergymen.[1] By this time (shortly before his journey to Italy) Milton was reading Dante in the original. But he was also reading (among much else) Foxe's *Ecclesiasticall History*, the seventh printing of which had appeared in 1632.[2] Hence his reinvention of the passage from *Paradiso* xxix is a reflection of the extensive debate about and reading of Dante in Reformation England.

1   On Milton's politics at this time see B. K. Lewalski, "How Radical Was the Young Milton?", in *Milton and Heresy*, edited by S. B. Dobranski and J. P. Rumrich (Cambridge, Cambridge University Press, 1998), pp. 49–72 (pp. 57–59, 69–70 nn. 29–33). On the anticlericalism of "Lycidas" see also p. 44 of T. N. Corns's essay in the same volume ("Milton's Antiprelatical Tracts and the Marginality of Doctrine", pp. 39–48).

2   See *Dante's Fame in England*, p. 194 (item 288). On Milton's citations of Foxe (from *Of Reformation* onwards) see J. C. Boswell, *Milton's Library* (New York–London, Garland, 1975), p. 105 (item 617).

"WOE TO THEE, SIMON MAGUS!": HENRY FRANCIS CARY'S TRANSLATION OF *INFERNO* XIX

Edoardo Crisafulli

This essay will focus on Henry Francis Cary's translation of Canto XIX of *Inferno*, which, because of the sheer emotion emanating from Dante's condemnation of simony, cannot but arouse strong feelings in the translator and therefore particularly lends itself to a comparative analysis.

Cary was born in Gibraltar in 1772 and was educated at Christ Church, Oxford, where he graduated in 1794. He then decided to follow an ecclesiastical career and took (Anglican) orders in 1796.[1] He was a scholar of both classical and modern European literature, with a particular interest in ancient Greek and the medieval poetry of France and Italy, and he himself wrote many poems and critical essays, some of which appeared in *The London Magazine*, one of the best-known journals of the time. His major achievement, however, was his translation of the *Commedia*. In 1805–06 he published his version of *Inferno* (with the Italian text facing the translation), and all three *cantiche* were published together in 1814 under the title *The Vision: Or Hell, Purgatory, and Paradise, of Dante Alighieri*. A second complete edition appeared in 1819, and a third in 1831. A final, revised, version of the whole translation was published in 1844.[2]

---

1   There are two main sources on Cary's life: *Memoir of the Rev. Henry Francis Cary, Edited by His Son*, 2 vols (London, Edward Moxon, 1847), and R. W. King, *The Translator of Dante: The Life, Work and Friendships of Henry Francis Cary (1772–1844)* (London, Secker, 1925).

2   In this essay all references are to the 1844 edition: H. F. Cary, *The Vision of Dante: Or Hell, Purgatory and Paradise* (London, William Smith, 1844). It is beyond the scope of the essay to consider the differences between the various editions of *The Vision*. The greater number of differences occur between the 1814 and 1844 texts and mainly concern stylistic questions,

The reception of Cary's work has erroneously been described as unfavourable, at least during an initial phase (1805–15).[1] It is true that *The Vision* was neglected and did not sell well for a considerable period of time, but it is not correct to state that Cary's early reviews were hostile or that *The Vision* was received at first with indifference or ignored.[2] In actual fact, a good number of reviews were published between 1805 and 1815 in leading journals such as *The Critical Review, The British Critic, The Literary Journal, The Monthly Review* and *The Gentleman's Magazine*.[3] During the first phase of Cary's reception most reviewers praised what they saw as his fidelity, or literalness, as well as the poetical quality of his style, while only a few minor blemishes were pointed out. Only *The Literary Journal* in 1805 and *The Critical Review* in 1814 dismissed his translation. Sales were indeeed slow to take off until the first

---

such as the use of elisions, apostrophes and punctuation. Although there are other, more significant differences between the 1814 and 1844 texts—on which see my *The Vision of Dante: A Case Study of Henry Francis Cary's Translation of the "Divine Comedy" in English* (unpublished doctoral dissertation, University College Dublin, 1999)—they do not affect the reading of *Inferno* XIX. My reason for basing this essay on the 1844 edition is simply that it has the advantage of being a more complete translation than the 1814 one. Ralph Pite produced the only edition of Cary's work which is still in print (based on the 1814 text): H. F. Cary, *The Divine Comedy: The Vision of Dante*, edited by R. Pite (London, Everyman, 1994). On Cary's intentions as a translator and the notion of textual criticism see my "The Translator as Textual Critic and the Potential of Transparent Discourse", *The Translator*, 5, i (1999), 83–107.

1 D. Sayers, "The Art of Translating Dante", *Nottingham Medieval Studies*, 9 (1965), 15–31 (p. 22).

2 W. P. Friederich, *Dante's Fame Abroad, 1350–1850* (Chapel Hill, NC, University of North Carolina Press, 1950), p. 231; P. Toynbee, *Dante in English Literature from Chaucer to Cary* (London, Methuen, 1909), p. xxxviii.

3 Rev. T. Price, review of Cary's *Inferno* I–XVII, *The Critical Review*, 6, ii (1805), 113–26; Rev. T. Price, review of Cary's *Inferno* XVIII–XXXIV, *The Critical Review*, 11, iii (1807), 267–73; anonymous review of H. F. Cary's *Inferno* I–XVII, *The British Critic*, 26, vii (1805), 18–26; anonymous review of Cary's translation of *Inferno* I–XVII, *The Literary Journal*, 5, vi (1805), 1088–90; anonymous review of H. F. Cary's *Inferno* XVIII–XXXIV, *The British Critic*, 29, vi (1807), 528–31; anonymous review of Cary's *Inferno*, *The Monthly Review*, 55, iv (1808), 438; anonymous review of Nathaniel Howard's translation of Dante's *Inferno*, *The British Critic*, 3, iv (1808), 436–38 (in which Howard and Cary are compared); anonymous review of H. F. Cary's *The Vision*, *The Critical Review*, 5, vi (1814), 647; anonymous "critical remark" on Cary's Dante, *The Gentleman's Magazine*, 84, iii (1814), 237; anonymous review of H. F. Cary's *The Vision*, *The Monthly Review*, 76, iii (1815), 322–24.

complete edition was published in 1819, but from the very start Cary's work achieved a considerable degree of critical acclaim. Even the reviews of his *Inferno*, which appeared as early as 1805–06, were on the whole favourable. The response was the same after the publication of *The Vision* in 1814, even though the work was not yet the commercial success it was to be in later years.[1]

One of the reasons for Cary's initial failure to impress all the reviewers may have been that he subscribed to a view of translation which was not widespread in the very early 1800s, and if we bear in mind that he had to compete with Henry Boyd's recently published translation (1785–1803), in pentameters arranged in six-line stanzas rhyming AABCCB, which was in keeping with the still dominant eighteenth-century mode of translating,[2] we shall realize that the reception of his translation was bound to be lukewarm in some quarters. In 1803, for example, a reviewer in *The Critical Review* had praised Boyd in the following terms: "The dullness of Dante is often enlivened by Mr Boyd with profuse ornaments of his own, by which he is rather elevated than degraded."[3] As we shall see, the Neoclassical policy of elevating or adorning the style of the original, when carried to excess, was quite alien to Cary's taste, though not to his alone. In later years, Boyd's liberties with the original fell completely out of favour, and from the early nineteenth century onwards critics and reviewers increasingly embraced a stricter notion of fidelity, therefore tending to become dismissive of Boyd's translation, which they began to consider, at

1   Previous (published) studies of *The Vision* consider only a handful of reviews, but in my doctoral dissertation (see above, p. 151 n. 2) I explore Cary's reception in depth by considering all the nineteenth-century reviews. The most important published studies of Cary's translation dealing with its reception (as well as other aspects) are: G. F. Cunningham, *The "Divine Comedy" in English: A Critical Bibliography, 1782–1900* (Edinburgh–London, Oliver and Boyd, 1965); W. De Sua, *Dante into English* (Chapel Hill, NC, University of North Carolina Press, 1964); W. P. Friederich, *Dante's Fame Abroad*; R. W. King, *The Translator of Dante*; R. Pite, *The Circle of Our Vision: Dante's Presence in English Romantic Poetry* (Oxford, Clarendon Press, 1994); D. Sayers, "The Art of Translating Dante"; V. Tinkler-Villani, *Visions of Dante in English Poetry* (Amsterdam, Rodopi, 1989); P. Toynbee, *Dante in English Literature*. See also the excellent study by A. Braida, *Henry Francis Cary's "The Vision": Its Literary Context and Its Influence* (unpublished doctoral dissertation, University of Oxford, 1997).

2   H. Boyd, *The Divina Commedia of Dante Alighieri*, 3 vols (London, Cadell-Davies, 1802). This was the first complete English translation of the *Commedia*.

3   R. W. King, *The Translator of Dante*, p. 90.

best, a loose paraphrase.[1] It was in this period that Cary's Dante finally met with considerable popular and critical acclaim, partly on account of its presumed respect for the original.

The Vision's initial lack of commercial success was also due to Cary's isolation in the world of letters, but his meeting in 1817 with Coleridge, who was to play a considerable role in promoting his work, marked a turning-point in its reception. Coleridge had been so impressed by the translation that he mentioned it in an important public lecture, the tenth in a series on literature which he delivered at the Philosophical Society of London in February 1818.[2] In the same month an article by Ugo Foscolo in praise of Cary's rendering of Dante appeared in *The Edinburgh Review*.[3]

The intervention of influential literary mentors such as Coleridge and Foscolo—not to mention other leading Romantic

1   Not only "fidelity" / "faithfulness" but also key terms such as "equivalence", "literal" and "free translation" tend to be used loosely in the critical liter-ature on Dante translations. All these terms in fact are "taxonomical shift-ers"—see D. Robinson, "Free Translation", in *The Routledge Encyclopedia of Translation Studies*, edited by M. Baker (London, Routledge, 1998), pp. 87–90 (p. 88)—, that is, their meaning varies diachronically and therefore can-not be defined *a priori* or in absolute terms, at least not from a historicist perspective. Here I shall use the terms "equivalence" and "equivalent" when target-language items are formally correspondent to the source-lan-guage segment (e.g. a given English noun corresponds to an Italian noun); in fact, in my theoretical perspective, which draws on Descriptive Translation Studies, the target text is equivalent to the source text by definition. On equi-valence in translation theory see my "Taboo Language in Translation", *Perspectives: Studies in Translatology*, 5, ii (1997), 237–56.

2   R. W. King, *The Translator of Dante*, p. 114; *Dante: The Critical Heritage, 1314(?)–1870*, edited by M. Caesar (London, Routledge, 1989), p. 439. There is no record of the remarks Coleridge made on that occasion, but, as we shall see, one may understand why he appreciated Cary's work if one considers his correspondence.

3   R. W. King, *The Translator of Dante*, p. 116. Foscolo's review was translated from the Italian. According to Samuel Rogers, who co-edited Foscolo's article, Cary owed his success to *The Edinburgh Review* rather than to Coleridge's lecture: see *Recollections of the Tabletalk of Samuel Rogers*, edited by A. Dyce (New Southgate, Rogers, 1887), p. 285. On Foscolo's article see B. Corrigan, "Foscolo's Articles on Dante in the *Edinburgh Review*: A Study in Collaboration", in *Collected Essays on Italian Language and Literature Presented to Kathleen Speight*, edited by G. Aquilecchia, S. N. Cristea and S. Ralphs (Manchester, Manchester University Press, 1971), pp. 211–25. According to Corrigan, Foscolo's article was manipulated by the periodical's English editors. Her discovery of the review's "multiple authorship" (p. 218) corroborates my contention that it epitomizes the prevailing attitude towards *The Vision* in English literary circles.

poets such as Wordsworth, who in later years referred to *The Vision* as "a great national work"—[1] secured Cary's fame and boosted the sales of the translation, all the more so as their praises were echoed by the vast majority of reviewers in the period between 1818 and 1824.[2] From then on *The Vision* was to enjoy long-lasting success. The revised edition published in 1844 (shortly before Cary's death) was to establish itself with such authority that for a long time it was a yardstick against which most translators of the *Commedia* into English measured their attempts. Not only was *The Vision* extremely successful in Cary's lifetime (four editions of the complete translation is no mean feat for the time), but his fame continued unabated until well into the twentieth century. His biographer, R.□W. King, claims that about twenty new editions of *The Vision* were published in England between his death and the 1920s—an achievement that no other translator of Dante has equalled.[3] It is therefore surprising that *The Vision*—the most successful version of Dante in the English literary tradition—has attracted only limited scholarly attention.

Before Cary, Dante had been neglected by English translators. In spite of the fact that a multitude of poets had been fascinated by single episodes of the *Commedia* (consider, for example, Chaucer's rendering of the Ugolino episode), the only complete rendering of Dante's poem had been Boyd's (1802). Particularly in the seventeenth and early eighteenth centuries literary translators and poets had failed to appreciate the *Commedia*; in the literary circles of the time Dante "appeared as the characteristic writer of an unenlightened age".[4] It was only towards the end of the eighteenth and

---

1   R. W. King, *The Translator of Dante*, p. 142; *Recollections of the Tabletalk*, p. 285.
2   These are the favourable reviews which appeared in the wake of Foscolo's article: anonymous "Observations on the Poetical Character of Dante", *The Edinburgh Magazine*, 3, ii (1818), 223–29; anonymous review of Nathaniel Howard's Translation of Dante's *Inferno*, *The British Critic*, 12, xii (1819), 584–97; anonymous review of H. F. Cary's *The Vision*, *The Eclectic Review*, 9, vi (1819), 556–72; anon., "Italian Poets: Frederick the Second and Piero delle Vigne", *The New Monthly Magazine*, 4, v, (1822), 455–62; T. B. Macaulay, "Criticism on the Principal Italian Writers: Dante", *Knight's Quarterly*, 2, i (1824), 207–33. Many more reviews were published from 1824 until shortly after Cary's death in 1844. Suffice it to say that after 1824 Cary's reception tended to be mixed, though on the whole it remained largely favourable.
3   R. W. King, *The Translator of Dante*, p. 285.
4   D. Sayers, "The Art of Translating Dante", p. 16; R. Pite, *The Circle of Our Vision*, p. 12. It does seem, however, that credit for the rediscovery of Dante

in the early nineteenth century, that is, during the Romantic period, that this tendency was reversed and Dante's journey through the afterlife became a source of inspiration for many English poets. Blake, for example, used quotations from Cary's translation for his illustrations to the *Commedia*.[1] Cary's role in this reversal of Dante's fortune in English literary circles should not be underestimated. According to R. W. King even some of Cary's contemporaries, such as Wordsworth, Scott, Landor, Hunt and Hazlitt, "failed, in greater or lesser degree, to conquer their prejudices in forming their opinions of Dante".[2] The only person to profess admiration for Dante openly (apart from Gray, who "had worshipped Dante in an age when he was neglected")[3] was Coleridge; but even he turned his attention to the *Commedia* only after reading Cary's translation.

The case against Dante was most effectively put by Miss Seward, a minor poet and a close associate of Cary's, who was quite influential in the early Romantic period. In a letter sent to one of her admirers, she was frankly critical of Cary's passion for Italian poetry: "I am chagrined to find our friend, Cary, grown an heretic to the high poetic claims of his country. His ear has been debauched by the luscious smoothness of Italian tones, till it delights no longer in the bolder and more majestic sounds of the English language."[4] In a passionate reply Cary defended his love of Italian poetry and reminded Miss Seward of the admiration for Dante that some of the greatest English poets had shown, which proved, he pointed out, that the current prejudices against the "sommo poeta" were bound to be ephemeral:

> I much wonder that you should listen to the idea, that a fondness for Italian poetry is the corruption of our taste, when you cannot but recollect that our greatest English poets, Chaucer, Spenser, and Milton, have been professed admirers of the Italians, and that the sublimer province of poetry, imagination, has been

in England belongs to eighteenth-century Neoclassicism (on which see my *The Vision of Dante*, pp. 163–76).

1   R. W. King, *The Translator of Dante*, p. 170. On the relationship between English Romantic poetry and Dante see R. Pite, *The Circle of Our Vision*, and S. Ellis, *Dante and English Poetry: Shelley to Eliot* (Cambridge, Cambridge University Press, 1983).

2   R. W. King, *The Translator of Dante*, p. 58.

3   R. W. King, *The Translator of Dante*, p. 88.

4   R. W. King, *The Translator of Dante*, p. 56.

more or less cultivated among us, according to the degree of estimation in which they have been held [...]. Give a few months to the acquisition of Italian; go and see the wonders of Dante's *Inferno, Purgatorio,* and *Paradiso;* remember what a vast interval of time there is between Homer and him; remember in what a state the country and age in which he lived, and how pure the language in which he wrote, and then abuse him, if you dare.[1]

Cary therefore played a significant role in the upsurge of interest in the *Commedia* among English poets, not to mention English-speaking translators, many of whom, following in his footsteps, were to find the task of translating Dante's masterpiece worth their efforts.[2] As Paget Toynbee put it, Cary "once and for all made Dante an English possession, and in so doing won for Dante as well as for himself a permanent place in English literature."[3]

One of the reasons for Cary's popularity and success was his decision to use naturalizing blank verse rather than foreignizing *terza rima;*[4] another was his diction, which was in keeping with nineteenth-century taste. Coleridge, whose position is fairly representative of Cary's contemporaries, wrote to him on 29 October 1817, extolling *The Vision*'s diction and verse form:

> In the severity and *learned simplicity* of the diction, and in the peculiar character of the Blank verse, [*The Vision*] has transcended what I should have thought possible without the *Terza Rima.* In itself the Metre is, compared with any English Poem of one quarter the length, the most varied and harmonious to my ear of any since Milton—and yet the effect is so Dantesque that to those, who should compare it only with other English poems, it

1   R. W. King, *The Translator of Dante,* p. 57; *Memoir of the Rev. Henry Francis Cary,* I, 42–43.

2   O. Kuhns, *Dante and the English Poets from Chaucer to Tennyson* (New York, Henry Holt, 1904), pp. 122, 140; W. P. Friederich, *Dante's Fame Abroad,* pp. 229–30; D. Sayers, "The Art of Translating Dante", p. 21. "According to Dr Paget Toynbee, who has compiled laborious statistics, there were produced in English between 1840 and 1920, twenty-three verse translations of the whole of the *Divina commedia*" (R. W. King, *The Translator of Dante,* p. 314).

3   P. Toynbee, *Dante in English Literature,* p. li.

4   It is interesting to note in passing that the debate on the issue of verse form among translators of Dante continued unabated well into the twentieth century, and that only recently has the dualism between *terza rima* and blank verse been superseded. Consider for example Steve Ellis's free-verse translation of *Inferno*: S. Ellis, *Hell* (London, Chatto and Windus, 1994).

would, I doubt not, have the same effect as the *Terza Rima* has compared with other Italian metres.[1]

But Cary's sudden popularity also depended on a variety of other factors, of which Foscolo's article in *The Edinburgh Review* highlights an important one, namely the translator's notion of fidelity:

> Of all the translators of Dante with whom we are acquainted, Mr Cary is the most successful; and we cannot but consider his work as a great acquisition to the English reader. It is executed with a fidelity almost without example; and though the measure he has adopted conveys no idea of the original stanza, it is perhaps the best for his purpose, and what Dante himself would have chosen, if he had written in English and in a later day.[2]

Foscolo, concurring with William Cowper's assertion that "a just translation of any ancient poet in rhyme is impossible", believed that the translator should not "forge fetters for himself [since] he has enough to wear already".[3]

To understand Cary's approach to translation we need to think of it in the context of Romanticism, where it set itself against the earlier, paraphrastic mode typical of Neoclassicism. The Romantics, as has already been pointed out, favoured a stricter notion of fidelity than that pursued by eighteenth-century translators. Pope's Homer and Boyd's Dante, for instance, were considered paraphrases by Cary's contemporaries, and in the nineteenth century the term "paraphrase" was used in the negative sense of loose or free translation, which is still current today. In actual fact, the differences between the Neoclassical (or paraphrastic) and Romantic (or literal) approaches to translation are only relative. Cary was simply more careful than Boyd had been in reproducing the original "literally line per line"—and, it should be said, word for word—, but as regards stylistic choices, it is difficult to distinguish in absolute terms between their respective versions of Dante.[4] Both

1   S. T. Coleridge, Letter 1079, to H. F. Cary (1817), in *Collected Letters of Samuel Taylor Coleridge*, edited by E. L. Griggs, 6 vols (Oxford, Clarendon Press, 1956–71), IV, 778–79 (p. 778).

2   U. Foscolo, review of Baglioli's *Dante* and *The Vision* of Dante by Cary, *Edinburgh Review*, 29, iv (1818), 453–74 (p. 469). On "fidelity" see above, p. 154 n. 1.

3   U. Foscolo, review of Baglioli's *Dante*, p. 470.

4   V. Tinkler-Villani, *Visions of Dante*, pp. 125, 183. Compare, for example, Cary's and Boyd's renderings of *Inferno*, XXI. 139, where Dante has recourse

consistently bowdlerize the source text and embellish their rewritings by means of poetic amplification, with the aim of elevating, whenever necessary, what was perceived to be Dante's coarse language or grotesque imagery. Yet, the differences between Boyd's approach and Cary's should not be glossed over. Although Cary's style is still influenced by the Neoclassical idiom (for example, he employs periphrases typical of eighteenth-century diction), his poetic interventions or embellishments are certainly less radical than his predecessor's.[1] Boyd had not hesitated on occasion to alter some facts of the narrative and freely to expand on the original imagery.[2] This is why Cary was, and still is, seen as having an uncommon respect for the source text. His version was considered to be the first attempt in the English-speaking world to naturalize the *Commedia* without completely distorting the original text.[3]

to taboo language to create a vivid scene. A devil in Malebolge uses his "cul" ["arse"] as a trumpet in order to catch the attention of his fellows: "ed elli avea del cul fatto trombetta" ["and he had of his arse made a trumpet"]: "Which [= the signal] he with sound obscene triumphant gave" (H. F. Cary, *The Vision*, p. 50); "And loud Aeolian fifes their [= the devils'] fury 'suage" (H. Boyd, *The Divina Commedia*, p. 274). Cary avoids the formal correspondent in English ("arse"), but Boyd departs more radically than Cary does from the original image. All instances of Dante's taboo language, together with Cary's choices, are considered at length in my "Taboo Language in Translation".

1   V. Tinkler-Villani, *Visions of Dante*, p. 183. It is beyond the scope of this essay to discuss the relationship between Neoclassicism and Romanticism in Cary's poetics. Various scholars, notably W. P. Friederich (*Dante's Fame Abroad*, p. 229) and W. De Sua (*Dante into English*, p. 28), label Cary a "Romantic" translator, mainly because his approach is consonant with the nineteenth-century advocacy of literalness, or word-for-word translation. On the other hand, because eighteenth-century translators took greater liberties in rewriting literary texts than the Romantics would have allowed, Boyd is considered to be a Neoclassical translator (W. De Sua, *Dante into English*, pp. 13–17, 26–28; B. Reynolds, "English Awareness of Dante", *Nottingham Medieval Studies*, 9 [1965], 4–14; D. Sayers, "The Art of Translating Dante", pp. 20–21). As regards translation practice and theory, one can only talk in very general terms about a Romantic, as opposed to a Neoclassical theory of translation, because this would imply a rigid notion of period, which is not consistent with translation practice: see S. Bassnett-McGuire, *Translation Studies* (London, Routledge, 1991), p. 42.

2   V. Tinkler-Villani, *Visions of Dante*, p. 125.

3   While Cary was much more successful in spreading Dante's fame than Boyd (which makes *The Vision* particularly interesting from the point of view of the sociology of reception), one cannot but agree with Tinkler-Villani that Boyd was the first translator of Dante and that his method of translating

Cary in fact conceived his work as an aid to Dante scholarship, for one of his professed intentions was to "facilitate the study of one of the most sublime and moral, but certainly one of the most obscure writers in any language".[1] In addition to being prefaced by a detailed "Life of Dante", *The Vision* is therefore accompanied by extensive notes, which constitute the first accurate commentary on the *Commedia* in the English language. And Cary made clear where his priorities lay when he stated:

> The first object of translation is to give you the clearest and most intimate acquaintance with the original. For this reason the strictest version may justly be called the best. Not but that I allow to paraphrases a large portion of merit; they may be even more finely executed than their copy, but a plainer if more true imitation is to be preferred.[2]

Nevertheless, when confronted with the task of rendering the *Commedia* Cary tended to allow himself certain liberties. In the preface to the 1814 edition of *The Vision* he argued that the translator has the right to intervene by imposing order on the conflicting readings of the original, thus to a certain extent taking on the function of the textual critic. In particular, we should note the following sentence in the preface:

> To those, who shall be at the trouble of examining into the degree of accuracy with which the task has been executed, I may be allowed to suggest, that their judgement should not be formed on a comparison with any single text of my Author; since, in more instances than I have noticed, I have had to make my choice

therefore deserves attention in its own right. Although my approach in this paper is to a certain extent influenced by W. De Sua, *Dante into English*, I do not agree with his evaluative stance. His position is well summarized by Tinkler-Villani: "Critics such as De Sua state that, like most eighteenth-century translators, Boyd distorts his original, first of all because he has no high regard for it, and secondly because of his desire to embellish poetry which is too stark for current taste" (*Visions of Dante*, p. 126). I believe that even if all literary translators—to a greater or lesser extent—manipulate the original text, one has to account for, and not condemn, their deviations, manipulations and distortions.

1 R. W. King, *The Translator of Dante*, p. 90.
2 *Memoir of the Rev. Henry Francis Cary*, i, 28; R. W. King, *The Translator of Dante*, p. 32.

out of a variety of readings and interpretations, presented by
different editions and commentators.[1]

"Accuracy" here means fidelity to the original, but although
Cary's choices were motivated by the existence of a number of
different versions of the source text itself, which meant he had to
take on the role of literary critic (and his originality as a translator
of Dante lies partly in this), the fact remains that the majority of his
interventions were not occasioned by conflicting readings of the
original. Even so, the translator's nineteenth-century admirers
praised *The Vision* for its fidelity—where modern subscribers to
the notion of fidelity would probably regard it as unfaithful. This
is a clear indication that the notion of faithfulness/fidelity is
historically determined and not absolute, and thus far from being
uncontroversial. And this brings us to a consideration of more
theoretical matters.

Translation theory should be of paramount importance in any
attempt to understand translated texts and the policies pursued by
translators. This discipline, also referred to as Translation Studies,
is still in its infancy, though the activity of translating has occupied
writers and other intellectuals for centuries. Here I shall attempt to
redress the balance, by linking the theoretical and practical sides
of the question.

The belief that theory is not relevant to understanding translation or to becoming a good translator is common among practition-
ers of the art, the assumption being that, by definition, the quiddity,
the peculiar quality of translation, cannot be grasped. However, if
we abandon the idea that it is feasible to define and prescribe what
an ideal translation should be like, and deal instead with what
translators actually do, we are more likely to discover basic truths
about the nature of translating. In order to do this, one has to
acknowledge that translations are not the unaccountable product
of idiosyncratic decisions on the translator's part, but the result of
particular tendencies, which are worth investigating in depth.
This idea, however, meets with considerable resistance in some
quarters. William Frawley, for example, rejects what he terms
"systematic semiotics", namely any framework that can account
for the choices made by a translator, on the grounds that a literary

---

1   H. F. Cary, *The Vision*, p. i.

translator is himself a poet and "poetic evaluation is too lugubrious a topic" for a systematic analysis.[1] But as the analysis in this essay will show, a systematic semiotics should indeed be possible. Cary is consistent in the strategies he adopts and this lays bare certain meaningful patterns.

Although there are differing (and conflicting) schools of thought among scholars dealing with translation, the most promising approaches stress the idea that translated texts should be upgraded to the status of originals and no longer seen as "second-hand and distorted versions of 'real' texts".[2] André Lefevere insists on this seminal concept when he states that translations should be regarded as rewritings. As he puts it, "The translation, quite simply, is the original."[3] This would suggest that the translator is an author in his own right and that his outlook or (to use Lefevere's word) ideology has therefore to be taken into account, as well as the "poetics dominant in the receiving literature at the time the translation is made".[4]

Lefevere's stress on ideology and poetics has two important implications. First, it means that the study of translated texts becomes highly relevant to literary critics who are interested in the translation's reception and/or in the source text's fortunes in foreign cultures. Indeed, these rewritings, by employing the language of the receiving reading public, are accessible to a wider audience than their originals, and so it is not surprising that translations "project images of the original work, author, literature, or culture that often impact many more readers than the original does".[5] Secondly, it means that the focus can now be on the receiving tradition and on the historically determined factors behind translation policies. Since translators belong to a given society and historical period and are influenced by the literary conventions of their time, the act of translating does not take place

1   W. Frawley, "Prolegomenon to a Theory of Translation", in *Translation: Literary, Linguistic and Philosophical Perspectives*, edited by W. Frawley (London–Toronto, Associated University Press, 1984), pp. 159–75.

2   M. Baker, "Corpus Linguistics and Translation Studies: Implications and Applications", in *Text and Technology: In Honour of John Sinclair*, edited by M. Baker, G. Francis and E. Tognini-Bonelli (Amsterdam–Philadelphia, Benjamins, 1993), pp. 233–50.

3   A. Lefevere, *Translation, Rewriting and the Manipulation of Literary Fame* (London–New York, Routledge, 1992), p. 110.

4   A. Lefevere, *Translation, Rewriting*, p. 41.

5   A. Lefevere, *Translation, Rewriting*, p. 110.

in a vacuum. As Gideon Toury puts it, translations are essentially features of the target culture. This means that translators "operate first and foremost in the interest of the culture into which they are translating".[1] Furthermore, Toury's view of a historically determined equivalence is inextricably linked with the notion of translation norms: translation is a norm-governed activity, that is, it is subject to various constraints which go beyond the source text (or source language) as such. It is translation norms, in fact, that "determine the (type and extent of) equivalence manifested by actual translations".[2] Overall Lefevere and Toury cast serious doubt on the received view of translation as being essentially a linguistic problem. To illustrate this, Lefevere makes the apparently paradoxical statement that "translation is not primarily 'about' language." One certainly deals with language all the time when one is translating, but whenever "linguistic considerations enter into conflict" with considerations which have to do with ideology and poetics, "the latter tend to win out."[3]

We may briefly relate these points to the debate on verse form among translators of Dante.[4] The argument of the advocates of blank verse is twofold. On the one hand they claim that *terza rima* is too foreign or exotic in English because English is poorer in rhymes than Italian. On the other hand, they consider blank verse to be the ideal verse form in which to translate epic poetry because the greatest epic poem in English, Milton's *Paradise Lost*, is written in blank verse. When Foscolo says that Dante himself would have used blank verse had he written in English, he is clearly expressing this aesthetic-poetic conviction. Yet literary translators are not fettered by language constraints, at least not as far as large-scale choices are concerned. The adoption of blank verse (or *terza rima* for that matter) depends more on the poetics of the translator than on objective properties of the English language. Cary's choice of verse form is in keeping with the poetic tradition established by William Cowper's blank-verse translation of Homer.[5]

---

1   G. Toury, *Descriptive Translation Studies and Beyond* (Amsterdam, Benjamins, 1995), pp. 29, 12.
2   G. Toury, *Descriptive Translation Studies*, p. 61.
3   A. Lefevere, *Translation, Rewriting*, pp. 57, 39.
4   On the blank verse versus *terza rima* debate see B. Reynolds, "Translating Dante in the 1990s", *Translation and Literature*, 4, ii (1995), pp. 221–37.
5   See T. R. Steiner, *English Translation Theory, 1650–1800* (Assen–Amsterdam, Van Gorcum, 1975). According to Steiner, "William Cowper (1731–1800)

Not even the notion of "literal" translation, as defined by Catford, is above constraints of ideology and poetics.[1] Although Catford's linguistic theory is the first attempt rigorously to account for "literal" (almost word for word) and "free" translation (*The Vision* would fall into the latter category), his framework is by no means neutral and totally objective. His notion of literalness is simply a translation strategy among others, albeit a popular one in some circles; and every translation strategy generates its own linguistic problems.

It is clear that the change of perspective suggested by the above-mentioned translation scholars implies discarding the source-oriented view of equivalence, because it projects an absolute, ahistorical concept of the original. The target-oriented view, which considers the relationship between source text and target text from the perspective of the receiving (target) literary tradition, banishes prescription from both the theory and the practice of translation: translators do not have to strive to reproduce an idealized and fixed original meaning, any more than translation scholars have to censure deviations from an allegedly perfect original. This change is a healthy one: the obsession with source-oriented equivalence explains why "instead of exploring features of translated texts as our object of study, we are still trying to justify them or dismiss them by reference to their originals." The trend is now for the translation to be studied for its own sake, and this is indeed a natural reaction to the "primacy of the source text".[2] In other words, prescription has been superseded by description. The risk in such a change of focus, however, is that the relationship between the source text and target text is no longer significant: it is the target text that now overshadows the source text and becomes the sole object of investigation. Peter Newmark rightly suggests that the new approaches in Translation Studies, by assigning pride of place to the study of translation reception, ignore "the values of the

followed in the Miltonic tradition" and "argued, against the authority of Pope, that faithful translation of classical poetry cannot be rendered in rhyme"; he believed that blank verse "is not Homer writing today, but it is the closest equivalent to Homer in English poetry" (p. 134). R. W. King, *The Translator of Dante*, contends that "Cary's rejection of the *terza rima* was based chiefly on considerations of literary tradition" (p. 315).

1   J. C. Catford, *A Linguistic Theory of Translation* (London, Oxford University Press, 1965).
2   M. Baker, "Corpus Linguistics", p. 235.

original" and are "limited to the sociology of translating".[1] But there may be a middle way. In analysing Cary's translation of Dante we shall see that an approach is possible which, while rejecting the primacy of the source text, acknowledges that the relationship between target text and source text is a meaningful one and therefore worth investigating.

The analysis to be undertaken here will focus on the central theme of *Inferno* XIX, the condemnation of simony; but first some general features of *The Vision*, which are representative of Cary's style, will be pointed out, even though confining the analysis to a single canto of *Inferno* makes it difficult to do full justice to the complexity of Cary's textual and translation strategies.

One of Cary's large-scale choices is that of enveloping the target text in an archaic patina by frequently using words such as *doth, hath, thee, thou* and *thy*, which are typical of the standard archaic usage of English poetry.[2] Cary naturalizes the *Commedia* into the receiving tradition by casting Dante's diction into the archaic mould of Elizabethan (and occasionally even pre-Elizabethan) English, borrowing many expressions from Spenser and Shakespeare.[3] This policy clearly has little to do with the language of the original. It is therefore hardly surprising that the Romantic reader of *The Vision* had a notion of Dante which was diametrically opposed to that of an Italian reader in the same period (or even later periods, for that matter). The Italian language had existed predominantly as a written language from the fourteenth century onwards, and as such it was preserved almost intact for centuries, so that, as De Mauro points out, the language of the major writers of the fourteenth century was not, by and large, remote and archaic for an educated Italian reader of the nineteenth century:

> A Frenchman, a Spaniard, a German or an Englishman in the nineteenth century, even if well educated, did not understand old texts in his language; for an Italian who had even a mediocre educational background it was not difficult to understand the *Novellino* [...]. The lexis of the writers of the Trecento was mostly

1   P. Newmark, *About Translation* (Clevedon–Philadelphia, Multilingual Matters, 1991), p. 172.
2   G. Leech, *A Linguistic Guide to English Poetry* (London, Longman, 1969).
3   R. W. King, *The Translator of Dante*, pp. 338–45.

alive and it was still almost entirely understandable in the nineteenth century.[1]

The contrast between Cary's archaic style and the relatively
modern state of Dante's language need hardly surprise us, given
that some archaic forms have been used by well-known translators
of the *Commedia*, such as Bynion, Bickersteth and Sayers, well into
the twentieth century, that is, even after many translators had
begun to modernize the linguistic make-up of original texts.[2]
Translators, it would seem, are conservative; they tend to conform
to (rather than challenge) established models and poetic repertoires
in the target literary system. The vast majority of them, whatever
the literary tradition, do not experiment with style or language.[3]
This goes some way towards explaining why one has to wait until
the 1990s (that is, well after Modernism had been canonized in the
English tradition) for a free-verse translation of *Inferno*, such as
Steve Ellis's, which, by accommodating informal English as well
as employing free verse, challenges the traditional approaches to
rendering the diction of the *Commedia*.

Cary's decision to wrap the target text in an archaic layer,
which achieves the stylistic effect of remoteness in time and fits in
with the nineteenth-century notion of poetic language, goes hand
in hand with the policy of embellishing the target text. Cary's
diction is characterized by a marked literariness. He uses literary
expressions more frequently than Dante does, so that the original
realistic imagery is considerably toned down. In the target text

1   T. De Mauro, *Storia linguistica dell'Italia unita* (Bari, Laterza, 1963), p. 29; my
     translation.
2   Dante Alighieri, *The Divine Comedy*, translated by L. Binyon (London,
     Agenda, 1947); Dante Alighieri, *The Divine Comedy*, translated by G. □Bicker-
     steth (Aberdeen, Aberdeen University Press, 1955); Dante Alighieri, *The
     Divine Comedy*, translated by D. L. Sayers (Harmondsworth, Penguin Books,
     1949).
3   "Normalization" or "conservatism", which seems to be a universal feature
     of translation, is "the tendency to conform to patterns and practices which
     are typical of the target language, even to the point of exaggerating them":
     M. Baker, "Corpus-based Translation Studies: The Challenges That Lie
     Ahead", in *Terminology, LSP and Translation*, edited by H. Somers (Amster-
     dam, Benjamins, 1996), pp. 175–86 (p. 176). For example, in translation there
     is more frequent recourse to fixed collocations and codified poetic repertoires.
     On translation conservatism see G. Toury, *Descriptive Translation Studies*,
     pp. 271–73.

there is no real plurilingualism or mingling of styles. Moreover, Cary frequently elevates his diction by expanding the original imagery through lexical additions. It must be stressed, however, that target-language renderings often solve more than one translation problem at once, so that it is not always easy to determine whether or not a given textual feature performs any one predominant function (such as poeticizing or metrical padding rather than clarification) at a specific point in the target text. This is especially the case with lexical additions, which provide the means not only to poeticize the target text but also to eliminate metrical irregularities and enhance the target text's intelligibility.

Let us consider the first textual example of poetic amplification (in all the examples adduced henceforth the source text will be followed by an equivalent translation of my own, that is, a formally correspondent or word-for-word rendering of the original within the constraints of English grammar and lexis, after which Cary's version will be reproduced):

> Non mi parean men ampi né maggiori
> che que' che son nel mio bel San Giovanni,
> fatti per loco d'i battezzatori.
> > (*Inferno*, XIX. 16–18)

> [They (= the holes) did not seem to me less wide nor larger
> than those which, in my beautiful St John's,
> are made the place for baptizers.]

> Nor ample less nor larger they appear'd
> Than, in Saint John's fair dome of me beloved,
> Those framed to hold the pure baptismal streams.
> > (*Hell*, XIX. 17–19)

These lines exemplify Cary's tendency to insert lexical items and constantly intrude in the narrative. "[Il] mio bel San Giovanni", which is so powerfully simple and direct, with the possessive "mio" conveying Dante's intimacy with his very own baptistery, becomes "Saint John's fair dome of me beloved"; and where the poet had let the reader infer that San Giovanni is a church, Cary feels it necessary to spell this out by inserting "dome". Moreover, Cary dissolves the compression of the source text by adding the participial phrase "of me beloved", which probably has the function of making up for the loss of the powerful impact, in his version, of the four words "mio bel San Giovanni".[1] Cary also creates an image where Dante, referring to the holes in which the simoniacal clerics are punished for their sins, likens them to those that are "fatti per loco d'i battezzatori". Since the topic is the lofty one of baptism, Cary decides to add the notion of "pure baptismal streams".

As was remarked above, Cary's policy of embellishment carries with it a tendency to tone down the original realism. We may see this, for example, where Dante introduces "the simoniacs' grotesquely appropriate punishment":[2]

> Lo buon maestro ancor de la sua anca
> non mi dipuose, sí mi giunse al rotto
> di quel che si piangeva con la zanca.
> (*Inferno*, XIX. 43–45)

> [The good master not yet from his hip
> did set me down, but brought me to the breach
> of the one who was weeping with his shank.]

> Nor from his side my leader set me down,
> Till to his orifice he brought, whose limb
> Quivering express'd his pang.
> (*Hell*, XIX. 45–47)

As Davis cogently explains, "the predicament of the simoniacs is an image of the way in which they have betrayed the heavenly purpose of their office. Planted upside down in the holes of the rock as if still seeking only earthly things [...], they frantically kick their feet, which are licked by flames that issue from those holes."[3] The grotesque element, which is central to the style of *Inferno* XIX, is toned down in the translation by the use of more abstract lexical items. By creating the image of a sinner weeping with his "shank" ("zanca"), Dante had wanted to suggest the condition of that sinner through language that has a concrete and almost physical

---

1   On the complex question of compensation in the translation process see
     K.□Harvey, "A Descriptive Framework for Compensation"*The Translator*,
     1, i (1995), 65–86, and my own "Dante's Puns in English and the Question
     of Compensation", *The Translator*, 2, ii (1996), 259–76.
2   C. T. Davis, "Canto XIX: Simoniacs", *Lecturae Dantis: Inferno*, edited by
     A.□Mandelbaum, A. Oldcorn and C. Ross (Berkeley, University of California
     Press, 1998), pp. 262–74 (p. 263).
3   C. T. Davis, "Canto XIX", p. 264.

quality. In Cary, the concrete act of weeping ("piangeva") is rendered by the less gripping "express'd his pang", and "limb" does not have all the realism of "zanca". Cary also adds a word, "quivering", which is not present in the Italian text.

Another *terzina* will show how Cary consistently elevates the poem's style:

> Io stava come 'l frate che confessa
> lo perfido assessin, che, poi ch'è fitto,
> richiama lui per che la morte cessa.
> *(Inferno*, XIX. 49–51)

> [I stood as the friar who confesses
> the perfidious assassin, who, once he's fettered,
> calls him back, wherefore death leaves off.]

> There stood I like the friar, that doth shrive
> A wretch for murder doom'd, who, e'en when fix'd,
> Calleth him back, whence death awhile delays.
> *(Hell*, XIX. 51–53).

Dante's "perfido assessin" is a collocation which is still current for the contemporary Italian reader and thus extremely compelling in its matter-of-factness, but Cary feels the need to embellish the original. This, together with the use of the archaic forms "doth" and "Calleth", would appear to mean the imposition of a poetic quality which is achieved differently in English, with the translator adopting a rendering ("A wretch for murder doom'd") that amplifies the text and is more distant from common speech, for which reasons it may be thought more literary.

In the following lines Cary again intervenes by poeticizing the target text:

> Per che lo spirto tutti storse i piedi;
> poi, sospirando e con voce di pianto,
> mi disse […].
> *(Inferno*, XIX. 64–66)

> [Wherefore the spirit fully contorted his feet;
> then, sighing and with a voice of lament,
> he said to me (…).]

> That heard, the spirit all did wrench his feet,
> And, sighing, next in woeful accent spake: [...].
> (*Hell*, xix. 66–67)

Here again Cary's tendency is to employ lexis which is literary or removed from everyday experience (the archaic past tense "spake"), while Dante's simple "voce di pianto" becomes the somewhat abstract "woeful accent".

I permit myself an example from outside *Inferno* xix to convey the full extent of Cary's toning down of the source text's forceful imagery. In *Paradiso*, xvii. 129 Dante famously writes, "e lascia pur grattar dov' è la rogna" ["And let them but scratch where the scabies is"], which Cary translates as "And let them wince, who have their withers wrung" (*Paradise*, xvii. 124). This rendering—which derives from Shakespeare: "Let the galled jade wince, our withers are unwrung" (*Hamlet*, iii. ii. 245–46)—[1] falls far short of capturing the coarse realism of the original image, of people scratching themselves because they have a skin disease. It is true that Cary plays with sounds and thereby brings these lines to the fore—consider the triple alliteration of "wince:withers:wrung", which may be an instance of compensation—, but the fact remains that the original realistic image is lost. As Valeria Tinkler-Villani observes: "Cary's translation is altogether more elevated in all its constituents: to wince is more genteel than to scratch, the dislocated shoulder of a horse is more acceptable in polite society than the disease of a dog."[2] These observations would, by and large, apply to the vast majority of those interventions in the target text where Cary deals with coarse or graphic imagery.

Clearly, there are also cases in the target text where Cary is constrained by translation norms (bowdlerization) or the literary conventions of his time, which prohibited the use of slang or taboo words in an epic poem. For example, he avoids a direct rendering of "merda" ["shit"] and "merdose" ["shitty"] in Canto xviii of *Inferno*: "un col capo sí di merda lordo" ["one with his head so smirched with shit"; *Inferno*, xviii. 116] becomes "One with his head so grimed" (*Hell*, xviii. 114), and "l'unghie merdose" ["shitty nails"; *Inferno*, xviii. 131] is rendered as "defiled nails" (*Hell*, xviii. 128).

---

1   R. W. King, *The Translator of Dante*, p. 345.
2   V. Tinkler-Villani, *Visions of Dante*, p. 227.

What is more, when Cary perceives the source text as being obscure, he intervenes by clarifying the original message, that is, he tries to enhance the text's immediate intelligibility. The tendency to make explanatory interventions, in fact, is so common among translators that it has given rise to the belief that translation displays universal features, which are "inherent in the translation process itself".[1] Among the most common are, precisely, "a marked rise in the level of explicitness" and a "tendency towards disambiguation and simplification",[2] though clearly they tend to manifest themselves differently depending on the beliefs and sensitivity of individual translators. An example of Cary's policy of clarification would be the following:

> l'un de li quali, ancor non è molt' anni,
> rupp' io per un che dentro v'annegava:
> e questo sia suggel ch'ogn' omo sganni.
> (*Inferno*, XIX. 19–21)

> [one of which, yet not many years ago,
> I broke for one who inside was drowning:
> and let this be the seal which disembroils every man.]

> One of the which I brake, some few years past,
> To save a whelming infant: and be this
> A seal to undeceive whoever doubts
> The motive of my deed.
> (*Hell*, XIX. 20–23)

Cary's explanatory stance is revealed in his rendering the line "rupp' io per un che dentro v'annegava" as "I brake [...] / To save a whelming infant." Dante had left it to the reader to infer that his action was aimed at saving a life, but Cary feels it necessary to spell this out and consequently inserts the explanatory verb "save". Not fully satisfied with this act of clarification, however, he goes on to specify that the object of Dante's attention is "a whelming infant". It is clear therefore that Cary imposes his own reading on the poem, and indeed in a footnote he reports that according to biographical sources Dante had broken a font to rescue a child who had fallen into it while playing. Clearly, Cary believes it to be the

---

1   M. Baker, "Corpus Linguistics", p. 246.
2   M. Baker, "Corpus Linguistics", pp. 243, 246.

translator's duty to clarify the source text, whether by adding an explanatory footnote or by rendering, for instance, Dante's vague "un" ["someone", "one"] as "a whelming infant". This tendency to explicitate the source text is carried further when the lexical item "sganni" is translated as "undeceive", a choice which then allows Cary to expand Dante's concise (and cryptic) message by means of the clause "whoever doubts / The motive of my deed".

Another typical instance of explicitation occurs in the following *terzina*, which deals with the simoniacs' grotesque punishment:

> Qual suole il fiammeggiar de le cose unte
> muoversi pur su per la strema buccia,
> tal era lí dai calcagni a le punte.
> (*Inferno*, XIX. 28–30)

> [As the flaming of anointed things
> is wont to move upwards along the outer rind,
> so was it there, from the heels to the tips.]

> As flame,
> Feeding on unctuous matter, glides along
> The surface, scarcely touching where it moves;
> So here, from heel to point, glided the flames.
> (*Hell*, XIX. 29–32)

Since the subject is punishment, Cary finds it necessary to emphasize the image by means of repetition: "glided the flames" in the last line makes explicit what is implicit in the source text. In other words, Cary, it would seem, aims to achieve two objectives: intensification (so as to make up at least partially for the loss of Dante's realistic imagery) and clarification.[1] Furthermore, he believes that an explanation would be appreciated and so expands the line by inserting the words "scarcely touching where it moves", regardless of the fact that no such words appear in the source text.

A final example will reveal quite clearly Cary's policy of making explicit the source text's compressed or elliptical message:

---

1   Cary himself pointed out that his additions had been intentional and were meant to perform various functions in the target text. When a contemporary critic, Miss Seward, criticized him for making lexical additions, he explained, in his reply, that he believed the insertion of new words "would add force" to his style, besides which they were "very convenient for filling up the verse" (*Memoir of the Rev. Henry Francis Cary*, I, 246).

Nuovo Iasón sarà, di cui si legge
ne' Maccabei; e come a quel fu molle
suo re, cosí fia lui chi Francia regge.
                              (*Inferno*, XIX. 85–87)

[A new Jason he will be, of whom one reads
in Maccabees; and just as to that one his king
was soft, so to him shall be he who rules France.]

He a new Jason shall be call'd, of whom
In Maccabees we read; and favour such
As to that priest his king indulgent show'd,
Shall be of France's monarch shown to him.
                              (*Hell*, XIX. 88–91)

Here a single lexical item, "molle" ["soft", "pliant"], which suggests the idea of weakness and surrender, is represented by two words ("favour" and "indulgent"); Cary must have thought that one word would not be sufficient for the English reader to grasp the notion expressed by Dante. The target text, in other words, should not retain any of the potential obscurities or ambiguities present in the source text. The same kind of consideration appears to lie behind the translation of "a quel" by the longer "to that priest", making overt the implied reference ("priest"). Similarly, "chi Francia regge" ["he who rules France"] becomes "France's monarch". Furthermore, Cary's policy of clarification leads him to make his version longer and repetitive: for example, the verb "show" is employed twice ("showed" and "shown"), despite the fact that it does not appear at all in Dante.

Having so far considered Cary's strategies as a translator, we may now turn to his ideology. The ideology of a translator is probably best revealed through stylistic analysis: although external sources such as letters and prefaces may reveal his attitude, one eventually has to verify whether the textual outcome is consistent with his declared intent. In Canto XIX of *Hell* the translation choices aim fully to reproduce Dante's condemnation of corrupt clergy. This, as we shall see, is extremely significant, given the times in which Cary was living. Being an Anglican clergyman, he was no doubt influenced by his religious outlook when he set out to translate the *Commedia*. In this connection, there is an interesting letter where Cary mentions Dante in relation to the unorthodox views of

certain contemporary Anglican clergymen who later entered the
Roman Church (he is probably referring to the Oxford Movement,
whose leader, the Anglican clergyman John Henry Newman,
eventually became a Roman Catholic in 1845):

> At this time [...] a leaning to some of the errors of the Church of
> Rome is but too apparent. In saying this, I do not mean to reflect
> on the motives and intentions of any. When a mind like Dante's,
> so vigorous and so impatient of any authority except that of
> truth, continued in some points still so enthralled, can we
> wonder that others should fall under the same delusions, even
> after all the efforts that have been made to undeceive them?[1]

Despite the fact that Cary is aware of the theological differences
between his views and Dante's, he ascribes to the latter a typical
Protestant belief: that the truth is independent of any authority (by
which he means the authority of the Church, since Anglicans
believe that only the Holy Scriptures are necessary for salvation).[2]
Cary does not, of course, believe Dante (still "enthralled [...] in
some points") to have been a Protestant before his time, but he
does consider him a forerunner of the spirit which produced the
Reformation; and his portrayal of Dante as an apostle of civil and
religious liberty clearly has its origin in his Anglicanism. In his
"Life of Dante", published as a preface to *The Vision*, he writes: "Of
what he considered the cause of civil and religious liberty, [Dante]
is on all occasions the zealous and fearless advocate."[3] The issue of
liberty—both political/civil and religious—was a central concern
for nineteenth-century Anglicans and Whigs,[4] and for the Whigs,
of whom Cary was one, the Roman Catholic Church was still very
much the Church Dante had attacked. They saw the Court of Rome

1   *Memoir of the Rev. Henry Francis Cary*, II, 334–35.
2   According to Article VI of *The Religion of the Anglican Faith* ("Of the Sufficiency
     of the Holy Scriptures for Salvation"), "Holy Scripture containeth all things
     necessary to salvation": *The Book of Common Prayer* (Oxford, Oxford Univer-
     sity Press, 1861), p. 314.
3   H. F. Cary, *The Vision*, pp. 10–11.
4   Anglicans consider their Church to be a spiritual authority which "recognizes,
     to the utmost extent, the right of every man to worship God according to his
     conscience". In fact, the Church of England "claims authority in controversies
     of faith, but it disclaims infallibility. Only Catholics think that they are in-
     fallible in matters of faith and morals": H. Marsh, *A Comparative View of the
     Churches of England and Rome* (London, Rivington, 1816), p. 171.

as a despotic government which, by claiming power in temporal matters, failed to render "unto Caesar the things that are Caesar's".[1]

The view establishing continuity between Dante's anticlerical stance and "the spirit which produced the Reformation" was quite common in the nineteenth century.[2] Ugo Foscolo, who was living as an exile in England, and John Taafe, the author of *A Comment on the "Divine Comedy" of Dante Alighieri* (1822),[3] were active in promoting a liberal reading of the *Commedia* (which was to influence both Shelley and Byron), whereby "Dante's dispute with political orthodoxies is [...] matched by his apparent dissent from Catholic orthodoxy."[4] In fact, "for Foscolo and other liberals, the spirit of liberty was opposed to 'the age of cloisters' as much as to 'tyrannical governments'. Political and religious opposition went hand in hand."[5]

This liberal, or Whig, reading of Dante is in keeping with the theory of another influential intellectual, Gabriele Rossetti, a Neapolitan émigré who, like Foscolo, had settled in England.[6] Rossetti portrayed Dante "as a defender of liberty",[7] and greatly emphasized the antipapal inspiration of the *Commedia* in his essay *Disquisitions on the Antipapal Spirit Which Produced the Reformation,* published in 1834.[8] He was appointed Professor of Italian at King's

1   One should bear in mind that in the nineteenth century "all government positions in the papal states were held by clerics": B. and M. Pawley, *Rome and Canterbury through Four Centuries* (London, Mowbray, 1974), p. 141.

2   It is interesting, for example, to consider the comment made by a reviewer of Gabriele Rossetti's *Disquisitions*: "It had been often shown before that the spirit which produced the Reformation was never wholly extinct in the ages preceding that event" (anonymous review of Rossetti's *Comento analitico* and *Disquisitions on the Antipapal Spirit, Edinburgh Review,* 55, vii [July 1832], 531–51 [p. 550]). For the Rossetti texts sees n. 8 on this page.

3   J. Taafe, *A Comment on the "Divine Comedy" of Dante Alighieri* (London, Murray, 1822).

4   R. Pite, *The Circle of our Vision,* p. 48.

5   R. Pite, *The Circle of our Vision,* p. 52.

6   On Rossetti see M. C. W. Wicks, *The Italian Exiles in London* (Manchester, Manchester University Press, 1937), and E. R. Vincent, *Gabriele Rossetti in England* (Oxford, Oxford University Press, 1936).

7   R. W. King, *The Translator of Dante,* p. 169.

8   This is an English translation (by Caroline Ward) of a book which had appeared in Brussels in 1832 under the title *Sullo spirito antipapale dei classici antichi d'Italia: disquisizioni di Gabriele Rossetti: Disquisitions on the Antipapal Spirit Which Produced the Reformation,* translated by C. Ward, 2 vols (London, Smith and Elder, 1834). Rossetti had written the book, and had it translated into English, in order to defend the esoteric ideas contained in his commentary

College, London in 1831, partly because his views were welcome in a Church of England institution (King's College had been established by conservative Anglicans in 1828).[1]

Cary, who had met Rossetti as early as 1825 (that is, long before Rossetti published his *Disquisitions*), had at once expressed reservations about Rossetti's politically biased interpretation of Dante, at least in its radical form, in a letter addressed to the Rev. Thomas Price:

> I have lately had an Italian staying with me, who thinks he has made great discoveries as to the political allusions in Dante, and wished for my opinion of them. I am inclined to believe them not altogether visionary; but that like other framers of hypotheses, he pulls down too much of what has been raised by others to erect his own fabric. His name is Gabriele Rossetti.[2]

Cary had confirmed his scepticism, without however rejecting Rossetti's theory altogether, in a letter addressed at the same time (January 1825) to Rossetti himself: "Your peculiar opinions [...] will meet with some opposition from the prejudices of the older readers of Dante like myself."[3] Cary was sceptical, first and foremost, of Rossetti's esoteric readings of Dante's allegories, for Rossetti maintained that Dante had been a member of a secret sect bent on overthrowing the tyranny of the Court of Rome, and that he had even prophesied the Reformation![4]

By contrast, Cary's "Protestant reaction" to the *Commedia* seems to have been quite mild, especially when compared with the radicalism of John Wesley Thomas, a translator of Dante who, in his *The Trilogy* (London, 1859–66) was to portray him "as a proto-Protestant, holding to the true faith amidst Catholic superstition".[5]

on *Inferno* published a few years earlier—*La "Divina commedia" di Dante Alighieri, con comento analitico di Gabriele Rossetti*, 2 vols (London, Murray, 1826–27)—, in which he had expressed similar views on Dante (see R. Pite, *The Circle of our Vision*, p. 52). On the reception of Foscolo's and Rossetti's theories in nineteenth-century English culture see my *The Vision of Dante*, pp. 180–220.

1   E. R. Vincent, *Gabriele Rossetti*, p. 21.
2   *Memoir of the Rev. Henry Francis Cary*, II, 120.
3   *Memoir of the Rev. Henry Francis Cary*, II, 122.
4   In his *Comento analitico* Rossetti draws the reader's attention to the fact that Veltro (*Inf.*, I. 101), a saviour or politico-religious (earthly) reformer, is an anagram of Luther (Lvtero)!
5   R. Pite, *The Circle of Our Vision*, pp. 51–52.

The truth is that Cary was not simply a translator but also a scholar well acquainted with the original text. Moreover, he seems to have been a historicist, for whom the *Commedia* had to be understood on its own terms, and this would explain why he was wary of modern theories not justified by an accurate appraisal of Dante's work. This is not to say that he does not have an ideological bias; indeed his Anglicanism seems to have influenced some at least of the choices he made as a translator. It is worth pointing out, however, that although translators are bound to express their opinions in their renderings, the pervasiveness of interventions of an ideological nature (whether overt or covert) seems to be inversely proportional to the presence of a modern, that is, philological attitude to fidelity and of a scholarly understanding of the source text; and this is certainly the case in Cary's *The Vision*.

Before turning to the textual evidence of Cary's ideological bias offered by Canto XIX of *Inferno*, it should be mentioned that the *Commedia* had been put on the Index in the sixteenth century, with the injunction that three passages in particular (*Inferno*, XIX. 48–117; *Purgatorio*, XIX. 106–18; *Paradiso*, IX. 136–43) "were to be expurgated from all editions whether with or without commentary".[1] The Latin translation of the *Commedia* by the Jesuit Carlo d'Aquino, published as late as 1728, was still affected by Counter-Reformation attitudes in that, in keeping with the papal injunction, it omitted "all controversial passages";[2] nor was papal censorship relaxed in the nineteenth century. Therefore the mere fact that Cary translated all the controversial passages from the source text without toning down their rhetorical strength was highly significant at the time. In itself it clearly signalled a strong anti-papal inspiration.

Let us take as our first example the opening of *Inferno* XIX, one of the passages which met with papal disapproval:

> O Simon mago, o miseri seguaci
> che le cose di Dio, che di bontate
> deon essere spose, e voi rapaci
> per oro e per argento avolterate [...].
>
> (*Inferno*, XIX. 1–4)

---

1   L. Martinelli, *Dante* (Palermo, Palumbo, 1973), p. 75; *Dante: The Critical Heritage*, pp. 31, 36.

2   W. P. Friederich, "Dante through the Centuries", *Comparative Literature*, 1 (1949), 44–54 (p. 49).

> [O Simon Magus, o wretched followers
> who the things of God, that of goodness
> must be spouses, and you rapacious ones,
> for gold and for silver adulterate (…).]

> Woe to thee, Simon Magus! woe to you,
> His wretched followers! who the things of God,
> Which should be wedded unto goodness, them,
> Rapacious as ye are, do prostitute
> For gold and silver in adultery.
>
> (*Hell*, xix. 1–5)

Clearly, the beginning of the canto is important since it sets the scene for its main theme: the condemnation of simony. As David Nolan pointed out, both the syntactical *non sequitur* ("e voi rapaci", with its powerfully arresting "e") and the profusion of relative clauses in lines 16–21 are essential to the quick flow of the rhythm in the original and the movement Dante wished to confer on the narrative.[1] This, however, is not preserved in the translation, though Cary does insert lexical items which are not present in the Italian text, presumably in order to capture the rhetorical strength of the invective; and the repetition of "woe" gives emphasis to his opening, as if he wanted to underline his personal indignation at the state of corruption in the Church. This point is proved by further lexical additions, such as that of the emphatic "as ye are" to "rapacious". The rendering of "avolterate" is also interesting. In modern Italian, *adulterare* (originally meaning "to conjoin illicit-ly") has lost its sexual connotation and is used metaphorically, but Cary insists on the sexual connotation of the expression by making two items, the verb "prostitute" and the noun "adultery", stand for "avolterate". The overall effect of the indictment in the target text is also conveyed by means of grammar, the auxiliary "do" which precedes "prostitute" adding further emphasis to the invective. Hence, when Cary deals with a topic he considers to be moment-ous, such as the corruption of the Roman Catholic Church, he is so keen to preserve the original's rhetorical strength that he does not hesitate to insert material of his own. A tendency of this kind is extremely significant because it runs counter to what Newmark dubs "the translator's occupational disease", namely a "tendency

---

1   D. Nolan, *"Inferno xix"*, in *Dante Commentaries: Eight Studies of the "Divine Comedy"*, edited by D. Nolan (Dublin, Irish Academic Press, 1977), pp. 7–42.

to water down words and metaphors, a fear of the truth in the source language", which would appear to be a universal feature of translation.[1] Cary's "Protestant reaction", that is, his reproduction of Dante's indictment, is all the more remarkable if we consider that he himself is not always immune to the translator's disease: as we have seen, elsewhere in the target text he is certainly capable of toning down Dante's realistic imagery.

It would seem that when translating "sappi ch'i' fui vestito del gran manto" ["know that I was dressed in the great mantle"; *Inferno*, XIX. 69] as "learn / That in the mighty mantle I was robed" (*Hell*, XIX. 70–71), Cary uses "mighty" for "gran" (and "robed" for "vestito", for that matter) in order to underline the earthly power of the papacy; and euphony is made to play the same role from a stylistic point of view, with the "mighty:mantle" alliteration serving to foreground the notion of the papacy's power—though admittedly this could also be an instance of compensation, to make up for the loss of the adjective "somme" ["mighty"] further on, where "E se non fosse ch'ancor lo mi vieta / la reverenza de le somme chiavi" ["And if it were not that reverence for the mighty keys still forbids it me"; *Inferno*, XIX. 100–01] is rendered as "If reverence of the keys restrain'd me not" (*Hell*, XIX. 104).

When confronted with the linguistic difficulty of rendering an unusual gerund ("simoneggiando") into English, Cary's choice is once again consistent with his policy of preserving Dante's condemnation of corrupt clergy:

> Di sotto al capo mio son li altri tratti
> che precedetter me simoneggiando.
> > (*Inferno*, XIX. 73–74)

> [Beneath my head are the others dragged,
> who preceded me, simonizing.]

> > Under my head are dragg'd
> The rest, my predecessors in the guilt
> Of simony.
> > (*Hell*, XIX. 75–77)

The Italian language allowed Dante to form a gerund from the noun *simonia*, a creative act which gives the line movement, for

---

1   P. Newmark, *About Translation*, p. 59.

"simoneggiando" suggests endless activity on the part of the popes and thus makes them seem even more despicable. On closer inspection, though, what appears to be a linguistic problem may not have been the only reason for Cary's choice. By introducing the notion of "guilt", which does not appear in the source text, he seems to have been determined not only to reproduce Dante's condemnation of the corrupt clergy but actually to add to it.

Cary's bias is further evidenced by his treatment of the following lines, which were among those censored by the Church because of the forceful language they contain:

> Di voi pastor s'accorse il Vangelista,
> quando colei che siede sopra l'acque
> puttaneggiar coi regi a lui fu vista.
> (*Inferno*, xix. 106–08)

> [Of you sheperds did the Evangelist take note
> when she who sits upon the waters
> whoring with the kings by him was seen.]

> Of shepherds like to you, the Evangelist
> Was ware, when her, who sits upon the waves,
> With kings in filthy whoredom he beheld.
> (*Hell*, xix. 109–11)

Here again Cary does not seek to tone down the impact of the original sexual imagery. According to Dante, lust for temporal power was the source of all perversion, and the Church (here symbolized by the whoring woman) was to concern itself only with the exercise of spiritual power, which was its sole rightful prerogative. Cary, for his part, not only translates "puttaneggiar" as "whoredom", but also inserts an adjective, "filthy", in order to make the sense of disgust even stronger; and the use of "filthy" is not without significance, for in *The Vision* the word never occurs as a direct translation of its Italian equivalent, "sozzo". Hence, it would seem that on the whole Cary waters down Dante's realistic, vernacular language—*unless* he wishes to emphasize the corruption of the papacy.

Cary also pursues his ideology, which I have termed "Protestant reaction", in his commentary, where the condemnation of the Roman Church is reinforced in a footnote to *Inferno*, xix. 106–09. Here the purpose is quite deliberately to influence the reader's attitude to the papacy. First Cary quotes Petrarch as a prestigious source in support of Dante's condemnation of the Roman Church, and then he rejects the contention of Richard Hurd, Bishop of Worcester, that Petrarch was not hostile to the papacy. From Hurd's *An Introduction to the Study of the Prophecies* he quotes the following:

> Numberless passages in the writings of Petrarch speak of Rome under the name of Babylon. But an equal stress is not to be laid on all these. It should be remembered, that the popes, in Petrarch's time, resided at Avignon, greatly to the disparagement of themselves, as he thought, and especially of Rome; of which this singular man was little less than idolatrous. The situation of the place, surrounded by waters, and his splenetic concern for the *exiled* [sic] church (for under this idea he painted to himself the popes' migration to the banks of Avignon) brought to his mind the condition of the Jewish church in the Babylonian captivity.[1]

Then, having quoted one of the epistles of Petrarch discussed by Hurd, Cary continues:

> Now a reference to the words printed in italics, which the Bishop of Worcester has omitted in his quotation, will make it sufficiently evident, that *Avignon*, and not *Rome*, is here alluded to by Petrarch. The application that is made of these prophecies by two men so eminent for their learning and sagacity as Dante and Petrarch is, however, very remarkable, *and must be satisfactory to those who have renounced the errors and corruptions of the papacy.* Such applications were indeed frequent in the middle ages, as may be seen in the "Sermons" above referred to. Balbo observes, that it is not Rome, as most erroneously interpreted, but Avignon, and the court there, that is termed Babylon by Dante and Petrarch.[2]

By thus emphasizing his belief that Petrarch supports Dante's condemnation of the corrupt papacy, Cary lays bare his own anti-Catholicism.

    This is also apparent in his translation of the lines dealing with the Donation of Constantine:

---

1   H. F. Cary, *The Vision*, p. 46.
2   H. F. Cary, *The Vision*, p. 46.

> Ahi, Costantin, di quanto mal fu matre,
> non la tua conversion, ma quella dote
> che da te prese il primo ricco patre!
> (*Inferno*, XIX. 115–17)

> [Ah Constantine, of what evil was mother,
> not your conversion, but that dowry
> which from you the first rich father took!]

> Ah, Constantine! to how much ill gave birth,
> Not thy conversion, but that plenteous dower
> Which the first wealthy Father gain'd from thee.
> (*Hell*, XIX. 118–20)

Cary introduces the adjective "plenteous" to modify "dower", in
spite of the fact that its equivalent, "dote", is not so modified in the
source text. This adjective was presumably added in order fully to
render the notion of a wealthy church. Interestingly, these lines
had attracted the attention of Milton—and this proves, incidentally,
that Rossetti was not the first to read into the *Commedia* a proto-
Protestant condemnation of the Roman Church. Indeed, in *Of
Reformation in England* (1641), Milton translates these lines alongside
Petrarch's Sonnet 107 and lines from Ariosto's *Orlando furioso*
(XXXIV. 72–79), all of which are condemnations of the Donation of
Constantine. This, then, is how Milton renders *Inferno*, XIX. 115–17,
in a manner which is remarkably similar to that of Cary (who, as
a matter of fact, quotes Milton's version in a footnote):[1]

> Ah, Constantine! of how much ill was cause,
> Not thy conversion, but those rich domains
> That the first wealthy pope receiv'd of thee![2]

Having assumed, as a starting-point, that Cary's solutions are not
the unaccountable product of idiosyncratic choices on his part, we
may now conclude—having looked for meaningful regularities in
the data yielded by the analysis and carefully considered even
those choices which at first sight might have appeared to be "mistranslations"—that his interventions do indeed show internal

---

1   H. F. Cary, *The Vision*, p. 47.
2   *Milton's Prose Writings*, edited by K. M. Burton (London, Dent; New York,
    Dutton, 1958), p. 19

consistency. As Lefevere put it, "An isolated mistake is, probably, just that, whereas a recurrent series of 'mistakes' most likely points to a pattern that is the expression of a strategy";[1] and textual strategies, one should add, might signal the existence of tendencies in translation behaviour which are particular to a given historical context (such as a norm like bowdlerization) or which span cultures and languages (such as universals of translation, for example clarification/explicitation).

Because Cary interpreted the *Commedia* as an epic poem in a modern (Miltonic) sense, he adhered to the norms governing the (re)writing of "serious" poetry in the target tradition. He subjected himself to various constraints in order to render his work acceptable in the receiving culture. He did not lack the linguistic means to rewrite Dante's taboo or coarse expressions, but he avoided them simply because in a nineteenth-century context they would have been perceived as utterly out of place in an epic poem. He drew inspiration from a codified poetic repertoire, the language of epic poetry (which has a distinctive archaic texture and is characterized by literary mannerisms). This is an unmistakable poetic decision. On the whole, the large-scale choices (verse form, diction) in *The Vision* are not linguistically constrained. Cary's embellishment of the original imagery, too, is a poetic decision, not a purely linguistic one (it is true that some of his additions might be explained in terms of metrical padding, but even this would be a general constraint determined by the exigencies of blank verse). In fact, bowdlerization and poetic embellishment were unmarked, that is, common strategies in the world of Anglo-American translation in the eighteenth and nineteenth centuries.[2]

The foregoing analysis also lends support to the view that translations belong to the target culture. If one is concerned with the relationships between single source and target texts, the receiving tradition appears to be the crucial dimension in which the translator's choices make sense. Ultimately, all the historically determined factors or norms affecting the stylistic make-up of the target text are rooted in the target tradition. This observation

---

1   A. Lefevere, *Translation, Rewriting*, p. 97.
2   T. R. Steiner, *English Translation Theory*, p. 42; L. Venuti, *The Translator's Invisibility* (London, Routledge, 1995), pp. 71–86; R. Ellis and L. Oakley-Brown, "British Tradition", in *The Routledge Encyclopedia of Translation Studies*, pp. 333–43 (p. 335).

applies to ideological considerations too: Cary inscribed his work within Anglican domestic concerns by upholding a Whig reading of Dante and opposing those intellectuals in the target culture who were "leaning towards the errors of Roman Catholicism".

A nineteenth-century Anglican clergyman with Whig leanings could hardly avoid portraying Dante as a defender of liberty, but clearly, if Cary had pursued this impulse with greater determination he would have defeated his purpose of illuminating the source text in its historical setting. To his credit, he achieved a balance between these two conflicting impulses. He did not endorse the radicalism of Rossetti and other Protestant interpreters of the *Commedia*. The result is a translation which sets Dante's poem in the Middle Ages (which Boyd's had not) while at the same time dressing the poet in English garb. Cary's ideological motivation should not blind us to the fact that by nineteenth-century standards he produced a linguistically "accurate" rewriting: *The Vision* is a historically determined and partisan reconstruction of Dante, but it is also the product of erudite scholarship.

Last but not least, my analysis suggests that *The Vision* is more than just a rendering of Dante. It is an act of literary criticism that expresses the poetics and the ideology of its author. Furthermore, by being an act of literary criticism of a special kind, namely a rewriting that recreates the original, *The Vision* contributes to the afterlife of the original, bringing some of its meanings to the fore.

True, it could be argued that Cary considerably tones down the rhetorical strength of Dante's style (and of his messages, for that matter). For example, one could claim that the condemnation of simony is more powerful in Dante because it is highly compressed and is conveyed in forceful language. Yet one has to consider Cary's fidelity to the source text in a specific context, the nineteenth century, when the *Commedia* was still censored in Italy. If we adopt a historicist perspective, Cary's fidelity is highly significant and discloses how important the indictment was to a nineteenth-century British readership. The corruption of the Church arouses the translator's emotions so greatly that his voice may clearly be heard. In the end, we are left with the conviction that Dante most certainly achieved his aim of moving and inspiring generations of his readers and interpreters.

DANTE THE POPULAR *CANTASTORIE*: PORTA'S DIALECT TRANSLATION OF THE *COMMEDIA*

Verina R. Jones

The nineteenth century witnessed numerous translations of the *Commedia* into a variety of Italian dialects, twenty-six altogether, excluding Porta's.[1] The underlying motivations for these translations appear to involve the fear of the diminution or destruction of dialect literature in Italy as a consequence of political and linguistic unification, the aim of making Dante's text more accessible to the uneducated, and also, not infrequently, the attempt to link Dante's poem to the "intrinsic qualities" of dialect, or of a particular dialect. The prevalent modes of approach are those of humorous deformation and what one might call the modernization of Dante, that is to say, a search for the relevance of Dante's message to the here and now.[2] It was one of the giants of Italian dialect poetry, Carlo Porta (1775–1821), who had opened the floodgates at the beginning of the century with his Milanese version of Dante.[3] This

1 On dialect translations of Dante see C. Salvioni, *La "Divina commedia", l'"Orlando furioso", la "Gerusalemme liberata" nelle versioni e nei travestimenti dialettali a stampa* (Bellinzona, Salvioni, 1902), and A. Stussi, "Fortuna dialettale della *Commedia* (appunti sulle versioni settentrionali)", in his *Studi e documenti di storia della lingua e dei dialetti italiani* (Bologna, Mulino, 1982), pp. 73–84.

2 Unintended humour is sometimes generated by such attempts to modernize Dante. A Bergamasque translation of *Inferno* published in 1864 took it for granted that the Veltro was none other than King Victor Emmanuel II ("e questo [the Veltro] l'istarà prope a Turì"); and another example of what Stussi calls "deliri esegetici" occurred in 1936, when a monk named Giovanni Ricci dedicated his Bolognese translation of *Inferno* "Al Duce Benito Mussolini—Padre della Patria—preconizzato dal Divin Poeta per il Veltro Salvatore d'Italia" (A. Stussi, "Fortuna dialettale", pp. 78–79).

3 Dante Isella has assigned the translation of the first two cantos to 1801–02 and the rest to no later than 1805: D. Isella, "Carlo Porta", in *Letteratura italiana: l'Ottocento* (Milan, Garzanti, 1969), pp. 513–60 (p. 533). All references

is the earliest known dialect translation of Dante: other Italian classics, especially Ariosto and Tasso, had been translated into various Italian dialects, but Dante had not.

Porta's Dante must have functioned to a certain extent as a model for the dialect translations of the *Commedia* that were to come later in the century. Not only were the vast majority of these nineteenth-century translations (nineteen out of twenty-six) into Northern dialects, and among these four into Milanese, but one also finds in Porta the modes of appropriation of Dante that will prevail later on: humour, modernization and defence of dialect, beside claims for the unique poetic qualities of the dialect in question, here Milanese. But it is imperative to add that the significance and the weight of Porta's translation are quite different from what comes later, not only because unlike many of his followers Porta is a great poet, but also because at the time of Porta's translation Italy was at a very different stage in its political and cultural development.

Porta's Dante is a product of Napoleonic Lombardy, of a city (Milan) which is intensely cosmopolitan, and of a particular cultural phase, at the crossroads between Enlightenment and Jacobinism, Classicism and Romanticism. There is as yet no sign of that process of closing in on itself which Dionisotti saw as a main characteristic of Italian culture in the nineteenth century—of that loss of cosmo-politanism which was perhaps the price that had to be paid for the achievement of independence. The translations of Dante that came later in the century exude something of the mean flavour of a narrow municipal culture, of a dialect literature that is in a state of limbo, that has clearly lost sight of its great historic role as the "language of reality" and has not yet discovered its modern role as the "language of poetry"; moreover, this insecure dialect literature attempts to come to terms with a Dante who has now become established as a national poet and acquired the status of precursor of the political and poetic *risorgimento* of Italy.[1] At the start of the

to Porta's poems will be to C. Porta, *Poesie*, edited by D. Isella (Florence, La Nuova Italia, 1955). The poems will be identified by numbers only. The translations of Porta's text are my own, as are all other translations from dialect texts. The Dante translations are from Dante Alighieri, *The Divine Comedy*, translated by C. S. Singleton, 3 vols in 6 (Princeton, Princeton University Press, 1970–75).

1   For Dionisotti's view of nineteenth-century Italy see especially his *Appunti sui moderni* (Bologna, Mulino, 1988). On the shifting connotations of dialect literature over the last century see *Il dialetto da lingua della realtà a lingua della poesia*, edited by M. Chiesa and G. Tesio (Turin, Paravia, 1978).

century, on the other hand, Milanese culture not only looked upon its own tradition with confidence and pride, but perceived Dante as a poet who was in some way in tune with that tradition.

Porta's translation covers only small sections of the *Commedia*, all of them in *Inferno*: the whole of Canto I, just over one-third of Canto II, some fragments of Canto III, two sections of Canto V (concerning Minos and Francesca respectively) and just over two-thirds of Canto VII. The translation of Canto I was first published in 1816, as part of what was to become a classic of Italian dialect literature, Francesco Cherubini's collection of works in Milanese from the early period to the present,[1] but it was only with the first posthumous edition of Porta's works in 1821 that the whole of his Dante translation was published.[2] Cherubini only included the translation of one canto because apparently that was all Porta was prepared to give him at that stage.[3] This seems to suggest that Porta viewed the translation of Canto I as something self-contained and complete, and the rest possibly only as fragments.

Both in the Cherubini edition and in later ones these translations are called "versioni", though Porta himself had used different designations. In the papers which accompany the various versions of his poems, he tends to refer to them as "frammenti" ["fragments"], but at the beginning of Canto I, in one of the variant versions, he claims that this is "il canto primo dell'*Inferno* di Dante travestito in lingua milanese" ["the first canto of Dante's *Inferno* clothed in Milanese"].[4] "Travestito" suggests something rather different from merely "translated", and the use of the term is significant on two counts. On the one hand it refers to the specific nature of the transposition of Dante's text into Porta's text, while on the other it appears to allude to a third text, which to all intents and purposes functioned as a powerful filter for Porta's dialect rendering of Dante.

Even a casual glance will reveal that Porta does not produce a systematic line-by-line or sentence-by-sentence translation, and,

1   F. Cherubini, *Collezione delle migliori opere scritte in dialetto milanese*, 12 vols (Milan, Pirotta, 1816).

2   *Raccolta di varie poesie di Carlo Porta*, edited by T. Grossi (Milan, Ferrario, 1821).

3   In the preface to volume XII (p. 6) of his *Collezione*, which consists of Porta's poems, Cherubini writes: "Non piú che il primo Canto ci è dato di presentarvi, perché questo solo ci concesse l'Autore, qual Saggio dell'opera intiera in cui egli è a questa ora di molto inoltrato."

4   C. Porta, *Poesie*, p. 154.

what is more, we also find the systematic insertion of new elements. This "unfaithfulness" to Dante increases progressively: while in Canto I we have an alternation of sets of lines which more or less render the equivalent sets of lines in Dante with one or two lines that are not in Dante at all, by Canto VII it is often very difficult to work out exactly what in Porta's text "translates" what in Dante's text. Clearly, these "translations" contain a strong element of rewriting as well as translating. As regards the "third text" to which the use of the expression "travestito" appears to allude, it is Domenico Balestrieri's translation into Milanese dialect of Tasso's *Gerusalemme liberata*, which had appeared some twenty-five years earlier but had remained a very strong presence in Milanese culture, especially in the Milanese dialect tradition. Its self-designation was precisely "travestimento".

The links between Porta's Dante and Balestrieri's Tasso will be discussed later, but first let us examine the very beginning of Canto I of Porta's Dante and compare it to the corresponding section of Dante's text.

Nel mezzo del cammin di nostra vita
mi ritrovai per una selva oscura
ché la diritta via era smarrita.
    Ahi quanto a dir qual era è cosa dura
esta selva selvaggia e aspra e forte
che nel pensier rinova la paura!
    Tant' è amara che poco è piú morte;
ma per trattar del ben ch'i' vi trovai
dirò de l'altre cose ch'i' v'ho scorte.
    Io non so ben ridir com' i' v'intrai,
tant' era pien di sonno a quel punto
che la verace via abbandonai.
                              (*Inferno*, I. 1–12)

A mitaa strada de quell gran viacc,
che femm a vun la voeulta al mond de là
me sont trovaa in d'on bosch scur scur affacc,
senza un sentee da podè seguità:
domà a pensagh me senti a vegnì scacc,
nè l'è on bosch inscì fazzel de retrà,
negher, vecc, pien de spin, sass, ingarbij
pesc che nè quell del barillott di strij.
    Quanto sia al cascià pussee spavent
in tra el bosch e la mort gh'è pocch de rid,
ma gh'eva anca el so bon, vel cunti, attent.
Com' abbia faa a trovamm in quell brutt sid,
no savarev mò nanch tirall in ment:
soo che andava e dormiva, e i coss polid
in sto stat no je fan in suj festin
squas nanca i sonador de viorin.
                              (L. 1–16)

[Midway in the journey of our life I found myself in a dark wood, for the straight way was lost. Ah, how hard it is to tell what that wood was, wild, rugged, harsh; the very thought of it renews the fear! It is so bitter that death is hardly more so. But, to treat of the good that I found in it, I will tell of the other things I saw there. I cannot rightly say how I entered it, I was so full of sleep at the moment I left the true way.]

[Halfway through that long journey which we make, one at a time, to the other world, I found myself in a proper dark wood, without a path that I could follow: just thinking about it I feel all scared, nor is it an easy wood to describe, black, old, full of thorns and stones, all tangled up, worse than the one where the witches hold their sabbath. / Which is going to give more fright, that wood or death, is no laughing matter, but it had good things as well, now I'll tell you, listen carefully. How I managed to find myself in that nasty place, now I couldn't even bring it

> back to mind: I know that I was walking and sleeping, and in that state even fiddlers can't manage to do things properly at all-night dances.]

What is most striking here is the change in metre. Apparently Porta did make an initial attempt to translate Dante using *terza rima*, but whatever he wrote in that form has been lost.[1] The verse he settled for is the *ottava*, with its ABABABCC rhyme-scheme. The *ottava*, as is well known, is the typical stanza of verse narratives, both the high literature of Ariosto's and Tasso's epic poems (which, as mentioned above, had been traditional objects of dialect translations in Italy) and the popular matter of oral storytellers. Porta's use of the *ottava* is more in line with the tradition of oral narration than with that of the learned epic poem: a line corresponds, almost always, to a syntactical unit (either a sentence or a clause), while *enjambements* are extremely rare (only three instances in all: L. 51–52, CXV. 31–32 and CXV. 36–37). But there are also other features of Porta's "transformation" of Dante which suggest the presence of an oral storyteller. One is the use of tenses: Dante's past historics ("mi ritrovai": line 2; "trovai": 8; "intrai": 10; "abbandonai": 12) are eliminated in favour of perfects ("me sont trovaa": 3; "abbia faa": 12), which is the typical tense of oral narration. The other is the formula used to announce the beginning of the narration: "vel cunti, attent" (11) implies the presence of silent bystanders and thus reinforces the construction of the narrator as *cantastorie*.

Another striking mode of transformation is what one might call a lowering of tone, which in its turn generates an effect of enhanced referentiality. A case in point is the treatment of the dark wood. Dante's "selva oscura" (2) becomes a rather scrubby wood ("negher, vecc, pien de spin, sass, ingarbij": 7), and a simile is used to describe it which is absent from the original and contains a clear allusion to popular culture: the "barillott di strij" (8), that is to say, the witches' dance or sabbath. This mode of approach is repeated at the end of the second *ottava*, where the state of sleepiness of the first-person narrator is compared to the mood of fiddlers at popular feasts who have to play all night long (15–16). This too is an addition to Dante containing an allusion to popular culture, though this time firmly anchored in the present. Finally, the word "scacc" □(5)

---

1   See D. Isella, "Carlo Porta", p. 532.

will be the first of many slang words used to render Dante's "paura" ("spaghett": L. 18; "folon": L. 25; "fôff": L. 64).

The practice of transformation used in the first two *ottave* is maintained and enhanced in the rest of the text. Throughout Porta's "translation" the matter of Dante's poem is systematically filtered through a process of enhanced referentiality, involving a lowering of the tone and what we might call a "modernization" of Dante. The three beasts which frighten Dante "al cominciar de l'erta" ["near the beginning of the steep"; I. 31], with their well-known allegorical connotations, are reduced to exclusively literal beasts in Porta. In particular, Porta's text latches on to the word "pelle" ["skin"; I. 42] in Dante to introduce completely new material. The first-person narrator invents the story of his having carried a pistol in his coat pocket and having therefore thought of making some money out of the animal's skin by shooting it, while at the same time saving his own skin:

sí ch'a bene sperar m'era cagione di quella fiera a la gaetta pelle. <div align="right">(*Inferno*, I. 41–42)</div>	e trattandes che gh'eva in la marsina un pistolott de fond, Sia pell per pell (hoo ditt intrà de mì), l'è mej zollagh; se la va a pell no poss che guadagnagh. <div align="right">(L. 53–56)</div>
[gave me cause for good hope of that beast with the gay skin]	[and seeing as I had in my coat a gun, skin for skin (I said to myself), it's best to shoot it; if it's a matter of skins I can only gain.]

In similar vein, the mountain, designated in Dante as "principio e cagion di tutta gioia" ["the source and cause of every happiness"; I. 78] is reduced in Porta to "paes de la cuccagna" ["land of milk and honey"; L. 104], an overt reference to what is probably the most powerful myth of popular culture, the myth of the land where everything is freely available and made of food. One could also mention the transformation of the invocation to the Muses (*Inferno*, II. 7–9; Porta, CV. 9–16), of the famous "Papè Satàn, papè Satàn aleppe!" (*Inferno*, VII. 1) into "Ara bell' Ara discesa Cornara" (CXVIII.□1)— which is a line from a children's rhyme traditionally used in the game of hide-and-seek—, and many more examples. Even Beatrice in Porta greets Virgil with a typical formula of everyday phatic conversation—"Oh el mè mantovan, che bona cera!/Stet ben?, la diss, gh'hoo propri gust davvera" ["Oh good Mantuan my friend, how well you look! You are well?, she says, I'm really pleased"; CXV. 87–88]—, instead of Dante's "O anima cortese mantoana" ["O courteous Mantuan spirit"; *Inferno*, II. 58], though it is only fair to add that Beatrice seems to have proved, not surprisingly, especially resistant to this kind of transformation, as is shown by the repeated changes in her designation in the variant versions: "on bell' tocch de Donna" ["a nice bit of skirt"; CXV⁴]; "ona Donna bella" ["a beautiful woman"]; "on tocch de donnin de Paradis" ["a nice bit from Paradise"; CXV⁶]; "on bel donnin" ["a nice bit"; CXV⁷]; "on bell donnin ma bell" ["a really nice bit"; CXV⁸]; "ona Donna" ["a woman"; CXV⁹]. What is more, the story narrated in Porta's text is placed in a framework which definitely suggests that the events have taken place in the here and now: the here of Milan and the now of French domination. We find clear references to "our own greedy rulers" (L. 141), and to the French government with its frenetic, ever-changing policies (CXV. 57–61), as well as to the multi-lingualism of Milan at the turn of the century (CXV. 80; CXVI². 6–8).

The "mask" of the oral storyteller which, as we have seen, marks the beginning of the narration is maintained throughout. The text employs not only formulas which suggest the presence of silent bystanders, but also direct addresses to a listening crowd (CXV. 8), formulas which imply gestures and therefore spectators (L. 121), narration through nominal phrases—"Bona nocc sur co-ragg!" ["Bye bye Mr Courage!"; L. 55]; "S'ciavo sor mascher" ["Cheerio folks!"; CXVI. 9]—, and narrative imperatives (CXVII³. 15–16). To this must of course be added the tenses of narration, with the systematic substitution of Dante's past historic by the perfect, and sometimes by the narrative present. The past historic does not, however, disappear completely. There are eight instances of it altogether in the whole translation, including two in connection with the she-wolf (in fact the narrative sequence concerning the she-wolf is framed by two past historics: L. 65 and L. 151), two in connection with Beatrice, and one in connection with God. By the early nineteenth century the past historic had become obsolete in both spoken and written Milanese, but it had been part of normal usage in earlier Milanese literature, from Maggi down to Balestrieri. It makes sense therefore to treat these rare occurrences in Porta as allusions or indeed acts of homage to the Lombard tradition. But I shall return to this point later.

The features of the transformation of Dante that have been examined so far undoubtedly suggest an element of humour, but it would be misleading to view Porta's remaking of Dante in Milanese dialect as a parody of Dante. In order to make sense of it, we need to look at a variety of different elements, and I should like to suggest that Porta's translation of Dante marks a significant episode in three separate, though overlapping areas of culture and tradition: in the first place, the strength of the Lombard dialect tradition, in particular the memory of the debates that had taken place just before Porta's own time; secondly, the tradition of dialect translations of the classics, especially Balestrieri's translation of Tasso; and lastly, elements which belong to the mainstream cultural debate rather than specifically to the dialect tradition, namely the particular way in which Dante was perceived and approached towards the end of the eighteenth century.

Like all dialect literature, Milanese dialect literature finds its *raison d'être* in the existence of literary texts in the standard language. If we accept Dionisotti's definition of dialect literature as one which chooses, self-consciously, to express itself through a linguistic medium that has connotations of inferiority, then we begin to understand the prevailing motivation of literatures written in dialect, that is to say, the notion that dialect, unlike the standard language, makes it possible to express the culture of ordinary people, to grasp reality, to tell the truth. This in its turn often goes hand in hand with the notion that dialect can and does reach as high as the standard language. Such notions acquired the status of myth within the Milanese dialect tradition, the so-called *linea lombarda* ["Lombard line"].[1]

1   C. Dionisotti, "Geografia e storia della letteratura italiana", in his *Geografia e storia della letteratura italiana* (Turin, Einaudi, 1967), pp. 23–45 (p. 35). On the status of dialect literature and its relation to literature in the standard language see also C. Segre, "Polemica linguistica ed espressionismo dialettale nella letteratura italiana", in his *Lingua, stile e società* (Milan, Feltrinelli, 1963), pp. 383–412; M. Corti, "Dialetti in appello", in her *Metodi e fantasmi* (Milan, Feltrinelli, 1969), pp. 111–17; E. Bonora, "Poesia letteraria e poesia dialettale", in his *Retorica e invenzione* (Milan, Rizzoli, 1970), pp. 255–99; A. Stussi, "Lingua, dialetto e letteratura", in *Storia d'Italia*, vol. I (Turin, Einaudi, 1972), pp. 680–728, reprinted in A. Stussi, *Lingua, dialetto e letteratura* (Turin, Einaudi, 1993), pp. 3–63; *Letteratura e dialetto*, edited by G. L. Beccaria (Bologna, Zanichelli, 1975); V. R. Jones, "Dialect Literature and Popular Literature", *Italian Studies*, 45 (1990), 103–17. On the Lombard tradition see D. Isella, "La cultura letteraria lombarda" and "Il teatro milanese del Maggi o la verità del dialetto", in his *I Lombardi in rivolta* (Turin, Einaudi, 1984), pp. 4–24, 25–47; also A. Stella, "Un 'filo' lombardo da Bonvesin, al Porta, al Manzoni", in *La poesia di Carlo Porta e la tradizione milanese: atti del Convegno di studi organizzato dalla Regione Lombardia* (Milan, Feltrinelli, 1976), pp. 34–70.

The most famous, and certainly the briefest expression of pride in the Milanese dialect tradition is the line "Varon, Magg, Balestrer, Tanz e Parin". This line, listing the classics of the *linea lombarda* from the seventeenth century to the early nineteenth, comes from a poem composed by Porta himself (xvi) at roughly the same time as the translations of Dante, in which he defends and celebrates the status of Milanese dialect as a language of literature. Carlo Maria Maggi, the seventeenth-century playwright, is the first great name in Milanese dialect literature. He is almost certainly the creator of Meneghino, who to this day has remained a symbol of the Milanese. Meneghino is often a servant, sometimes simply a man of the people, who has all the supposed characteristics of the Milanese temperament: he is sensible, down-to-earth, humble, wise in the earthy way of ordinary people, moderate and also rather scared of dangerous situations. After Maggi he became one of the main signs of the *linea lombarda*, so much so that he appears repeatedly in different Milanese dialect writers, one of whom was Domenico Balestrieri, the Milanese translator of Tasso's *Gerusalemme liberata*. If we examine the characterization of the first-person narrator in Porta's translation of Dante, we shall find that he is another re-incarnation of the figure of Meneghino. Inasmuch as he is constructed as a character, we notice that he is not at all the same as Dante the character in Dante's own text. Indeed the Lombard Dante who tells the story in Porta's version is a politically moderate Milanese of lowish extraction, a poor devil of a poet, who has taken a lot of beatings at the school of the grammarians, would much rather avoid trouble and is somewhat impatient to get to Heaven, as opposed to simply wanting to see Heaven and Hell. In short, he is another Meneghino.

Balestrieri had also been one of the two main figures (the other having been Parini) involved in the dispute over the literary value of the Milanese dialect which had raged in Milan just before Porta had arrived on the scene. And Parini had also been the key figure, as far as Milan was concerned, in the debate on Dante. The dispute on literature and Milanese had taken place in 1759–60 and had become known as the Brandana, after the man who had started it.[1]

---

1   On the Brandana see G. Salinari, "Una polemica linguistica a Milano nel sec. XVIII", *Cultura neolatina*, 4–5 (1944–45), 61–92; M. Sansone, "Relazioni fra la letteratura italiana e le letterature dialettali", in *Letterature comparate*, edited by A. Viscardi (Milan, Marzorati, 1948), pp. 261–327.

Onofrio Branda had attacked dialect in general and Milanese in particular, saying that one ought to write in Tuscan only, that is, in the standard language, for by using Tuscan one could avoid affectation and write with naturalness, while Milanese was simply the language of the kitchen, the stockpot and such like. The counter-attack from the Milanese intelligentsia had come immediately, with Balestrieri and Parini taking leading roles. The most cogent arguments in defence of Milanese, however, were Parini's. He did not simply defend dialects but stated that dialects are in fact superior to the standard language because of their naturalness and spontaneity; in particular he exalted the special nature of the Milanese dialect. He took it for granted that each language, and therefore each dialect, has its own *carattere* ["character"], and stated that Milanese above all was characterized by simplicity, clarity and naturalness, and was the ideal language in which to express the true nature of things, without the unnecessary filter of rhetorical devices.[1] What Parini was in fact doing was restating, within a new context, the principle which had been the slogan of the *linea lombarda* ever since the time of Maggi in the seventeenth century. It is in one of Maggi's plays that we find the maid Beltramina uttering the statement which was thenceforth quoted whenever the Lombard tradition needed to be reaffirmed. Milanese, says Beltramina, is "una lengua correnta, averta e ciæra, / che apposta la pær fæ / par dì la veritæ" ["a fluent, open, and clear language, which seems as if it had been made on purpose just to tell the truth"].[2] This image of the Lombard tradition was strongly present in the Milanese cultural milieu when Porta began to write.

It was Parini too who had made some of the most interesting remarks on the status and importance of Dante. In the eighteenth century Dante, far from being despised and neglected as some have claimed, was mostly regarded as a great poet, sometimes also a great thinker, though it was generally considered that he was a great poet in spite of some unfortunate shortcomings. On the whole, most writers who engaged with the Dante question agreed that Dante's main defect was the way he wrote: he was messy, incomprehensible and lacking in good taste; to put it bluntly, he

---

1   G. Parini, *Prose*, edited by E. Bellorini, 2 vols (Bari, Laterza, 1913), I, 71, 54–55.

2   *Il concorso de' Meneghini*, in C. M. Maggi, *Il teatro milanese*, edited by D. Isella, 2 vols (Turin, Einaudi, 1964), I, 820.

wrote badly.[1] Parini, though, went a step further than this. While regretting that Dante had not written better than he had and stating that in fact good taste in Italian literature had begun only with Petrarch, he nevertheless acknowledged that Dante had the great merit of having rebelled against the barbarous Latin of his times; he had dared to use his own vernacular, the Tuscan vernacular, not just for mundane everyday things but for lofty things as well. It was Dante, says Parini, who helped Italians to realize that all languages and not just Latin, and certainly not the barbarous Latin of the Middle Ages, could be used to talk of sublime matters.[2]

What Parini says about Dante, particularly as it comes from someone so closely and visibly associated with the defence of the Lombard tradition, should perhaps help us make sense of at least some of the rationale behind Porta's decision to translate Dante into Milanese. Porta's systematic filtering of the matter of Dante's *Inferno* through a process which lowers the tone but also enhances its referentiality, with the effect of making things more concrete, more literal and in a sense more "real", should be linked both to the belief that Milanese, with its special characteristics of simplicity and naturalness, was the ideal medium for such a process, and to the notion that Dante actually needed this kind of improvement, clarification and rationalization. Furthermore, I would suggest that, as well as an element of "improvement" of Dante, and therefore of critique of Dante, Porta's translation also contains an element of emulation of Dante. By translating Dante from what had become the language of the high literary tradition into the language of the people, one could be doing something very similar to what, according to Parini, Dante himself had done in moving away from the Latin of his own day and daring to use the Tuscan vernacular for the treatment of lofty matters. In this respect it may be significant that the only instance of overt discourse on dialect in Porta's translation opposes the Milanese dialect not to Italian but to Latin.

1   On views of Dante in the eighteenth century see: A. Vallone, *La critica dantesca nel Settecento ed altri saggi danteschi* (Florence, Olschki, 1961); R. Frattarolo, *Studi su Dante dal Trecento all'età romantica* (Ravenna, Longo, 1970); *Dante: The Critical Heritage*, edited by M. Caesar (London–New York, Routledge, 1989); D. Pietropaolo, *Dante Studies in the Age of Vico* (Ottawa, Dovehouse, 1989); and above all, C. Dionisotti, "Varia fortuna di Dante", in his *Geografia e storia*, pp. 205–42.

2   G. Parini, "Principi generali e particolari delle belle lettere", in his *Poesie e prose*, edited by L. Caretti (Milan–Naples, Ricciardi, 1951), pp. 723–29.

This is filtered through Virgil, at the point where the latter speaks for the first time, his famous "Poeta fui" being rendered as "ho faa el Bosin". Virgil, that is to say, is made to identify with the traditional Lombard plebeian poet. He then goes on to express his regret at not having written his poem in Lombard dialect. While a literal reading would take us no further than this, a metrical reading clearly reveals the opposition between "lattin" and the Lombard dialect tradition, whose signs, "bosin" and "meneghin", are made to frame the name of Virgil's language:

Poeta fui, e cantai di quel giusto
figliuol d'Anchise che venne di Troia,
poi che 'l superbo Iliön fu combusto.
(*Inferno*, I. 73–75)

Voeutt de pù?... Te diroo ch'hoo faa el Bosin
e che hoo scritt on poemma, ma sul sciall,
sora Eneja e el foeugh d'Illi in vers lattin,
e te diroo che voreva anch brusall
per ghignon de no avell faa in meneghin.
(L. 97–101)

[I was a poet, and I sang of that just son of Anchises who came from Troy after proud Ilium was burned.]

[Do you want to know more?... I'll say that I was a storyteller and that I wrote a poem, but a swanky one, on Aeneas and the fire of Troy in Latin verses, and I'll say that I even wanted to burn it, because I was angry for not writing it in Milanese.]

As may be seen, the section which contains the rhyme "lattin:meneghin" is a completely new insertion, not present in Dante at all. It is however present in another piece of Milanese poetry, written some ten years earlier than Porta's text and which Porta knew very well—the introductory poem to the Milanese translation of the ancient *Batrachomyomachia* by Alessandro Garioni:[1]

> On poemma compost in gregh de Omer,
> d'on Villeri tradott in vers Latin,
> in vers toscan d'on Dolci, d'on Malpier,
> d'un Ricci, d'un Del Sart, Ridolf, Salvin:
> possibel mò che un Magg, on Balestrer,
> no se sien miss a trall in meneghin!

[A poem written in Greek by Homer, translated into Latin verses by a Villeri, and into Tuscan verses by a Dolci, a Malpiero, a Ricci, a Del Sarto, Ridolfi, Salvini: how come a Maggi, a Balestrieri did not set out to turn it into Milanese?]

---

1   Published in vol. x (pp. 7–40) of Cherubini's *Collezione*, this is a partial translation of the pseudo-Homeric parody epic. It was originally published in 1793.

Garioni was one of the Milanese writers mentioned in Porta's poem which celebrates the Lombard dialect tradition ("Varon, Magg, Balestrer, Tanz e Parin": XVI), and his Lombard *Batraco-miomachia di Omero* is listed among the books in Porta's own library.[1] All the available evidence in fact points to Porta's thorough familiarity with the recent translations of classics into Milanese. His library included not only Garioni's *Batracomiomachia* but also, according to Cherubini, part of the manuscript of Francecso Bellati's 1773 translation of *Orlando furioso*,[2] in addition, as one would expect, to a copy of Balestrieri's translation of Tasso's *Gerusalemme liberata*. What emerges from all this is a picture of Porta constructing his Lombard Dante as something new and original but also as something firmly linked to a well-known and well loved-tradition.

There is no doubt that Balestrieri was Porta's most immediate model on this count. In fact the very first line of Porta's translation of Canto I ("A mitaa straa de quel gran viacc"), apparently so close to Dante's original, turns out to be an almost literal quotation from Balestrieri, not from his *Gerusalemme liberata* in this case, but from one of his own poems (*Rime*, V. 55); and at the end of Porta's first Dante *ottava* the description of the frightening wood in terms of the fear induced by the witches' sabbath ("pesc che nè quell del baril-lott di strij") is again a near-quotation from Balestrieri, this time from the description of Ismeno's wood in *Gerusalemme liberata* ("i strij [...] al barilott": XIII. 4. 1–4). A detailed textual comparison between Porta's Dante and Balestrieri's Tasso has yet to be carried out,[3] but even a cursory examination reveals frequent borrowings, often in those very sections of Porta's text which add something "new" to Dante's text, as indeed is the case with the comparison between the dark wood and the witches' sabbath at the end of the first *ottava*. Such is the case too with the addition of "Tucc dormiven: nè gh'eva in tutt Milan/fors gnanch cent lengu de Dònn, che se movess" ["All slept: and in the whole of Milan there were perhaps

1   The content of Porta's library is known from a handwritten list entitled "Elenco e stima dei libri del Sig. Carlo Porta", kept at the Archivio Storico Civico in Milan (RP I 5a.4, c. [5]r). I am extremely grateful to Pierantonio Frare for providing me with a print of the relevant microfilm.

2   "Due [of the cantos of *Orlando furioso* translated by Bellati] di fatto se ne tro-vano ancora manoscritti nella libreria del valente poeta milanese il Sig. Carlo Porta" (F. Cherubini, *Collezione*, II, 73).

3   A brief but penetrating comparative analysis is to be found in F. Milani, "Balestrieri e Porta traduttori", in *La poesia di Carlo Porta e la tradizione mila-nese*, pp. 119–27.

not even a hundred women's tongues wagging"] to the description of the end of the day at the beginning of the translation of Canto II (CXV. 3–4), which reproduces II. 96. 1–6 of Balestrieri's *Gerusalemme liberata*. It is also the case with the designation of God's mind as the "scervell de quell che stà dessora ai tecc" ["the brain of him who lives above the roofs"; CXV. 37—from *Gerusalemme liberata, XIV*. 82], with Pluto making "on rabadan del trenta para" ["one hell of a din"; CXVIII. 3—from *Gerusalemme liberata, I*. 37), and many more.

Balestrieri's is the closest and most visible of Porta's intertexts, but not the only one. I suggested earlier that Porta's sporadic use of the past historic, obsolete in his own day, represents an act of homage to the Lombard tradition of the past. Archaisms of all kinds, lexical and grammatical as well as metrical, are present in Porta's text, and many of them may be traced to Maggi, for example "s'cess" for "pity" (CXV. 6), "marmoria" for "memory" (CXV. 15), "tiatter" for "theatre", which in its turn rhymes with "scarpiatter" ["blunder"; CXV. 17 and 21], as in Maggi's *Concorso dei Meneghini* (604 and 605). Porta's Milanese translation of *Inferno*, then, would appear to be filtered through quotations from, allusions to and echoes of that *linea lombarda* which provides the very rationale for such a translation, with Balestrieri as his immediate model, and further in the background the classic figure of the founding father of the Lombard tradition, Carlo Maria Maggi.

DANTE AND GEORGE ELIOT

Andrew Thompson

George Eliot might not immediately be linked with Italy in the minds of her readers, who would tend to think of her as the author of *Adam Bede*, *The Mill on the Floss* and *Middlemarch*, all set in parts of rural England. Yet she had a keen interest in Italy and Italian literature. She learned Italian at an early age and was reading in Italian by the summer of 1840.[1] She visited Italy on five occasions, spending a total of about five months on Italian soil, and also wrote an "Italian novel", *Romola*, set in the fifteenth-century Florence of Savonarola. In her mature novels—those written and published after 1861, namely *Romola*, *Felix Holt, the Radical*, *Middlemarch* and *Daniel Deronda*—there is an increased interest in Italy and its literature, and as we shall see she comes increasingly to draw upon the works of Dante, to the point where in her last book Dante becomes an essential part of the novel's organization.

We do not know when Eliot first read Dante. The letters tell us that she re-read *Purgatorio* in Italian from the autumn of 1862 to January 1863.[2] Works in the George Eliot/G. H. Lewes Library include *Dante, opere minori* (published in 1855–57), *The Divine Comedy* (in John A. Carlyle's translation of 1865), Cesare Balbo's *Vita di Dante* and Ozanam's *Dante et la philosophie catholique au treizième siècle*. It is likely, however, that Eliot read far more on Dante than the material in her own library would indicate, and she probably became acquainted with his work sometime in the early to mid-1850s.[3] The first definite reference to Dante I have found in the novels is in *The Mill on the Floss*, published in 1860.[4]

1   *The George Eliot Letters*, edited by G. S. Haight, 9 vols (New Haven–London, Oxford University Press, 1954–78), I, 53.
2   F. Bonaparte, *The Triptych and the Cross: The Central Myths of George Eliot's Poetic Imagination* (New York, New York University Press, 1979), p. 26.
3   F. Bonaparte, *The Triptych and the Cross*, p. 26.
4   George Eliot, *The Mill on the Floss*, edited by A. S. Byatt (Harmondsworth, Penguin, 1985). There is only one explicit reference to Dante in this novel,

The present essay will examine some of the ways in which George Eliot uses Dante and her purposes in doing so, by focusing in some detail on parts of three of her novels, *Romola*, *Middlemarch* and *Daniel Deronda*.[1] In her use of Dante Eliot has recourse to a number of techniques: parallel scenes (mirroring those in the *Commedia*), echoes (often in the choice of one or two words or phrases inserted into a passage), paraphrase (which may be serious or comic in its intent) and direct quotation (often as epigraphs, or "mottoes" as Eliot herself called them). Sometimes she follows Dante's narrative scheme closely or employs Dantesque imagery, which is often assimilated into her text without direct reference to Dante. It seems, too, that she had a few favourite images and scenes from Dante which she drew on more than once and which appear to have had particular significance for her. We may look to Eliot's notebooks and "quarries", in which she made notes on her reading and which she "mined" for material for the novels, as evidence of her sustained interest in and integration of Dante into her novels.[2] There are also a number of references to Dante in the late essays, where her comments throw some light on Eliot's own relationship to Dante.

Romola is George Eliot's "historical" novel, set in Florence at the end of the fifteenth century, the time of Savonarola's Florentine Republic.[3] One might have expected to find Dante as an imposing presence in this novel, but apart from three early references and a comic paraphrase, *il divino poeta* seems curiously absent. In the Proem to the novel Eliot invokes the spirit of a fifteenth-century Florentine and has him muse on the events in his city after his

---

to the account of Ugolino in *Inferno* XXXIII: "Does not the Hunger Tower stand as the type of the utmost trial to what is human in us?" (pp. 430–31).

1   I have discussed Eliot's use of Dante in *Felix Holt, the Radical* in my "George Eliot, Dante and Moral Choice in *Felix Holt, the Radical*", *The Modern Language Review*, 86 (1991), 553–66.

2   Many of these notebooks have been published. Of particular interest for Eliot's use of Dante are: *Some George Eliot Notebooks: An Edition of the Carl H. Pforzheimer Library's George Eliot Holograph Notebooks MSS 707–711* edited by W. Baker, 4 vols (Salzburg, Universität Salzburg, 1976–85), especially vols II and III; *George Eliot: A Writer's Notebook 1854–1879*, edited by J. Wiesenfarth (Virginia, University of Virginia, 1981); *George Eliot's "Middlemarch" Notebooks: A Transcription*, edited by J. C. Pratt and V. A. Neufeldt (Berkeley–Los Angeles–London, Univesity of California Press, 1979).

3   All quotations are from George Eliot, *Romola*, edited by D. Barrett (London, Penguin, 1996).

death: "What famous scholar is dictating the Latin letters of the Republic—what fiery philosopher is lecturing on Dante in the Duomo [...]?" (p. 7). Chapter 1 opens:

> The Loggia de' Cerchi stood in the heart of old Florence, within a labyrinth of narrow streets behind the Badia, now rarely threaded by the stranger, unless in a dubious search for a certain severely simple door-place, bearing this inscription:
>
> QUI NACQUE IL DIVINO POETA
>
> To the ear of Dante, the same streets rang with the shout and clash of fierce battle between rival families; but in the fifteenth century, they were only noisy with the unhistorical quarrels and broad jests of wool-carders in the cloth-producing quarters of San Martino and Garbo.
>
> (*Romola*, p. 11)

Later in the same chapter there is a conversation in a barber's shop about the death of Lorenzo de' Medici: "'It appears the Magnifico is dead—rest his soul!—and the price of wax will rise?' [...] 'Ah! a great man—a great politician—a greater poet than Dante'" (p. 18). Finally, there is a jocular exchange between one of the main characters, Tito Melema, and Nello the barber. A comic paraphrase of Dante is used by Nello to ask what brings Tito to Nello's shop: "'Let me see the very needle's eye of your desire, as the sublime poet says, that I may thread it.' 'That is but a tailor's image of your sublime poet's,' said Tito" (pp. 130–31). The reference here is to Dante the character's comment on a question put to him by Virgil in *Purgatorio*, XXI. 37–38: "Sí mi diè, dimandando, per la cruna / del mio disio" ["By his question he so threaded the needle of my desire"].[1]

All these references appear to be little more than "local colour" which, as Andrew Sanders has observed, is "laid on with a trowel" in *Romola*;[2] but it has been convincingly argued that the presence of Dante (along with references to Homer and Virgil) is an indication of Eliot's intentions in *Romola*, for her project is to write a modern epic "to explore the present in the context of the past, and to probe,

---

1   Translations of passages from the *Commedia* are taken from Dante Alighieri, *The Divine Comedy*, translated by J. D. Sinclair, 3 vols (New York, Oxford University Press, 1971).

2   A. Sanders, Introduction to G. Eliot, *Romola*, edited by A. Sanders (London, Penguin, 1980), p. 16.

at the same time, the eternal human condition".[1] She embodies
"the progress of western civilization" symbolically in her main
characters: Greece in the Dionysian Tito Melema, Rome in Romola's
Stoic father (a Renaissance scholar), the Christian world in Romola's
brother Dino and in Savonarola, and the modern world in Romola
herself, who comes under the influence of each of the other characters, assimilates them in her own synthesis and thus represents
Eliot's (somewhat Positivist) modern world view. Eliot's "epic
project" is akin to that of Dante. Dante was the "locus" of the meeting of pagan and Christian worlds, and could be seen as the
spokesman for the world view of the modern Christian vision.
Like Dante, Eliot was trying to express universal truths through
particular experience.

There are signs that a larger role in the book was being prepared for Dante. Eliot had planned to use "mottoes" appropriate
to the theme of each chapter, and had chosen them for the first nine
chapters. One of these was to have been taken from Dante,[2] but in
the end they all remained unused owing to the problems of serial
publication in the *Cornhill Magazine*. There is however one scene in
Romola where Dante's influence may be clearly felt. At the end of
the book Tito, who has betrayed everybody, including his wife
Romola, is captured by an aroused mob. He escapes by throwing
himself off the Ponte Vecchio into the Arno. The river carries him
along unconscious, but he is thrown up on the bank at the feet of
Baldassare, the old man who had raised him as his own child and
whom Tito had subsequently robbed and left a prisoner of the
Turks. Baldassare, who has tracked Tito down, waits for him to
regain consciousness before taking his revenge: "He pressed his
knuckles against the round throat [...]. He would never loose his
hold till some one came and found them. [...] he [...] would declare
that he had killed this traitor, to whom he had once been a father.
[...] then he would desire to die with his hold on this body, and
follow the traitor to hell that he might clutch him there." Baldassare
dies holding Tito and the two are found later: "The aged man had

1   F. Bonaparte, *The Triptych and the Cross*, p. 29.
2   The "mottoe" originally intended for Chapter 2 of *Romola* is taken from *Pur-
    gatorio* XXXIII and was to provide a comment on the impressionable nature of
    Tessa, a peasant girl, whom Tito has promised to marry: "Come anima gen-
    til, che non fa scusa, / ma fa sua voglia de la voglia altrui / tosto che è per se-
    gno fuor dischiusa" (lines 130–32).

fallen forward, and his dead clutch was on the garment of the other. It was not possible to separate them" (p. 548). Eliot's scene is a parallel to that of the traitors Ugolino and Ruggieri in *Inferno* XXXIII: the dramatic visual image, so redolent of Dante's, at once points up Tito's essential inhumanity and also conveys Eliot's own final judgement on him.[1]

In *Middlemarch* George Eliot chose two quotations from Dante to serve as epigraphs: one is taken from the *Vita nuova*, the other from the *Commedia*. The epigraph to Chapter 19 of the novel comes from *Purgatorio* VII—"L'altra vedete ch'ha fatto alla guancia / Della sua palma, sospirando, letto" ["See the other, who couches his cheek on his hand and sighs"; lines 107–08]—, while the one to Chapter 54 is the sonnet ("Negli occhi porta la mia donna Amore") in Chapter XXI of the *Vita nuova*.[2] The image from *Purgatorio* is one which is repeatedly used by Eliot as a striking static image of suffering.[3] In *Middlemarch* it precedes a chapter in which we meet Dorothea standing before a statue of Ariadne in the Vatican Museum in Rome, where she is seen by Will Ladislaw and his painter friend, Naumann:

> They were just in time to see another figure standing against a pedestal near the reclining marble: a breathing, blooming girl, whose form, not shamed by the Ariadne, was clad in Quakerish grey drapery; her long cloak, fastened at the neck, was thrown backward from her arms, and one beautiful ungloved hand pillowed her cheek, pushing somewhat backward the white beaver bonnet which made a sort of halo to her face around the simply braided dark-brown hair. She was not looking at the

1   A similar scene in which a father betrays a son is present in *Felix Holt, the Radical* (London–Melbourne–Toronto, Dent, 1983), pp. 561–63.

2   Note that in the former case Eliot changes the gender of the person referred to in the quotation, from the masculine "l'altro" to the feminine "l'altra", in order to fit her heroine, Dorothea. "L'altro" in Dante's *Purgatorio* is Henry of Navarre.

3   Twice in *Middlemarch* (edited by W. J. Harvey [London, Penguin, 1971]: the epigraph to Chapter 19; and Chapter 55, pp. 592–93), once in *Felix Holt, the Radical*, (p. 432; see also my "George Eliot, Dante and Moral Choice", p. 557) and in *Daniel Deronda* in relation to Gwendolen: "She rose from the low ottoman where she had been sitting purposeless, and walked up and down the drawing-room, resting her elbow on one palm while she leaned down her cheek on the other, and a slow tear fell" (edited by B. Hardy [London, Penguin, 1967], p. 335). All subsequent quotations from *Middlemarch* and *Daniel Deronda* are taken from these editions.

sculpture, probably not thinking of it: her large eyes were fixed
dreamily on a streak of sunlight which fell across the floor.

(Middlemarch, p. 220)

Dorothea has begun to realize her mistake in marrying Casaubon
(whom she admired for his intellect and his scholarly endeavours),
and the image of Dantean suffering prefigures her suffering in the
next chapter, where we find her "sobbing bitterly" when left alone
(p. 224). George Eliot also employs her own light imagery (which
reminds us of Dante's in the canto from which the epigraph is
taken) when talking of Dorothea's "eyes [...] fixed dreamily on a
streak of sunlight". Again in the following chapter: "Her view of
Mr Casaubon and her wifely relation, now that she was married to
him, was gradually changing [...]. [...] whatever else remained the
same, the light had changed, and you cannot find the pearly dawn
at noonday" (pp. 226–27).

It is important to note that the quotation from Dante comes
from *Purgatorio*. Not always does Eliot give the sources of her
epigraphs in the chapters themselves, but here the origin is clearly
indicated. We are thus made aware that Dorothea's suffering is
purgatorial, intimating hope and growth, rather than infernal, like
that of Mrs Transome in the previous novel, *Felix Holt, the Radical*,
where the same image is used, but where the woman to whom it
applies remains unredeemed.[1] In *Purgatorio* VII, the canto which
represents the Valley of the Princes, containing the souls of rulers
who repented at the last moment, Virgil tells the Christian poet
Sordello:

> Non per far, ma per non fare ho perduto
> a veder l'alto Sol che tu disiri
> e che fu tardi per me conosciuto.
>
> (Purgatorio, VII. 25–27)

[Not for doing, but for not doing, I have lost the sight of the Sun
above for which thou longest and which was known by me too
late.]

The sun in the *Commedia* represents the face, the promise, of God.
Locally, the light imagery associated with Dorothea in *Middlemarch* may be "negative", but the promise of redemption is there
in the epigraph from *Purgatorio*, to be fulfilled at the end of the

---

1   See my "George Eliot, Dante and Moral Choice", pp. 553–66.

novel (Book VIII), when Dorothea renounces wealth and position to marry Will Ladislaw. The strands of sun and light imagery are drawn together in the title of Book VIII, "Sunset and Sunrise". Thus the image and the echoes (in the light imagery) from *Purgatorio* VII are allowed to bear a precise significance locally within the novel (Dorothea's realization of her mistake in marrying Casaubon) but they also take on significance in the wider context of the novel as a whole, where—to use one of Eliot's favourite metaphors—a web of connections is created stretching outwards from the initial image.

The second of Eliot's Dante epigraphs bears a close relation to the first and also becomes part of the web of Dante connections in the novel. The sonnet from Chapter XXI of the *Vita nuova* which appears, in its entirety, much further on in *Middlemarch*, as an epigraph to Book VI, entitled "The Widow and the Wife", is one of the poems in which Dante discovers his "praise style"; it thus marks a moment of poise in the central section of the *Vita nuova*. On one level, Eliot's choice gives us a simple indication of the fact that Will is in love with Dorothea. The possessive adjective "mia" and the noun "donna" of "Negli occhi porta la mia donna Amore" are easily equated with Will and Dorothea respectively, who appear in the chapter which follows. The position of this sonnet in the *Vita nuova*, however, is such that it prefigures Dante's loss of Beatrice, for in the next chapter Dante has the shocking realization (provoked by the death of Beatrice's father) that she herself must die and will thus be unreachable. An immediate connection between Eliot's novel and Dante's poem is the *vite nuove* embarked upon by Dorothea in being newly widowed and Will in renouncing any claim to Dorothea, and the seemingly eternal separation of the two caused by the "dead hand" of the jealous Casaubon, who has had a clause inserted into his will stipulating that if Dorothea should marry Will she shall be disinherited. Indeed, in this chapter Will comes to say goodbye to Dorothea, and for most of Book VI they are apart. But we may also link this epigraph to Chapter 19, where, as we have seen, Dorothea was portrayed in the Dantean attitude of suffering.

In that earlier chapter a number of attempts are made by the male observers to figure Dorothea. The painter Naumann represents her as "the most perfect young Madonna" and then as "a sort of Christian Antigone—sensuous force controlled by spiritual passion". Will Ladislaw, however, refuses to accept the merely visual representation: "As if a woman were a mere coloured superficies!

You must wait for movement and tone." To this the painter retorts:
"I see, I see. You are jealous. No man must presume to think that
he can paint your ideal" (pp. 221–22). By the end of the chapter, and
after Naumann's joke that Dorothea, in being married to Will's
second cousin (Casaubon) is in fact Will's great-aunt, Will is "conscious of being irritated [...]. [...] he felt as if something had
happened to him with regard to her" (pp. 222–23). Now, Dante's
sonnet dwells on the power of Beatrice's eyes to affect men:

> Ne li occhi porta la mia donna Amore,
> per che si fa gentil ciò ch'ella mira;
> ov' ella passa, ogn' uom ver lei si gira,
> e cui saluta fa tremar lo core.
>
> (*Vita nuova*, XXI. 2)

> [Love is encompassed in my Lady's eyes
> Whence she ennobles all she looks upon.
> Where'er she walks, the gaze of everyone
> She draws; in him she greets, such tremors rise,
> All pale, he turns his face away and sighs.][1]

It also dwells on the power of her voice:

> Ogne dolcezza, ogne pensero umile
> nasce nel core a chi parlar la sente.
>
> (*Vita nuova*, XXI. 3)

> [All gentleness and all humility
> When she is heard to speak in hearts unfold.]

In his commentary on the sonnet, Dante says:

Ne la prima parte dico sí come virtuosamente fae gentile tutto ciò
che vede, e questo è tanto a dire quanto inducere Amore in potenzia là ove non è; ne la seconda dico come reduce in atto Amore
ne li cuori di tutti coloro cui vede.

> (*Vita nuova*, XXI. 6)

[In the first I speak of her miraculous power of ennobling
everything she sees, and this amounts to saying that she calls

---

1   The English translations given are from Dante Alighieri, *Vita Nuova* (*Poems
     of Youth*), translated by Barbara Reynolds (London, Penguin, 1969), pp. 60–
     61.

Love into potentiality where he is not; in the second I say how she actualizes Love in the hearts of all whom she sees.]

When Dorothea is standing against the background of the Ariadne statue, "her large eyes [...] fixed dreamily on a streak of sunlight", and the men are discussing how she should be represented, Will says, "How would you paint her voice, pray? But her voice is much diviner than anything you have seen of her" (p. 222). So in Will's irritation and his feeling that "something had happened to him with regard to her" we may see that Dorothea, too, has the power to "inducere Amore in potenzia" and "reduce[re] in atto Amore". Dante's *Vita nuova* (and the Dante/Beatrice relationship) is also just below the surface in Chapter 19, therefore, though we only obtain confirmation of this 350 pages later in the book. It seems, moreover, that we have a replaying of Dante's experience in the character of Will Ladislaw, or possibly a structuring of Will's experience through that of Dante in the *Vita nuova*. But "literary readings" are not altogether to be trusted in *Middlemarch*. The appearance of the sonnet at the beginning of Book VI and the promising opening line "Negli occhi porta la mia donna Amore" lead us to expect some development in the Will/Dorothea relationship: we naturally think of the poem as referring to the couple and accept it as an expression of Will's sentiments. But George Eliot is merely leading us on a false trail, for Book VI ends as it begins with Will—who is unable to stay away—coming back to take his leave of Dorothea once again.

Barbara Hardy has drawn attention to Will's tendency to read life through literature and to allow literature to structure his emotions to the point where he is ultimately "misguided and let down by literary expectation" and led to make "a simplification about the nature, place and power of feeling" in the world of *Middlemarch*, where George Eliot tries to deal plainly with unideal existence.[1] Will, who also composes his own poetry ("O me, O me, what frugal cheer/My love doth feed upon!": p. 512), was "educated in the passions of literature",[2] and "was conscious of a generous movement, and of verifying in his own experience that higher love-poetry which had charmed his fancy. Dorothea, he said to himself, was for ever enthroned in his soul: no other woman could

1   B. Hardy, "*Middlemarch* and the Passions", in her *Particularities: Readings in George Eliot* (London, Peter Owen, 1982), pp. 88, 95, 100.
2   B. Hardy, "*Middlemarch* and the Passions", p. 96.

sit higher than her footstool" (p. 510). But, as Hardy points out, his motives are anything but pure. The source of his love for Dorothea is connected to Casaubon's jealousy: part of his design in going to church, ostensibly in the hope of seeing Dorothea, is the thought of annoying Casaubon, who has made it clear that he wants no contact with Will. In a similar incident in Chapter 37—prefaced this time by a sonnet by Spenser ("Thrice happy she that is so well assured / Unto herself, and settled so in heart")—Will devises a plan to go sketching near Dorothea's house on the path where she often walks, but his stratagem is foiled by the weather, for it begins to rain. The everyday world of the novel is forever intruding into Will's literary world of sonnets, and this prompts Eliot to comment: "However slight the terrestrial intercourse between Dante and Beatrice or Petrarch and Laura, time changes the proportion of things, and in later days it is preferable to have fewer sonnets and more conversation" (p. 397)—which makes the appearance of Dante's sonnet seventeen chapters later seem rather ironic.

Will's courtly mode of loving and of controlling his passions is therefore anachronistic and his "worship, adoration, higher love-poetry, [enthroned] queens and footstools are innapropriate images —says Hardy—for love in the quotidian world of *Middlemarch*". And she concludes: "In a way George Eliot seems to know this, or at least to glimpse the deficiency of those troubadour images."[1] I would in fact go further than this and say that Eliot is fully aware of their inappropriateness, but that she actually wants to encourage multiple interpretations of the text even if her readers are, like Will, temporarily misled by the literary expectations arising from Dante's sonnet.

The use of "Negli occhi porta la mia donna Amore" as the epigraph to Chapter 54 is in some senses highly inappropriate, then, and Eliot, I believe, knows this. It both continues and undermines the courtly form of worship chosen by Will—continues, in that it allows one to predict and holds out the hope of a final union of the two lovers, and undermines, in that this love takes place in the world of *Middlemarch*, where motives are mixed and expectations thwarted. It may be said, therefore, that Eliot's selections from Dante in *Middlemarch* present a (rather unsuccessful) attempt to reconcile the ideal, timeless moment of pure passion to the everyday world of the novel. The web of connections, the

---

1   B. Hardy, "*Middlemarch* and the Passions", p. 98.

echoes and resonances built around the Dante epigraphs and allusions stretch both backwards and forwards through the novel and contribute to the multiple readings which Eliot encourages.

In her last novel, *Daniel Deronda*, George Eliot has echoes, allusions, parallel scenes and direct references to Dante running through the book, especially in the second half. Dante serves to illustrate the moral growth through suffering of the heroine, Gwendolen, and the world of the *Commedia* is translated into the psychological world of the novel. The large body of allusions to Dante centres principally on Gwendolen and her relationship with her husband Grandcourt and her mentor Daniel Deronda. It is not possible to do justice to all of it here, so I shall try to illustrate how Dante is employed in four identifiable stages of Gwendolen's journey. These stages are:

1   Gwendolen's sin in marrying the rich Grandcourt for wealth and position, without the least sentiment of love on either part and in the knowledge that Grandcourt has a mistress;
2   Gwendolen's relationship with her husband Grandcourt (which marks the advent of the Dantean *contrapasso*);
3   Gwendolen's dependence on Daniel Deronda (cast in the role of a Virgil figure) and her oscillation between infernal and purgatorial states;
4   Daniel Deronda's abandoning of Gwendolen.

The book opens with a gambling scene in which Gwendolen pawns a necklace; the action is emblematic of her gambling away her moral integrity by marrying Grandcourt, after the loss of her own family fortune and the prospect of becoming a governess, even though she knows he has a mistress, Mrs Glasher. On returning from their honeymoon, Gwendolen receives a package containing some diamonds, which Grandcourt has asked his former mistress to return to him for his wife, as well as a letter to Gwendolen from Mrs Glasher, to whom she had previously promised not to marry Grandcourt. The letter contains both a Dante-like judgement on Gwendolen and a terrible prophecy of the future awaiting her, a prophecy which will be fulfilled in the novel:

> These diamonds, which were once given with ardent love to Lydia Glasher, she passes on to you. You have broken your word to her, that you might possess what was hers [...]. The man you have married has a withered heart. His best young love was mine; you could not take that from me when you took the rest.

It is dead; but I am the grave in which your chance of happiness is buried as well as mine. You had your warning. You have chosen to injure me and my children [...]. He would have married me at last, if you had not broken your word. You will have your punishment. I desire it with all my soul [...]. Shall you like to stand before your husband with these diamonds on you, and these words of mine in his thoughts and yours? Will he think you have any right to complain when he has made you miserable? You took him with your eyes open. The willing wrong you have done me will be your curse.

(*Daniel Deronda*, p. 406)

This curse will echo through the pages of the novel, holding out the prospect of a damnation on the lines of Dante, for indeed what distinguishes the sinners in Dante who go to Hell from those who do not is that the former actively will and continue to desire their sins.

In Lydia Glasher's letter Gwendolen's sins are described as being those of betrayal and theft ("You have broken your word to her, that you might possess what was hers"), and when describing the opening of the jewel case which contains the diamonds, George Eliot subtly introduces the imagery which characterizes these sins in *Inferno* (imagery which will then recur throughout the novel): "She felt no doubt that she had the diamonds. But on opening the case, in the same instant that she saw their gleam she saw a letter lying above them. She knew the handwriting of the address. It was as if an adder had lain on them" (p. 406). In a spasm of terror Gwendolen consigns the letter to the flames of the fire in her mirror-filled dressing room before falling "back in her chair again helpless. She could not see the reflections of herself then: they were like so many women petrified white [...]. She sat so for a long while, knowing little more than that she was feeling ill, and that those written words kept repeating themselves in her" (p. 407). Along with the flames of the fire in Gwendolen's dressing room (the archetypal symbol of the Christian Hell), adders and multiple reflections of people petrified white, which set up echoes of the serpents in the thieves' *bolgia* and of the betrayers compelled to look upon their own reflections in the frozen ice of Cocytus, are the first fleeting glimpse of the punishments to come. They signal the onset of the Dantean *contrapasso*.[1]

---

1   A similar scene, in which the betrayer sees himself in the mirror at the moment of betrayal, occurs in *Felix Holt, the Radical*, where the lawyer☐Jermyn

The relationship between Gwendolen and her husband Grandcourt is described as one of mastery and subjection. Grandcourt
likes to exert his power over his pet dogs by making them feel
jealous, and his manservant talks of him, behind his back, as a
"tyrannous patron". Of his future wife Grandcourt thinks that "to
be worth his mastering it was proper that she should have some
spirit" (p. 195), and only seven weeks into their marriage the
narrator comments:

> Her husband had gained a mastery which she could no more
> resist than she could have resisted the benumbing effect from the
> touch of a torpedo. Gwendolen's will had seemed imperious in
> its small girlish sway; but [...] she had found a will like that of a
> crab or a boa-constrictor which goes on pinching or crushing
> without alarm at thunder. [...] Grandcourt [...] had a surprising
> acuteness in detecting that situation of feeling in Gwendolen
> which made her proud and rebellious spirit dumb and helpless
> before him.
>
> (*Daniel Deronda*, pp. 477–78)

Here again we have the serpent imagery, and Grandcourt is further described as "a handsome lizard of a hitherto unknown☐species,
not of the lively, darting kind" (pp. 173–74) and as looking "as
neutral as an alligator" (p. 195). We also have images of serpents
crushing (pp. 477–78), of Gwendolen's hair being gathered up to
make a coil (p. 340), of strangling and throttling (p. 651) and of
Gwendolen being throttled by Grandcourt: "The thought of his
dying would not subsist: it turned as with a dream-change into the
terror that she should die with his throttling fingers on her neck
avenging that thought" (p. 669). And at the end of the book Gwendolen comes to see her experience as "a long Satanic masquerade,
which she had entered on with an intoxicated belief in its disguises,
and had seen the end of in shrieking fear lest she herself had
become one of the evil spirits who were dropping their human
mummery and hissing around her with serpent tongues" (p. 831).

All this imagery is deliberately evocative of *Inferno* xxv, where
Dante recounts with horror and disbelief the transformation of
human forms into those of serpents winding around one another.
Gwendolen's world (and her relationship with her husband)

betrays Mrs Transome in revealing to her son that he is his true father. See
my "George Eliot, Dante and Moral Choice", pp. 561–63.

becomes like that of the thieves, where all bonds of human honesty
and trust are dissolved. Grandcourt prefers mastery to love, while
Gwendolen, seemingly unable to love, betrays Lydia Glasher.
With the inexorable progress of the *contrapasso*, the diamonds too
become a coil around Gwendolen's neck when she is compelled to
have Grandcourt fasten them for her and to wear them in public
(p. 482). Moreover, Dante's horror, disbelief and confusion, in *Inferno* xxv, at witnessing the transformation of human forms is
shared by Gwendolen, who, in far more immediate danger of
being caught up in the scene herself than is Dante the character,
vividly imagines her husband "dropping [his] human mummery".
From the outset, Grandcourt is portrayed as having little or no
personality. He displays perennial boredom with life, having "left
off" (p. 147) doing most of the things that a gentleman of means
usually does. Yet his apparent lethargy hides the serpent's traditional cunning, and Eliot's image of him as a "lizard [...], not of the
lively, darting kind" (p. 174) and as a "sleepy-eyed animal" (p. 465)
is suggestive of Dante's description of the transforming serpents in
Inferno:

> Lo trafitto 'l mirò, ma nulla disse;
> anzi, co' piè fermati, sbadigliava
> pur come sonno o febbre l'assalisse.
> (*Inferno*, xxv. 88–90)

[The one transfixed stared at it, but said nothing, only stood still
and yawned, as if sleep or fever had come upon him.]

Throughout this process of transformation Gwendolen herself
remains passive: she never becomes a serpent, but imagines herself
being attacked by her husband as one serpent attacks another in
Dante's scene. It is Grandcourt who throttles and crushes and who
is imagined as a lizard, like Dante's serpents, with legs and claws.
And in the same way as Dante's serpents present an obscene
parody of sexual union, the only union (indeed any kind of
physical contact) between husband and wife in Eliot's novel is this
imagined throttling, coiling and crushing. So too, just as during the
transformation process in *Inferno* xxv there is no sound other than
the hissing of the serpents, Gwendolen realizes that her unnatural
"marriage had nullified all [...] interchange, and Grandcourt had
become a blank uncertainty to her" (p. 480). Eliot thus applies
Dante's imagery to Grandcourt's union with Gwendolen and

registers the same breakdown of communication as accompanies the sinners' total absorption with their sins in the lower regions of Hell. Although Gwendolen herself is saved, she imagines with horrific immediacy that she is participating fully in this transformation. Yet she too undergoes a visible, dehumanizing transformation of sorts. There are clear signs of a withering of the most valuable human qualities in her. "Deronda now marked some hardening in a look and manner which were schooled daily to the suppression of feeling" (p. 667), and on another occasion "there was an indescribable look of suppressed tears in her eyes" (p. 624), which seem to suggest the frozen tears of Cocytus. Finally, there is the complete breakdown in communication between Gwendolen and her husband ("She was dumb": p. 667), which is also possibly reminiscent of Dante's sinners imprisoned in the ice of Cocytus. This imagery is introduced gradually in the second half of the book but begins to crystallize and impinges increasingly on the reader's consciousness. Thus, the second stage in Gwendolen's journey, the *contrapasso*, involves her passing through Dante's thieves' *bolgia* for the sin of theft, before descending lower still into the silence and the frozen human emotion typical of Cocytus. Dante's punishments for these crimes are also Eliot's.

Even when Gwendolen appears to be in the depths of her "Inferno", there are signs that she is not actually damned, for although she has chosen her sin, after the letter from Lydia Glasher she does not actively desire it, and herein lies the crucial difference between those of Dante's sinners who are eternally damned and those who are redeemed. As Moldstadt has noted, Gwendolen is unable to give up the fruits of her sin, but she does not actively desire it.[1]

From the very first scene, where she pawns a necklace to pay for her last game, the figure of Daniel Deronda, the titular hero of the novel, is present to Gwendolen. He redeems the necklace and gives it back to her, thus establishing a bond between them. Indeed, in this act we have a preview of the whole tenor of their relationship, for Deronda is to act as spiritual guide and mentor to Gwendolen, who evidently feels a strong attraction towards him and accepts his counselling. There are many echoes of Dante in this

---

1   D. Moldstadt, "The Dantean Purgatorial Metaphor in *Daniel Deronda*", *Papers on Language and Literature*, 19, i (Winter 1983), 183–98. I am indebted to Moldstadt's article for stimulating a number of the ideas contained in the present essay.

relationship. Deronda is at one point characterized thus: "He had a wonderful power of standing perfectly still, and in that position reminded one sometimes of Dante's *spiriti magni con occhi tardi e gravi*" (p. 500). Here Eliot puts together parts of two lines in *Inferno* IV, referring to the first circle of Hell, the Limbo of the virtuous heathen: "Genti v'eran con occhi tardi e gravi" ["(There) were people with grave and slow-moving eyes"; line 112] and "mi fuor mostrati li spiriti magni" ["There (…) were shown to me the great spirits"; 119]. Foremost among these "spiriti magni" are Homer, Horace, Lucan, Ovid and Virgil. Thus in Eliot's lines we have a connection established between them and Deronda, which five pages later becomes even more specific. Gwendolen, who is on a walk through the grounds of Sir Hugo Mallinger's manor with her husband and others, seeks an opportunity to talk with Deronda alone before she leaves: "[taking] advantage of the winding road to linger a little out of sight, and then set off back to the house, almost running when she was safe from observation. […]. 'I thought you were far on your walk,' said Deronda. 'I turned back,' said Gwendolen" (pp. 504–05). The parallel between *Inferno* I and this scene is clear, with Gwendolen turning back and meeting Deronda as Dante had met Virgil, and effectively choosing the difficult path in asking for Deronda's guidance.

There is a similar scene two hundred pages later. The setting is Genoa, in Italy, where Grandcourt and Gwendolen, who is now in the depths of her infernal suffering, are to stay on his yacht: "She was waked the next morning by the casting of the anchor in the port of Genoa—waked from a strangely-mixed dream in which she felt herself escaping over the Mont Cenis […], till suddenly she met Deronda, who told her to go back" (p. 740). Again, there is the parallel with Dante's rushing down the slope only to be stopped by Virgil, whose presence signifies the "altro viaggio" ["other road"; *Inferno*, I. 91].

Gwendolen's proud nature has not allowed her to "say to the world, 'Pity me'" (p. 482), but in these two scenes which parallel *Inferno* I we cannot but be reminded of Dante's first words to Virgil when he encounters him on his headlong descent back the way he has come: "'*Miserere* di me,' gridai a lui, / 'qual che tu sii, od ombra od omo certo!'" ["'Have pity on me, whoever thou art,' I cried to him, 'shade or real man!'"; lines 65–66], and this sets up resonances for the Deronda/Gwendolen relationship. Gwendolen herself comes to think of Deronda as "a terrible-browed angel from whom she could not think of concealing any deed so as to win an ignorant regard from him: it belonged to the nature of their relation that she should be truthful, for his power over her had begun in the raising of a self-discontent which could be satisfied only by genuine change" (p. 737). Here Gwendolen also appears to be projecting a Beatrice role onto Deronda. Just as Dante undertakes his journey to become worthy of Beatrice, so the impulse to confess, to be worthy of Deronda, becomes stronger in Gwendolen as the novel progresses.

George Eliot is careful to mark the moment when Gwendolen's purgatorial ascent begins. It is at the point where she appears to be in her lowest spirits—the "dual solitude" of the Genoa yachting trip—and Eliot sets up an explicit parallel with Dante's Pia in *Purgatorio* v:

> Ricordati di me, che son la Pia;
>   Siena mi fé, disfecemi Maremma:
> salsi colui che 'nnanellata pria
> disposando m'avea con la sua gemma.
>   (*Purgatorio*, v, 133–36)

[Remember me, who am La Pia. Siena gave me birth, Maremma death. He knows of it who, first plighting troth, wedded me with his gem.]

In Eliot's version the scanty details given by Dante are imaginatively expanded:

> Madonna Pia, whose husband, feeling himself injured by her, took her to his castle amid the swampy flats of the Maremma and got rid of her there, makes a pathetic figure in Dante's Purgatory, among the sinners who repented at the last and desire to be remembered compassionately by their fellow-countrymen. We know little about the grounds of mutual discontent between the Siennese couple, but we may infer with some confidence that the husband had never been a very delightful companion, and that on the flats of the Maremma his disagreeable manners had a background which threw them out remarkably; whence in his desire to punish his wife to the uttermost, the nature of things was so far against him that in relieving himself of her he could not avoid making the relief mutual. And thus, without any hardness to the poor Tuscan lady who had her deliverance long ago, one may feel warranted in thinking of her with a less sympathetic

interest than of the better known Gwendolen who [...] is at the
very height of her entanglement in those fatal meshes which are
woven within more closely than without.

(*Daniel Deronda*, pp. 731–32)

However much of Pia's story Eliot herself may have invented, "the
poor Tuscan lady" is offered as the type of suffering that Gwendolen
herself is undergoing. Only a few paragraphs later Gwendolen too
has "her deliverance" and repents at last. The realization of the
magnitude and the consequences of her actions is expressed with
a clarity which reflects that of her mind in this moment of "revelation" on the yacht:

> She had a root of conscience in her, and the process of purgatory
> had begun for her on the green earth: she knew that she had been
> wrong. [...] she found herself [...] [in] the domain of the husband
> [...] to whom she had sold her truthfulness and sense of justice,
> so that he held them throttled into silence, collared and dragged
> behind him to witness what he would, without remonstrance.
>
> (*Daniel Deronda*, p. 733)

Gwendolen has her physical deliverance too (and here Eliot departs
from Dante's Pia episode), for it is Grandcourt who falls overboard
and drowns. After his death she is once more able to weep, though
not for her husband but for her own past sins, and she feels
impelled to confess to Deronda:

> I will tell you everything as God knows it. I will tell you no
> falsehood; I will tell you the exact truth [...]. I knew it all—I knew
> I was guilty. [...] everything held a punishment for me—every-
> thing but you. I always thought that you would not want me to
> be punished—you would have tried and helped me to be better.
>
> (*Daniel Deronda*, p. 757)

As well as a Virgil role, then, Gwendolen also projects a Beatrice
role onto Deronda, for it is Beatrice who requests Virgil to guide
Dante the character, since she does not wish him to be punished.

Eliot herself gives her hero something of the qualities of both
Dante the character and Dante the poet, which had so much impressed her in the *Commedia*. She had noted that "to balance Dante's severity, there are many signs of tenderness and compassion:
e.g. in the wood of the suicides [...] he begs Virgil to ask questions
for him of Pietro de' Vigni—'Ch'io non potrei: tanta pietà m'acco-

ra.'"[1] And again: "Throughout the *Inferno* I find only three instances of what can be called cruelty in Dante. Everywhere else, the sufferings of the damned fill him with pity" (p. 44). In Deronda too there is this great capacity for pity and compassion for the suffering of the sinner:

> [Gwendolen's] words of insistence that he "must remain near her—must not forsake her"—continually recurred to him with the clearness and importunity of imagined sounds, such as Dante has said pierce us like arrows whose points carry the sharpness of pity: "Lamenti saettaron me diversi / Che di pietà ferrati avean gli strali."[2]
>
> (*Daniel Deronda*, p. 684)

For her part, Gwendolen becomes like a child dependent upon Deronda's support for her actions.[3] Like Dante the character, she wishes to keep her guide near and fears being forsaken. She learns to see her inner mental actions through the impression she imagines they would make on Deronda. But through her suffering she will become more perfect and will have a greater capacity for future pleasure: "Her remorse was the precious sign of a recoverable nature; it was the culmination of that self-disapproval which had been the awakening of a new life within her; it marked her off from the criminals whose only regret is failure in securing their evil wish" (p. 762). Once again we note that Eliot's theme of moral growth through suffering in the world finds expression in terms of Dante's moral universe: in judging Gwendolen, she has been working within and through Dante's moral framework.

Whereas earlier there were running parallels with Dante's scheme in the *Commedia*, in the final stage of Gwendolen's journey there is apparently a major divergence from Dante, for Deronda,

---

1   *George Eliot: A Writer's Notebook*, p. 43.
2   "Strange lamentations assailed me that had their shafts barbed with pity" (*Inf.*, xxix. 43–44). Eliot here quotes directly from Dante's Italian. The passage is also copied into her Folger notebook (*George Eliot: A Writer's Notebook*, p. 43). She uses the same image to characterize Deronda's feeling towards Gwendolen later: "The sight pierced him with pity" (p. 753). She had previously used the same two lines as the epigraph to Chapter 22 of *Felix Holt, the Radical*.
3   "If she cried towards him, what then? She cried as the child cries whose little feet have fallen backward—cried to be taken by the hand, lest she should lose herself" (p. 842).

who has played Virgil to Gwendolen's Dante-the-character, abandons her after her ordeal, marries Mirah Lapidoth and leaves England to promote Zionism. Thus Gwendolen is excluded from the "Paradiso" of marriage at the end of the book. This has led a number of commentators to remark that Gwendolen's salvation seems a rather fragile affair and that there appears to be little hope that her resolve to be better will hold under pressure. Yet if we take account of the Dantean subtext as we read the novel we shall see that there is indeed hope for Gwendolen. Eliot, it may be argued, intended the body of allusion and metaphor from Dante's *Purgatorio* to sustain our hope in Gwendolen's future and allow us to withstand the immediate shock of Deronda's departure, and if we cannot believe in the power of Gwendolen's resolve at the end of the book, this may be through a failure on our part to appreciate the extensive but often subtly presented Dantean subtext to the full.

In terms of Dante's framework, Gwendolen is already saved when Deronda abandons her. She has entered upon her purgatorial journey, and the loss of Deronda is to form part of her purgatorial testing. Deronda himself gives what is essentially a Dantean interpretation of the preceding events in the novel (and of his part in them) with regard to Gwendolen:

> What makes life dreary is the want of motive; but once beginning to act with that penitential, loving purpose you have in your mind, there will be unexpected satisfactions [...]. You will find your life growing like a plant. [...] think that a severe angel, seeing you along the road of error, grasped you by the wrist, and showed you the horror of the life you must avoid. And it has come to you in your spring-time. Think of it as a preparation. You can, you will, be among the best of women, such as make others glad that they were born.
>
> (*Daniel Deronda*, pp. 839–40)

The image of Gwendolen's life growing like a plant echoes a similar image at the very end of *Purgatorio*. Eliot had copied these lines into her notebook, deliberately marking the passage as being the "End of Purgatorio":[1]

> Io ritornai da la santissima onda
> rifatto sí come piante novelle

---

1   *George Eliot: A Writer's Notebook*, p. 45.

> rinovellate di novella fronda,
> puro e disposto a salire a le stelle.
> (*Purgatorio,* XXXIII. 142–45)

[From the most holy waters I came forth again remade, even as new plants renewed with new leaves, pure and ready to mount to the stars.]

Thus Dante's image of purification, pointing onwards and upwards, is subtly worked into the text, which in fact has Dante very close to its surface at this point. A final epigraph taken from Dante (with an indication, this time, of the source) is used in Chapter 64, and again it is one intended to reinforce our confidence in Gwendolen's ability to sustain moral growth:

> "Questa montagna è tale,
> Che sempre al cominciar di sotto è grave,
> E quanto uom piú va su e men fa male."
> — DANTE: *Il Purgatorio.*

["This mountain is such that it is always hard at the start below and the higher one goes it is less toilsome"; *Purgatorio,* IV. 88–90]

Although Deronda ultimately refuses to carry through the Virgil role which he himself took on in redeeming the necklace at the beginning of the novel, Eliot sees him as having successfully completed his mission, for in *Daniel Deronda* she is interested in showing the workings of the human (moral) sanctions which hold together the moral fabric of society in the absence of divine sanctions. She says of Gwendolen: "Would her remorse have maintained its power within her […] if it had not been for that outer conscience which was made for her by Deronda? […] In this way our brother may be in the stead of God to us, and his opinion which has pierced even to the joints and marrow, may be our virtue in the making" (pp. 832–33).

As we have seen, Eliot does not present a strictly chronological sequence in drawing on Dante's *Commedia* in *Daniel Deronda.* For a time she allows the infernal and purgatorial sets of allusions and imagery to co-exist, and this is indicative of Gwendolen's inner mental torment. But ultimately there is no doubt that the purgatorial metaphor points in the direction of the heroine's development beyond the novel's close. Part of Eliot's purpose in including Dante in the novel is surely to judge and to make present to the reader the nature of Gwendolen's "sins". But Dante is also present, in the form of the human sympathy and compassion which Gwendolen encounters in Deronda, to soften this judgemental aspect. These two aspects of Dante are also to be found in the young Deronda: "A too reflective and diffuse sympathy was in danger of paralysing in him that indignation against wrong and that selectness of fellowship which are the conditions of moral force; [...] what he most longed for was either some external event, or some inward light, that would urge him into a definite line of action, and compress his wandering energy" (p. 413).

In a late essay Eliot expresses the same sentiment in similar words and links it explicitly with Dante:

> I respect the horsewhip when applied to the back of Cruelty, and I think that he who applies it is a more perfect human being because his outleap of indignation is not checked by a too curious reflection on the nature of guilt—a more perfect human being because he more completely incorporates the best social life of the race, which can never be constituted by ideas that nullify action. This is the essence of Dante's sentiment (it is painful to think that he applies it very cruelly)—"E cortesia fu, lui esser villano"[1]—and it is undeniable that a too intense consciousness of one's kinship with all frailties and vices undermines the active heroism which battles against wrong.[1]

George Eliot's own view of morality depends heavily on these qualities of human sympathy and compassion, which she found in Dante. And her view of how morality may be sanctioned in a godless society led her to assign great importance to and place great responsibility upon Virgil-like figures such as Daniel Deronda, or Felix Holt in the novel of that name.

---

1   "How We Come to Give Ourselves False Testimonials, and Believe in Them", in *Impressions of Theophrastus Such: Essays and Leaves from a Note-book* (Edinburgh–London, Blackwood, 1901), pp. 122–23. Eliot gives the line reference at the foot of p. 123 thus: "[1] *Inferno*, XXXIII. 150" ["and it was courtesy to be a churl to him"]. The comment refers to Ser Branca d'Oria, who murdered his father-in-law Michele Zanche.

FRANCESCA DA RIMINI
FROM ROMANTICISM TO DECADENCE

Deirdre O'Grady

Critics have consistently argued that Dante's purpose in creating the star-crossed lovers Francesca da Polenta and Paolo Malatesta was literary, moral and political. *Inferno* v has been afforded diverse interpretations over seven centuries.[1] The fact that during the nineteenth century, along with the Ugolino episode (*Inferno* XXXII–XXXIII), it topped the popularity charts, not only in Italy but also in France and England, resulted in an abundance of critical and creative material, with the lovers emerging as the subjects of translations, poems, operas and dramas. Before taking a critical look at the reception of Francesca da Rimini from Romanticism to Decadence, some general reference to the popularity of the figure in Italy, France and England is necessary. This will illustrate the interest and enthusiasm she aroused.

Italian Neoclassicism in the wake of the French Revolution provided an aspiration towards artistic order, harmony and symmetry, along with a growing sense of national identity. The major writer of the period, Ugo Foscolo (1778–1827),[2] reflects its entire spirit in his epistolary novel *Le ultime lettere di Jacopo Ortis*, begun in 1796 and first published in complete form in 1801. In this work Foscolo establishes an identification between Francesca and Venice, which he regarded as his fatherland. He is thus the first to introduce a nationalistic dimension into the reading of the canto. This was followed and brought to the stage by Silvio Pellico (1789–

---

1   For a detailed bibliography see my "Women Damned, Penitent and Beatified in the *Divine Comedy*", in *Dante Readings*, edited by E. Haywood (Dublin, Irish Academic Press, 1987), pp. 73–106 (pp. 104–05).

2   For a critical account of Foscolo's artistic achievement see M. Fubini, *Ugo Foscolo* (Bari, Laterza, 1962), and D. Radcliff-Umstead, *Ugo Foscolo* (New York, Twayne, 1970).

1854) in his tragedy *Francesca da Rimini* (1814).[1] Pellico's patriotic fervour, and his contribution to the Risorgimento as editor of *Il conciliatore*, its journalistic mouthpiece, was rewarded with arrest and eight years' confinement in the Austrian prison of Spielberg in Moravia. His Francesca is a dramatization of wronged innocence, which proved influential for many Romantic critics; Francesco De Sanctis, in this spirit, perceives her as an expression of the pure poetry of sentiment.[2] In nineteenth-century Europe, Pellico's drama proved more influential than its source, *Inferno* v. In 1820, it was reduced to two acts by the librettist Felice Romani,[3] and between 1823 and 1882 it was set to music by fifteen composers, including Saverio Mercadante (1795–1870) and Feliciano Strepponi (1767–1832).[4] Further dramatized versions in imitation of Pellico appeared between 1830 and 1838. These include works by the little-known writers Ulivo Bucchi, Luigi Bellacchi and Antonio Viviani. With the passing of the period of High Romanticism in Italy, Dante's work became the subject of ridicule and satirical treatment. The episode of Paolo and Francesca was parodied dramatically in 1867 by Antonio Petito, and in 1887 by Giovanni Marchetti.[5] The lovers

1   Pellico's memoirs of this period provide the material for his most famous work, *Le mie prigioni*. He also wrote twelve tragedies, only eight of which were published during his lifetime.
2   See F. De Sanctis, *Lezioni sulla "Divina commedia"*, edited by M. Manfredi (Bari, Laterza, 1955), pp. 137–47.
3   A lawyer by profession, Romani (1788–1865) attained the peak of his popularity at the time of his collaboration with Vincenzo Bellini, for whom he wrote the texts of the operas *Norma* (1831), *Il pirata* (1827), *La straniera* (1829), *I Capuleti ed i Montecchi* (1830), *La sonnambula* (1831) and *Beatrice di Tenda* (1833). While editor of the Turin *Gazzetta piemontese* from 1834 to 1849, he published several books of verse in imitation of Pietro Metastasio (1698–1782).
4   Further musical versions are by the following composers: Carlini (Naples 1825), Quilici (Lucca 1829), Generali (Venice 1829), Staffa (Naples 1831), Fournier-Gorre (Livorno 1832), Tamburini (Rimini 1836), Borgatta (Genoa 1840), Brancaccio (Venice 1844), Franchini (Lisbon 1857), Marcarini (Bologna 1870). There is also a musical version in the Milan Conservatory dated 1841. This list was compiled by Bingham: see *"Francesca da Rimini": A Tragedy of Silvio Pellico*, translated by the Rev. J. F. Bingham, 5th edition (London etc., Frowde, 1905), pp. xxix–xxx. See too U. De Maria, "Francesca da Rimini nel teatro", *La Romagna*, 2–5 (1906).
5   Antonio Petito (Naples 1822–78), best known as the actor responsible for the refinement of the mask of Pulcinella, carried the Neapolitan improvised theatre towards reform. Although barely literate, he wrote several comedies, the best-known being *Palummella Zompa*. His autobiography was published

were then introduced to twentieth-century Italian audiences by Gabriele d'Annunzio. His tragedy *Francesca da Rimini* (1902) is the source of the opera by Zandonai,[1] which was produced twelve years later, with a libretto by Tito Ricordi, the Milanese music publisher, and to which a section of the Act III love duet was added by d'Annunzio himself.

The individualism and strong political ideals of Dante held no appeal for Revolutionary France. In 1805, however, a translation of the Francesca episode by Carion de Nizas was published.[2] This was followed by three translations of the entire *Inferno*. The first was a verse translation of 1817 by Henri Terrasson;[3] in 1823 a second verse translation followed, by Brait Delamathe,[4] and a year later a French translation in prose was published in London. The pathos of Francesca's plight obviously appealed to French Romantic writers. The lines, "Nessun maggior dolore / che ricordarsi del tempo felice / ne la miseria" ["There is no greater sorrow than to recall, in wretchedness, the happy time"; *Inferno*, v. 121–23] are adapted by de Vigny at the opening of his *Servitude et grandeur militaires*.[5] In "Le Saule" (1830) Alfred de Musset paraphrases the same lines; he pays tribute to Francesca in *Le Poëte déchu* and also refers to her in "Souvenir", though disputing the statement that there is no greater pain than to recall happiness in times of misery.[6] In 1848 Silvio Pellico's *Francesca da Rimini* was translated into

posthumously in Naples in 1895. Giovanni Marchetti (1790–1852), poet and Dante scholar, collaborated with P. Costa over a commentary on the *Commedia* (1819). In 1824 he wrote *Cenno intorno allo stato presente della letteratura in Italia*.

1   D'Annunzio's *Francesca da Rimini* (1902) is a tragedy in five acts dedicated "alla Divina Eleonora Duse".

2   W. P. Friederich, *Dante's Fame Abroad, 1350–1850* (Chapel Hill, University of North Carolina Press, 1950), p. 120.

3   W. P. Friederich, *Dante's Fame Abroad*, p. 127.

4   W. P. Friederich, *Dante's Fame Abroad*, pp. 127–28.

5   "S'il est vrai, selon le poète catholique, qu'il n'y ait pas de plus grande peine que de se rappeler un temps heureux dans la misère, il est aussi vrai que l'âme trouve quelque bonheur à se rappeler, dans un moment de calme et de liberté, les temps de peine ou d'esclavage": see W. P. Friederich, *Dante's Fame Abroad*, p. 130. My Dante translations are taken from Dante Alighieri, *The Divine Comedy*, translated by C. S. Singleton, 3 vols in 6 (Princeton, Princeton University Press, 1970–75).

6   "Écoute, moribonde! il n'est pire douleur / Qu'un souvenir heureux dans les jours de malheur" ("Le Saule"); "Dante, pourquoi dis-tu qu'il n'est pire misère / Qu'un souvenir heureux dans les jours de douleur?" ("Souvenir"); see W. P. Friederich, *Dante's Fame Abroad*, pp. 136–38.

French by Vannoni. In 1850, Victor de Méri de la Canorgue published a dramatic work entitled *Françoise de Rimini,* which he called an imitation of Silvio Pellico.[1] In 1882 the operatic composer Ambroise Thomas, best remembered for his operas *Mignon* (1866) and *Hamlet* (1868), adapted Romani's libretto, based on Pellico, and produced it at the Paris Opéra with the title *Françoise de Rimini.*

Although late starters, the English-speaking peoples have been the most prolific translators of the *Commedia.* Between 1782 and 1900 they produced more versions than any other European nation—forty in all.[2] These include efforts in rhyme, prose, blank *terzine* and triple rhyme. The best known are those by Henry Francis Cary (see the essay by Edoardo Crisafulli in this volume), John Aitken Carlyle (a prose translation of *Inferno,* of 1849) and Henry Wadsworth Longfellow (a translation of the whole *Commedia,* of 1867). There were also three translations by Irishmen published during the nineteenth century. The first was by Edward N. Shannon, under the pseudonym Odoardo Volpi (1836); a prose translation by E. O'Donnell, a Roman Catholic priest, appeared in 1852, and a further prose translation came from the pen of Sir Edward Sullivan, a lawyer, in 1893. The century, however, can boast only one woman translator, Claudia Hamilton Ramsay, who translated *Inferno* in 1862 and *Purgatorio* and *Paradiso* in the following year. A further interesting piece of information is the fact that Sir John Russell translated the Francesca episode into heroic couplets in 1844, just two years before he became British Prime Minister.

The influence of Silvio Pellico on the English poets Byron and Leigh Hunt is considerable;[3] his work appears to have provided a stimulus for a closer study of Dante on their part. Two years after the first production of Pellico's tragedy, Leigh Hunt wrote the verse novel *The Story of Rimini,* and in a letter of 21 January 1821 Pellico, writing to his father, claimed that Byron had translated his play (though he had in fact translated Canto v of *Inferno*). Pellico writes:

1   W. P. Friederich, *Dante's Fame Abroad,* p. 159.
2   For a detailed study of Dante's English translators see G. F. Cunningham, *The "Divine Comedy" in English: A Critical Bibliography, 1782–1900* (Edinburgh–London, Oliver and Boyd, 1965).
3   On Leigh Hunt see A. Blainey, *Immortal Boy: A Portrait of Leigh Hunt* (London–Sydney, Croom Helm, 1985), and E. Blunden, *Leigh Hunt: A Biography* (London, s.n., 1930).

Ho buoni libri e traduco un poema inglese. È giusto ch'io retri-
buisca agli Inglesi la cortesia che hanno per me, giacché hanno
fatto conoscere con molta lode la mia *Francesca da Rimini* al loro
paese; si legge su questa tragedia un articolo lusinghiero nel
Quarterly Review di dicembre, con degli squarci della traduzione
che ne ha fatta lord Byron.[1]

[I have good books and am translating an English poem. It is
right that I return to the English the courtesy they have done me
in making known to their country with much praise my *Francesca
da Rimini*. There is a flattering article in the *Quarterly Review* of
December, with some excerpts of the translation which Lord
Byron has made of it.]

As early as 1814, moreover, Byron had adorned three cantos of *The
Corsair* with Dantesque mottos from *Inferno* v: "Nessun maggior
dolore" ["No greater sorrow"; 121]; "Conosceste i dubbiosi desi-
ri?" ["Did you know the dubious desires?"; 120]; and "Come vedi,
ancor non mi abbandona" ["As you see, it does not leave me even
now"; 105].[2]

In addition to Leigh Hunt's and Byron's acquaintance with the
Francesca episode through Pellico, other English Romantics identified with the "gentler" aspects of Dante's writing. Alfred Lord
Tennyson, at the tender age of eleven, in a letter to his aunt, in 1820,
alludes to "Nessun maggior dolore", while in "Locksley Hall" he
states:

> This is truth the poet sings,
> That a sorrow's crown of sorrow is remembering happier things.[3]
> ("Locksley Hall", lines 75–76)

For their part Shelley and Keats, two of England's most celebrated
nineteenth-century poets, display a sensitive appreciation of
Dante's romantic disposition as demonstrated in Canto v. John
Keats, in a letter of 1819, wrote:

1 See *"Francesca da Rimini"*, pp. xxx–xxxi. Bingham cites evidence suggesting
   that Byron did not write the article in the *Quarterly Review*. See also
   H. Kaeger, "Lord Byron and Francesca da Rimini" *Archiv für das Studium
   der neueren Sprachen*, 98 (1897), p. 403.
2 See M. Renzulli, *Dante nella letteratura inglese* (Florence, La Via, 1925), p. 84.
3 W. P. Friederich, *Dante's Fame Abroad*, pp. 304, 307.

The fifth canto of Dante pleases me more and more. It is that in
which he meets Paulo and Francesca. I had passed many days in
rather a low state of mind, and in the midst of them I dreamt of
being in that region of Hell [...] "where mid the gust of whirlwind
and the flow / of rain and hailstones, lovers need not tell / their
sorrows. / Pale were the lips I saw / pale were the lips I kissed and
fair the form / I floated with, about the melancholy storm."[1]

In that same year Percy Bysshe Shelley, a friend of both Leigh Hunt
and Byron, proved his acquaintance with the dove simile of
Canto Ⅴ (lines 82–87). The following lines from "Prometheus
Unbound" illustrate the point:

> Behold'st thou not two shapes from the east and west
> Come, as two doves to one beloved nest,
> Twin nurslings of the all-sustaining air
> On swift still wings glide down the atmosphere?
> ("Prometheus Unbound", Act ɪ, lines 752–55).[2]

Another close friend of Byron, the Irish poet Thomas Moore, best
known to Irish readers for his *Irish Melodies*, writes in his "Imitation
of Dante":

> I turn'd my steps, and lo, a shadowy throng
> Of ghosts came fluttering tow'rds me—blown along.[3]

It was the themes of love, betrayal and damnation, then, which
particularly appealed to English nineteenth-century taste. When
Romanticism gave way to Realism and Decadence, the central
section of *Inferno* v continued to appeal, with only the tone and
treatment of the tale having altered, as will be illustrated later. At
the close of the nineteenth century, almost fifty years after the
completion of the first translation into English of Pellico's *Francesca
da Rimini*, the performance took place of Stephen Phillips's tragedy
in four acts, *Paolo and Francesca*,[4] which, on its title page, carries the
supreme expression of Dantean *pietà*:

1   W. P. Friederich, *Dante's Fame Abroad*, pp. 267–68.
2   W. P. Friederich, *Dante's Fame Abroad*, p. 263.
3   W. P. Friederich, *Dante's Fame Abroad*, p. 268.
4   S. Phillips, *Paolo and Francesca: A Tragedy in Four Acts*, sixth edition (London–
     New York, John Lane, The Bodley Head, 1900).

Oh lasso,
quanti dolci pensier, quanto disio
menò costoro al doloroso passo!
(*Inferno*, v. 112–14)

[Alas! How many sweet thoughts, what great desire, brought
them to the woeful pass!]

Francesca da Rimini thus proved to be one of the most popular
figures in European literature in the nineteenth century, providing
material for poetry, plays and music; and to this day she remains
a challenging enigma. The enigma is due, in part, to the drama and
mystery surrounding her life and death. In 1275 Giovanni Malatesta
of Rimini, a daring but deformed warrior, also known as Giovanni
the Lame, contracted a political marriage with Francesca, daughter
of Guido da Polenta of Ravenna. Following the marriage, Francesca
lived in Ravenna, where she fell in love with Giovanni's handsome
brother Paolo. In about 1286, Giovanni surprised them together
and killed them both. The history of these events was first told by
three medieval commentators on the *Commedia*, the so-called Ano-
nimo Fiorentino, Giovanni Boccaccio and Dante's son Pietro.[1] The
most detailed account is by Boccaccio, who claims that Paolo was
sent to Ravenna to marry Francesca by proxy, thus leading people
to believe that it was he and not his deformed brother who was to
be Francesca's husband. This detail, however, is not present in
Inferno v. Later accounts place the lovers' death at the beginning of
1289. By then Francesca had been married for at least ten years and
was the mother of a nine-year-old daughter, while Paolo, who was
also married, was the father of two grown-up sons. In 1282, when
Dante was a youth of seventeen, Paolo had been *capitano del popolo*
in Florence; and during his years of exile Dante was the guest, in
Ravenna, of Francesca's nephew Guido Novello. It is highly likely,
therefore, that he knew more than he actually reveals in *Inferno* v.
    In the *Commedia* the story of Francesca is set against a backdrop
of literary references and associations.[2] Prior to Dante the pilgrim's
conversation with her, the evocation of knights and ladies of

1   For an account of the commentaries see Dante Alighieri, *La Divina commedia*,
      edited by T. Casini (Florence, Sansoni, 1921), pp. 46–47n.
2   For a further critical account of the canto see the section devoted to France-
      sca in my "Women Damned, Penitent and Beatified", pp. 75–84.

antiquity instils in him a feeling of compassion ("pietà": line 72), which serves as an introduction to this theme in the canto and forms a prelude to the association of Francesca and Paolo with the chivalric romance. The world of chivalry is then highlighted in Francesca's narrative (121–38), as she relates the circumstances of her death, establishing a link with Lancelot and Guinevere, of whom she and Paolo had been reading and who, like them, were overcome by passion (127–36). The book they were reading is personified and he who wrote it called a Galeotto, the Italian version of the name of the person who acted as go-between for Lancelot and Guinevere (137). In his presentation of the figure of Francesca, Dante the poet juxtaposes the image of the temptress and the angelic woman of medieval love poetry. Francesca thus represents the antithesis of the *donna gentile* symbolizing love as a spiritual force. Although the lines spoken by her contain some of the poetic devices of the *dolce stil novo* (100–06), as a character in Hell she cannot act as a guide to Heaven, but can merely tempt those in proximity to her. The power of all-consuming love is associated with the "cor gentil", which in Italian medieval poetry belongs only to the sinless lover. Francesca's passionate experience, relived by her as she speaks to Dante the pilgrim, leads only to death and damnation and not to a *vita nuova*. In the tradition of the *dolce stil novo* it was the lady who chose her lover. Francesca, on the contrary, implies that Paolo chose her. In medieval love poetry, the praises of the lady were sung by the knight. In *Inferno* v it is Francesca who speaks. So Dante, it would appear, is presenting unbridled passion garbed in the conventions of the literary school to which he belonged in order to portray one who subjugated reason to passion ("ragion […] al talento": line 39).

From the purely lyrical point of view, however, Francesca is most certainly the personification of beauty and pathos of expression. She is tossed by the winds of passion, having abandoned reason for emotion. She answers Dante's call in dove-like fashion, and her greeting takes the form of a hypothetical prayer:

> Se fosse amico il re de l'universo
> noi pregheremmo lui de la tua pace,
> poi c'hai pietà del nostro mal perverso.
> (*Inferno*, v. 91–93)

[If the King of the universe were friendly to us, we would pray Him for your peace, since you have pity on our perverse ill.]

If the lovers had indeed been the friends of the king of the universe, however, Dante's pity would not have been necessary, which certainly makes the situation ambiguous; but what is clear is that the literary and moral notions underlying the story are at cross purposes. To deny Francesca's guilt would be to plunge the moral system of *Inferno* into confusion. It is Dante the pilgrim, as yet unversed in the full implications of evil, who feels pity.

The lyricism of the episode of unhappy love and death was what touched Romantic writers. It also afforded them an opportunity to explore a psychological factor—the relationship between guilt and innocence, and the point at which the latter yields to the former. It is this aspect of the episode that is dramatized by Silvio Pellico and which the English poet Leigh Hunt adapts in order to defend romantic love and freedom of expression. But before proceeding to consider these writers, it is necessary to refer briefly to Ugo Foscolo.

In *Le ultime lettere di Jacopo Ortis*, which consists of letters by a politically fired young man caught up in a hopeless love affair who sees death by suicide as an act of both sacrifice and escape, we read the following lines, in a letter dated 17 March 1798: "Piango la patria mia, 'che mi fu tolta, e il modo ancor m'offende'" ["I weep for my fatherland that was taken from me, and the manner in which it was done still offends me"].[1] The object of Foscolo's indignation is the passing of the Venetian Republic to Austria on 17 October 1797, as agreed in the Treaty of Campoformio. The origin of the lines is *Inferno*, v. 102. Foscolo, however, alters the original context to suit his own political designs. In his hands, Francesca becomes a political symbol, and like her, the Venetian Republic is sought after by two "suitors" and finally betrayed. Foscolo's use of this episode, albeit briefly, marks the association between the theme of love and (Italian) politics, and heralds Silvio Pellico's symbolic dramatization of the two lovers' plight in 1814.

Pellico's tragedy *Francesca da Rimini*,[2] although maintaining the story's medieval setting, falls into the category of patriotic Romantic literature. Paolo is presented as a medieval warrior

---

1 See U. Foscolo, *Le ultime lettere di Jacopo Ortis, Poesie*, edited by M. Puppo (Milan, Mursia, 1988), p. 46. The translation is mine, as are subsequent ones from authors other than Dante.

2 S. Pellico, *Francesca da Rimini*, edited by P. Gobbi (Milan, Signorelli, 1951).

fighting for a foreign emperor; yet his political utterances are intended as invectives against Austria. What is more, Pellico adds a subtle dimension to the tragedy, not found in Dante: he makes Paolo the killer of Francesca's brother. In this way the theme of brotherhood is introduced. The term "brother" and the concept of brotherhood recur throughout the drama, to underline the fact that Paolo and Lanciotto (as he is called by Pellico) are brothers; and the yearning for fraternity, leading to reconciliation, is also stressed throughout. The following passages serve to illustrate these points:

> PAOLO   Per chi di stragi si macchiò il mio brando?
>   Per lo straniero. E non ho patria forse
>   cui sacro sia de' cittadini il sangue?
>   Per te, per te che cittadini hai prodi,
>   Italia mia, combatterò se oltraggio
>   ti moverà la invidia.
>   (Pellico, *Francesca da Rimini*, I. 5, p. 28)

[For whom was my sword stained with slaughter? For the foreigner. Have I no fatherland whose citizens' blood is sacred? For you, for you who have courageous citizens, oh Italy, I shall fight, if envy shall move insults against you.]

The theme of brotherhood is developed through exchanges between the principal characters. Paolo, for instance, says to Lanciotto: "U-niti/sempre saremo d'or innanzi" ["From now on we shall be united"; I. 5, p. 28]. Lanciotto says to Francesca, "Ah, pensa/ch'ei t'è cognato" ["Ah, bear in mind that he is your brother-in-law"; II.□3, p. 36] and, "O donna, /il fratello abborrità non potrai!" ["Oh lady, you cannot abhor your brother in such a manner!"; II. 3, p. 36]. Lanciotto further exclaims, "Fratello m'è; più orribile è il delitto" ["The crime is all the more horrible, since he is my brother"; IV. 2, p. 49].

The theme of betrayal also runs throughout the work, as does the theme of pretence, with Francesca feigning hatred of Paolo in order to mask her true feelings for him. This attitude of hers serves to dramatize the question of innocence and guilt, and by introducing such psychological probings into a story whose implications had been primarily literary, moral and political, Pellico turns Francesca into a true Romantic heroine, whose moral dilemma is expressed as follows: "Dovere è il fingere; dovere/il tacer; colpa il dimandar conforto; / colpa il narrar" ["It is my duty to use pretence, to remain silent. It is wrong to seek consolation, wrong to speak"; II. 1, p. 33]. Her human need for self-expression leads her, paradoxically, to desire a cloistered existence, where she might find silent fulfilment: "liberi dal seno / sariano usciti i miei gemiti a Dio" ["my mournful cries would have been freely expressed to God"; I. 2, p. 23].

Pellico, like Foscolo, is a tragedian in the tradition of Vittorio Alfieri (1749–1803), whose revitalization of classical tragedy sought to dramatize both political and philosophical thought, and whose characters symbolically demonstrate eighteenth-century rational behaviour and the conflict between reason and emotion. Pellico has Francesca combine reason and emotion in an internal struggle, which cannot be truthfully expressed:

> Lunga battaglia fin ad ora io vinsi;
> ma questi di mia vita ultimi giorni
> tremar mi fanno.
> (Pellico, *Francesca da Rimini*, II. 1, p. 34)

[In long battle, I have hitherto been victorious. But these last days make me tremble.]

And the inability of the individual to do away with emotional response is proclaimed by Lanciotto: "Rea non ti tengo… involontari sono / spesso gli affetti" ["I do not hold you guilty… love is often involontary"; I. 2, p. 24].

Thus Francesca, in Pellico's treatment, is completely innocent of any adulterous act. She is nevertheless guilty of pretence, which she adopts as a weapon in her battle for self-control. She discards truth and embraces falsehood, in order that feelings, for which she does not feel responsible, may be concealed.[1] This prompts one to wonder how independent this Francesca is of Dante's. In *Inferno* v Francesca da Rimini is among the sinners "che la ragion sommettono al talento" ["who subject reason to desire"; line 39]. In a post-Enlightenment interpretation of Francesca's personal dilemma Pellico creates a tragedy of opposites, in which love and hatred, youth and

---

1 Like Alfieri, Pellico recognizes one's inability to eliminate emotions, but he illustrates the virtue of self-control: "I nostri padri crudi / hanno in note di sangue in noi scolpito / scambievol odio. In me ragion frenarlo / ben può; ma nulla nol può spegner mai" (*Agamennone*, edited by V. Branca [Milan, Rizzoli, 1996], III. 3, p. 139).

age, action and contemplation, war and peace, and innocence and guilt are juxtaposed.

Pellico's imitators made no effort to alter the story-line of his work. Mario Rapisardi, who in 1875 became Professor of Italian Literature in the University of Catania, wrote his own *Francesca da Rimini* in the form of an intermezzo to his work *Le ricordanze*. It depicts Paolo and Francesca, in Hell, upbraiding their killer. When an angel appears in order to free Francesca, she refuses to leave without her lover, for Heaven would be comfortless in his absence. The work thus appears to parody the sonnet by Giacomo da Lentini, "Io m'aggio posto in core a Dio servire", where the poet proclaims that he would not wish to go to Heaven without his lady:

> ché sanza lei non poteria gaudere,
> estando da la mia donna diviso.[1]

[because without her I could not rejoice, since I would be separated from my lady.]

Pietro Gobbi calls this *Francesca da Rimini* "povera cosa, che non si può leggere senza pena",[2] which is well illustrated by the following lines from the chorus of devils, where awkward metre and banality of concept provide a grotesque deformation of Dante's "bufera infernal":

> Urlate, urlate, urlate,
> voi, che d'adultero
> foco d'amor bruciate!
> Noi per quest' aria nera
> tessiamo la ridda agli orridi
> fischi de la bufera.[3]

[Howl, howl, howl, you who burn with adulterous fire. We in this black air weave the maze to the horrid whistles of the infernal gale.]

As early as 1811 Leigh Hunt had toyed with the idea of writing a narrative poem on the subject of *Inferno* v. He was visiting Italy

1   *Sonetti della scuola siciliana*, edited by E. Sanguineti (Turin, Einaudi, 1965), p.□22.
2   S. Pellico, *Francesca da Rimini*, p. 14.
3   M. Rapisardi, *Francesca da Rimini* (Catania, Giannotta, 1869). See M. Apollonio, *Lirici minori dell'Ottocento* (Milan, Vita e Pensiero, 1943).

when Pellico's drama was favourably received, and seized on the emotional aspect of the work as the subject-matter for his own poem. The early version, of 1816, is a justification of the love of Paolo and Francesca. In 1844 some revisions were made to allow the story to conclude, like Dante's, with the double murder of wife and lover. This version, *The Story of Rimini*, is a poem consisting of 1,700 lines and divided into four cantos, with the following titles: "The Coming to Fetch the Bride from Ravenna", "The Bride's Journey to Rimini", "The Fatal Passion" and "How the Bride Returned to Ravenna".[1] Charles Lamb called it "an ill judged subject for a poem", whereas Hazlitt, in the *Edinburgh Review*, commented favourably on it.[2] Canto III is regarded by most critics as its finest section. Unlike that of Cantos I and II, the inspiration here comes from Francesca's narrative in *Inferno* V. Paolo and Francesca are shown reading together in a summer-house:

> And o'er the book they hung, and nothing said,
> And every lingering page grew longer as they read.
> (*The Story of Rimini*, III: "The Fatal Passion", p. 77)

Having thus created the desired atmosphere of suspense, Hunt momentarily adopts a more light-hearted and amusing tone. This is achieved by his use of rhyme and image:

> Only he felt he could not more dissemble,
> And kissed her mouth to mouth, all in a tremble.
> Sad were those hearts, and sweet was that long kiss:
> Sacred be love from sight whate'er it is.
> (*The Story of Rimini*, III: "The Fatal Passion", p. 78)

The finality of Francesca's words, "Quel giorno piú non vi leggemmo avante" ["That day we read no farther in it"; line 138], is echoed in Hunt's expression of dramatic ambiguity:

> The world was all forgot, the struggle o'er,
> Desperate the joy. That day they read no more.
> (*The Story of Rimini*, III: "The Fatal Passion", p. 78)

---

1   J. H. L. Hunt, *The Story of Rimini, 1816*, introduced by J. Woodworth (Otley–Washington, DC, Woodstock, 2001.

2   For the background to *The Story of Rimini* and its reception see A. Blainey, *Immortal Boy*, pp. 75–79. For Hazlitt's comments see *Edinburgh Review*, 26 June 1816, pp. 476–91.

Hunt, in his later critical study, *Dante's "Divine Comedy"*, remarks that the alternation of anger and tenderness in Francesca's expression had been explained to him by Foscolo,[1] but Francesca's story may well have struck a personal note in him, and his affection for her could be due to a similarity of situation in his own life. Ann Blainey points out that the story of two brothers in love with the same woman presented a mirror-image of Hunt's own dilemma. He was in fact in love with two sisters, Marianne and Bess Kent. After his marriage to Marianne in 1809 he affirmed that Bess was "linked with all the interest and hopes of my life".[2] In an attempt to convince both himself and the world of the innocence of this relationship, he transformed it into *The Story of Rimini*. Whether or not Hunt achieved all his aims is a matter for speculation, though the poem was considered highly original, both by his contemporary critics and by later readers, in spite of its Italian source and the popularity of its theme.

As one reaches the turn of the nineteenth century one notices a shift in emphasis in the treatment of the two lovers' tale. The dramatic works of Stephen Phillips and Gabriele d'Annunzio are examples of realistically charged accounts where spontaneity of expression is sacrificed to calculated theatrical effect.[3] Both plays are products of artistic Decadence, which attempts to give permanence to splendour by over-emphasis and exaggeration. D'Annunzio follows the cult of the "superman" in his artistic endeavour, and as a "super-artist", combining a multiplicity of expressions and techniques, he constructs the artificial in an attempt to transcend all art forms. His *Francesca da Rimini* was first produced in 1902, carrying the lovers and their plight into the twentieth century.

Like d'Annunzio, Phillips may be said to create literature in which effects, impressions and the fusion of genres form the framework within which the action takes place. His *Paolo and Francesca* was commissioned and accepted for production at the St James's Theatre, London in 1900, by George Alexander. It

1   L. Hunt, *Dante's "Divine Comedy": The Book and Its Story* (London, Neunes, n.d.), p. 75n.
2   A. Blainey, *Immortal Boy*, p. 76.
3   Stephen Phillips, the English actor, poet and dramatist, has been compared to Rossetti for his impassioned love poetry.
4   S. Phillips, *Paolo and Francesca*, Appendix, p. 123.

opened to superlative reviews. *The Times* reported: "Simple, direct, concerned with the elemental human passions, and presenting its story in the persons of three strongly defined characters of the first rank, it should appeal to the dramatic sense, as well as to the sense of poetic beauty."[1] *The Daily Chronicle* was even more effusive in its praise: "Mr Phillips has achieved the impossible. Sardou could not have ordered the action more skilfully, Tennyson could not have clothed the passion in words of purer loveliness."[2] *Punch* referred to "a combination of glamour and romance, with the restraint of classic traditions". The greatest tribute was paid by *The Morning Leader* in its claim that "Mr Phillips has succeeded where Leigh Hunt, Silvio Pellico and many others failed. He has performed a feat from which even Byron shrank. He has taken three beautiful spirits out of their everlasting pain and passion and shown us afresh their exultations and their agonies."[3] While the subject is Dante's, the influence of Pellico is reflected particularly in the presentation of the themes of brotherhood, innocence and guilt; but Phillips displays an original flair, not found in either Pellico or Hunt. To the chivalric world he adds the popular one of the tavern (Act II Scene 2) and the shop (that of Pulci, the drug-seller in Act III). The influence of Shakespeare is evident in the character of Francesca, where traces of Miranda's innocence (*The Tempest*) and Juliet's joy (*Romeo and Juliet*) are blended with the contained emotion of Pellico's Francesca. Phillips's most outstanding achievement lies in the combination of opposites, resulting in a "bitter-sweet" effect typical of the later nineteenth century. A good example of this is the work's conclusion, where the macabre revelation of the two corpses is tempered by Giovanni's comparison of them to two sleeping children (IV. 1, p. 120).

The theme of brotherhood is first introduced, symbolically, in Act I, when Paolo calls Francesca "sister", since she is his brother's wife:

> And, therefore, sister, am I glad that you
> Are wedded unto one so full of shelter.
>   (*Paolo and Francesca*, I. 1, p. 17)

---

1   S. Phillips, *Paolo and Francesca*, Appendix, p. 123. The critic was Mr William Archer.
2   S. Phillips, *Paolo and Francesca*, Appendix, p. 125. The critic was Mr James Douglas.
3   S. Phillips, *Paolo and Francesca*, Appendix, p. 120.

For his part Giovanni, with reference to his relationship with his brother Paolo, states, "We are, Francesca, / A something more than brothers—fiercest friends", to which Francesca replies, "Sir, I will love him: is he not my brother?" (i. 1, p. 18). Francesca's childlike innocence at the beginning of the drama contrasts with her later recognition of guilt in her mind (Act ii) and final admission of moral guilt (Act iv). She at first declares:

> I
> Am innocent as yet of this great life;
> My only care to attend the holy bell,
> To sing and to embroider curiously.
> (*Paolo and Francesca*, i. 1, p. 13)

But later she believes that, in thought at least, she has sinned: "O, I had not thought! / I had not thought! I have sinned, and I am stained!"; to which her maid Nita replies, "Lady, you have done nothing" (ii. 1, p. 43). Guilt, though, is finally admitted:

> FRANCESCA   Ah, Paolo! if we
> Should die to-night, then whither would our souls
> Repair? There is a region which priests tell of
> Where such as we are punished without end.
> PAOLO   Were we together, what can punish us?
> (*Paolo and Francesca*, iv. 1, p. 111)

Decadence, effected by exaggeration, repetition and over-loading of light and fire imagery, is the keynote of the final act, where Paolo and Francesca, by overindulging in their sensual experience, bring about a poetic rapture which is unbearable in its intensity and a herald of death. The terms "sweet sound", "too sweet", "sweetly" and "mortal sweetness" are later enhanced by the introduction of light effects:

> FRANCESCA   Thy armour glimmered in a gloom of green. [...]
> PAOLO   And in that kiss our souls
> Together flashed, and now they are one flame,
> Which nothing can put out, nothing divide. [...]
> Let me with kisses burn this body away,
> That our two souls may dart together free.
> [...] For what ecstasy
> Together to be blown about the globe!
> What rapture in perpetual fire to burn
> Together—where we are is endless fire.
> (*Paolo and Francesca*, iv. 1, pp. 109–12)

The unity of Paolo and Francesca in death is celebrated as a wedding ceremony, with a call for lights, music and dancing from the wronged husband:

> GIOVANNI Rouse up the house and bring in lights, lights, lights!
>   There shall be music, feasting and dancing.
>   Wine shall be drunk. Candles, I say! More lights!
>   More marriage lights!
>   (*Paolo and Francesca*, IV. 1, p. 117)

As the corpses are carried in full view of the servants, Giovanni's desire for ceremonial exhibition yields to contained sorrow:

> I did not know the dead could have such hair.
> Hide them. They look like children fast asleep!
>   (*Paolo and Francesca*, IV. 1, p. 120)

The final image of the two lovers thus paradoxically conveys life and death, the beautiful and the macabre.

A wallowing in poetic effects for sensual ends is also a feature of d'Annunzio's *Francesca da Rimini*.[1] This draws together aspects of the many versions of and variations on the tale of Francesca. The art of storytelling is combined with dramatic exposition. Boccaccio's version of the story is contained in the plot.[2] The adventures of Tristan, which are communicated by means of visual, literary and musical devices in the text, are also depicted on the wall-panels of the set, as well as being related in verse and song. Dante and Boccaccio, however, both rise above the level of mere sources to become active forces within the drama: Paolo recalls his friendship with Dante when he was *capitano del popolo* in Florence, and Francesca echoes Dante's heroine when she states that she will pray for him who introduced Paolo to love:

> FRANCESCA   Sia
>   benedetto colui che v'insegnò
>   tal pianto! Io pregherò per la sua pace.
>   (d'Annunzio, *Francesca da Rimini*, III. 5, p. 637)

[Blessed be he who taught you such sorrow! I will pray for his peace.]

1   G. d'Annunzio, *Francesca da Rimini*, in his *Tragedie, sogni e misteri*, edited by E. Bianchetti, 2 vols (Milan, Mondadori, 1945), I, 463–712.
2   See *La Divina commedia*, edited by T. Casini, pp. 46–47n.

Furthermore, Francesca's foreboding is depicted as a nightmare, in which she identifies with the maiden in Boccaccio's story about Nastagio degli Onesti (*Decameron*, ɪɪ. 8). In the pine forest of Ravenna, she is pursued by two dogs and a dark knight, who cuts out her heart and throws it to the dogs. She asks the meaning of the nightmare. It is not spelled out in the text and the audience is left to decipher it. Symbolically, it depicts the pursuit of Francesca by two men, as a result of which her heart is torn out.

The love poetry throughout the tragedy reveals d'Annunzio at his most inspired. A short example from the final act will demonstrate how lyricism is brutally destroyed, as Paolo attempts to escape his brother's anger, catches his cloak on a spike and is grasped by his hair:

> FRANCESCA   E non è l'alba;
>   le stelle non tramontano sul mare;
>   la state non è morta; e tu sei mio,
>   et io son tutta tua,
>   e la gioia perfetta
>   è nell'ardore della nostra vita. [...]
>   GIANCIOTTO   Sei preso nella trappola,
>   ah traditore! Bene ti s'acciuffa
>   per queste chiome!
> (d'Annunzio, *Francesca da Rimini*, v, 4–5, pp. 701, 706)

[FRANCESCA: And it is not dawn. The stars do not sink into the sea. The summer is not dead, and you are mine, and I am all yours, and perfect joy is in the ardour of our life. (...) GIANCIOTTO: Ah traitor, you are trapped! I grab you firmly by these locks.]

The treatment of Francesca da Polenta by the writers considered in this essay reflects the personal, political and artistic aspirations of the Romantic period, as well as a desire to preserve emotional content within a realistic framework, which became the hallmark of late nineteenth-century and early twentieth-century Decadence. Translators carried the tragic tale to new literary climes, and in many cases their versions achieved the status of artistic works in their own right. The pathetic features of Dante's episode were immortalized by the English Romantics Tennyson, Shelley, Keats and Leigh Hunt. Byron in his poem "The Corsair" quoted lines from *Inferno* v to create an atmosphere of amorous pathos. In Italy

Foscolo used the figure of Francesca to illustrate the political upheaval of his own times, while Pellico carried Dante's heroine to a new set of readers, theatre-goers and musicians. It could be said that his interpretation of the story, in the light of events and ideological innovations of his day, served to highlight some of the outstanding features of Dantean art and allegory; and his imitators provided new material for the great tragedians of the Italian and English stage at the dawn of the twentieth century.

INDEX OF REFERENCES TO DANTE'S WORKS

A name between square brackets after an entry indicates an alternative form under which that entry may occur in the text.

INDEX OF NAMES

An asterisk indicates a character appearing or mentioned in the *Commedia*. The symbol ° indicates a character appearing or mentioned in some other work; the work's author is indicated in parenthesis. A name between square brackets indicates an alternative form in which the entry may occur in the text.